THE AENEID

VIRGIL

THE
AENEID

A New Prose Translation by David West

PENGUIN BOOKS

PENGUIN BOOKS

Published by the Penguin Group
Penguin Books Ltd, 27 Wrights Lane, London w8 5TZ, England
Penguin Putnam Inc., 375 Hudson Street, New York, New York 10014, USA
Penguin Books Australia Ltd, Ringwood, Victoria, Australia
Penguin Books Canada Ltd, 10 Alcorn Avenue, Toronto, Ontario, Canada M4V 3B2
Penguin Books India (P) Ltd, 11, Community Centre, Panchsheel Park, New Delhi – 110 017, India
Penguin Books (NZ) Ltd, Private Bag 102902, NSMC, Auckland, New Zealand
Penguin Books (South Africa) (Pty) Ltd, 5 Watkins Street, Denver Ext 4, Johannesburg 2094, South Africa

Penguin Books Ltd, Registered Offices: Harmondsworth, Middlesex, England

This translation first published 1990
Published in this edition 2001

1

Set in 10.25/14 pt Palatino
Typeset by Rowland Phototypesetting Ltd, Bury St Edmunds, Suffolk
Printed in England by Bath Press Ltd, Bath

Contents

TO THE GREAT DEAD
WHO WILL NOT DIE

Introduction

1. A POEM FOR OUR TIME

The *Aeneid* is the story of a man who lived three thousand years ago in the city of Troy in the north-west tip of Asia Minor. What has that to do with us?

Troy was besieged and sacked by the Greeks. After a series of disasters Aeneas met and loved a woman, Dido, queen of Carthage, but obeyed the call of duty to his people and his gods and left her to her death. Then, after long years of wandering, he reached Italy, fought a bitter war against the peoples of Latium and in the end formed an alliance with them which enabled him to found his city of Lavinium. From these beginnings, in 333 years, in 753 B.C., the city of Rome was to be founded. The Romans had arrived in Italy.

The *Aeneid* is still read and still resonates because it is a great poem. Part of its relevance to us is that it is the story of a human being who knew defeat and dispossession, love and the loss of love, whose life was ruled by his sense of duty to his gods, his people and his family, particularly to his beloved son Ascanius. But it was a hard duty and he sometimes wearied in it. He knew about war and hated the waste and ugliness of it, but fought, when he had to fight, with hatred and passion. At the end of the twentieth century the world is full of such people. While we are of them and feel for them we shall find something in the *Aeneid*. The gods have changed, but for men there is not much difference:

Pitiless Mars was now dealing grief and death to both sides with impartial hand. Victors and vanquished killed and were killed and neither side thought of flight. In the halls of Jupiter the gods pitied the futile anger of the two armies and grieved that men had so much suffering . . .

10.755–9

But the *Aeneid* is not simply a contemplation of the general human predicament. It is also full of individual human beings behaving as human beings still do. Take the charm and humour of Dido putting the Trojans at their ease at 1.562–78; the grief of Andromache when she meets the Trojan youth who is the same age as her son Astyanax would have been if he had been allowed to live – we do not need to be told that Astyanax is the name on the second altar at 3.305; the cunning of Acestes and Aeneas as they shame the great old champion back into the ring at 5.389–408; the childish joke of Iulus at 7.116 and its momentous interpretation; the aged hero feasting his eyes on his old friend's son at 8.152 or realizing at 8.560 that he can do nothing now except talk; the native's abuse of the foreigners from 9.598; the lying harridans at the beginning of Book Ten or the death of Mezentius and his horse from 10.858; the growling of Aeneas and the fussing and fumbling of the doctor as he plies his mute, inglorious art from 12.387.

The *Aeneid* presents a heroic view of the life of man in all its splendour and anguish, but it is also full of just observation of the details of individual behaviour. It is not yet out of date.

2. THE *AENEID* IN ITS OWN TIME

Virgil was born seventy years before Christ. In 44 B.C., after a century of civil war and disorder, Julius Caesar was assassinated by Brutus and Cassius in the name of liberty. His heir was his nineteen-year-old grand-nephew and adopted son, Octavian, astute, ruthless and determined. In 42 B.C. Brutus and Cassius were defeated and the fortunes of Virgil were at their lowest ebb. His family estates at Mantua were confiscated by the victors to provide land for their soldiers to settle on. But he won the patronage of Maecenas, one of the two chief aides of Octavian, and published his pastoral *Eclogues* in 37 B.C. In 29 B.C., after Octavian had made himself master of the known world by defeating Antony and Cleopatra at Actium, Virgil finished what Dryden called 'the best poem of the best poet', the *Georgics*, on the agriculture of Italy. Throughout the twenties Virgil was at work on his *Aeneid*, a poem in imitation of Homer's *Iliad* and *Odyssey* and in praise of Augustus, the name Octavian had taken on 16 January 27 B.C. Virgil died before finishing it, on his way back from Athens with Augustus in 19 B.C. To qualify for membership of the Senate, a Roman had to be extremely wealthy. When Virgil died, he owned property ten times that requirement. He left instructions that the *Aeneid* was to be burned. These instructions were countermanded by Augustus.

It is therefore clear that Virgil wrote and wrote acceptably in praise of his patron, the ruler of Rome. The *Aeneid* is successful panegyric.

It would be easy to despise or dislike the poem for that. But wrong, for the following reasons:

(1) Rome had endured a century of violence, discord, corruption and insecurity of life and property. Augustus, after intense effort and suffering, notably in his disastrous campaign in Sicily in 37 B.C., by his victory at Actium promised

peace, order, prosperity and moral regeneration. He even, according to Suetonius (*Life of Augustus* 89), fostered the talents of his generation in every possible way. It was the promise of a Golden Age, and in this euphoria Virgil and his friend Horace, another client of Maecenas and Augustus, wrote their great patriotic poems. In that day it was not foolish to hope and to believe.

(2) Although Virgil wrote in praise of Augustus and the ideal of empire, he was no Chauvin. He loved country people and country ways, their traditions and their stubborn independence. He responded to human love, between man and woman, between father and son, between men and their homes (consider only 6.450ff., 12.435ff., 10.779ff.), and he knew that empire had to be bought with the coin of human suffering and deprivation. He also knew the other side – the hard work and danger, the dedication and sacrifice which empire demanded of those who had made it and who maintained it, notably Augustus. Virgil does not solve the problems inherent in all this. He does not even pose them. The *Aeneid* is a story. But behind that story we have all the issues which would have moved a contemporary Roman, and may still move us.

(3) Praise is one thing. Flattery is another, and the *Aeneid* is not flattery. The action of the epic is set a thousand years before Augustus and it praises him in two ways: first, by telling the story of his great ancestor, the first founder of Rome, in such a way as resembles the story of Augustus himself, its third founder. The resemblances are not pointed out. The reader is left to observe and ponder them for himself if he wishes. The second mode of praise is direct allusion to Augustus in prophecies and visions, notably near the beginning and end of the poem, in the descent of Aeneas to consult his father in the underworld at the end of Book Six and on the great shield of Aeneas at the end of Book Eight.

The *Aeneid* is, among other things, a search for a vision of peace and order for Rome and for humanity. To see its outlines through the mists of time nothing is more helpful than the family tree of the Julians on page 335. Allusions to these names in the *Aeneid* are often to be heard as praise of Augustus, the contemporary Julian.

3. THIS TRANSLATION

Received wisdom, as represented by *The Proceedings of the Virgil Society* 19(1988)14, states that 'to translate poetry into prose is always a folly'. Leaving aside the fact that I am not a poet, I have had to reject this because I know of nobody at the end of our century who reads long narrative poems in English, and I want the *Aeneid* to be read. I believe also that this view does less than justice to the range, power and music of contemporary English prose. As written by our best novelists and journalists and even sometimes by ordinary letter-writers, it daily moves us towards pity, terror or laughter, and does so at least as effectively as the voices of contemporary poets. Further – this is ungentle but the argument requires that it be said – the English poets who have translated the *Aeneid* since Dryden have not done well. We may accept that poetic transla- tion need not be true to the tone or detail of the original. A poet's first concern is with his own poem. But if we grant this freedom, we must then judge their works as poems, and as such the poetic translations of the *Aeneid* are low in interest and inspiration.

The ruling prose version is Jackson Knight's Penguin Classic of 1956. This is lovingly faithful to the author's vision of Virgil but the language is dated. It would be difficult to disagree with Sandbach's judgement in *The Proceedings of the Virgil Society* 10(1970–71)35 (reprinted in *Meminisse Iuvabit* (1989), ed. F. Robertson): '. . . too often the attempt to grasp and represent each of Virgil's words has pushed aside the need to give the sentence rhythm and cohesion and the emphasis that goes with form.'

The present version has two objectives. When Peter Schidlof died, one of the other members of the Amadeus Quartet was asked what their approach had been, and he replied: 'Loyalty to the spirit and the letter.' As a translator I think of the letter and the spirit. I have tried to be utterly faithful to everything I see and hear in the Latin, the rhetoric, nuances, colour, tone, pace, passion, even the peerless music of Virgil's verse, which Tennyson thought 'the stateliest measure ever moulded by the lips of man'. This, of course, is impossible, as Neruda well realizes:

> Now it is clear this couldn't be done –
> that in this net it's not just the strings that count
> but also the air that escapes through the meshes.
>
> Pablo Neruda, 'Isla Negra', trs. Alastair Reid

My second aim has been to write readable English which does honour to the richness and sublimity of Virgil's language – ebullient, for example in the utterances of Aeneas at the games in Book Five, charged with grief for the death of Marcellus at the end of Book Six and ringing with the courage and cruelty of war in the four great last books. Another impossible task. But if it is to be attempted, the translator must be ready to jettison the idiom of Latin and search for the English words that will carry as much as possible of the spirit of the Latin.

By this creed there are two great sins: to fall short of Virgil through sloth or ineptitude or self-love; and to write what is dull. If it is dull, it is not a translation of Virgil. This version admits defeat in every line, but where it seems to abandon some feature of the Latin, I hope it is always in an attempt to respond in living English to the poetic eloquence of its great original.

FURTHER READING

Anyone who is new to Virgil and would like to learn more about him would be well advised to start with W. A. Camps, *An Introduction to Virgil's 'Aeneid'* (1969), Oxford, and the Penguin translations of the *Georgics* and the *Eclogues*.

Acknowledgements

The text used, with very few exceptions, is the Oxford Classical Text by Sir Roger Mynors. This translation is of course based on such of the vast scholarly literature as I have been able to read. Previous translations have been plundered. Standard commentaries have been consulted, notably R. G. Austin on Books 1, 2, 4 and 6, R. D. Williams on 3 and 5, C. J. Fordyce on 7 and 8. Particularly valuable have been E. Norden on 6, P. T. Eden on 8 and Stephen Harrison who gave me access to his forthcoming commentary on 10 and corresponded vigorously with me for a whole summer. The *Aeneidea* of James Henry have been an inspiration.

For years now my friends have been set to work daily on Virgilian problems, and have saved me from many errors. Rosemary Burton and E. L. Harrison criticized the whole translation. Stephen Harrison, James Morwood and Nicholas Horsfall have commented on whole books or extended passages. Pamela West, Janet Watson and Jane Curran have been shrewd and generous consultants. To all of these I owe a debt that cannot be paid, as I do to my wonderful colleagues in the best of all imaginable university departments of Classics.

DAVID WEST
Newcastle upon Tyne

THE AENEID

₧ ₨

Paris, son of Priam, king of Troy, has judged Venus to be more beautiful than Juno and Pallas Athene, and claimed his reward, Helen, wife of Menelaus, king of Sparta. The Greeks have gathered an army and sacked the city of Troy. Aeneas has escaped with his son Ascanius Iulus and his father Anchises. Driven by the jealous hatred of Juno, he has wandered across the Mediterranean for six years, trying to found a new city. At the beginning of the poem, his father has just died in Sicily and Aeneas is sailing at last for Italy . . .

CR 1 RD

STORM AND BANQUET

I sing of arms and of the man, fated to be an exile, who long since left the land of Troy and came to Italy to the shores of Lavinium; and a great pounding he took by land and sea at the hands of the heavenly gods because of the fierce and unforgetting anger of Juno. Great too were his sufferings in war before he could found his city and carry his gods into Latium. This was the beginning of the Latin race, the Alban fathers and the high walls of Rome. Tell me, Muse, the causes of her anger. How did he violate the will of the Queen of the Gods? What was his offence? Why did she drive a man famous for his piety to such endless hardship and such suffering? Can there be so much anger in the hearts of the heavenly gods?

There was an ancient city held by colonists from Tyre, opposite Italy and the distant mouth of the river Tiber. It was a city of great wealth and ruthless in the pursuit of war. Its name was Carthage, and Juno is said to have loved it more than any other place, more even than Samos. Here the goddess kept her armour. Here was her chariot, and this was the city she had long favoured, intending to give it sovereignty over the peoples of the earth, if only the Fates would allow it. But she had heard that there was rising from the blood of Troy a race of men who in days to come would overthrow this Tyrian citadel; a people proud in war and rulers of a great empire would come to sack the land of Libya; this is the destiny the Fates were unrolling. These were the fears of the daughter of

3

Saturn, and she had not forgotten the war she had fought long since at Troy for her beloved Argos, nor had her bitter resentment and the reasons for it ever left her mind. There still rankled deep in her heart the judgement of Paris and the injustice of the slight to her beauty, her loathing for the whole stock of Dardanus and her fury at the honours done to Ganymede, whom her husband Jupiter had carried off to be his cup-bearer. With all this fuelling her anger she was keeping the remnants of the Trojans, those who had escaped the savagery of Achilles and the Greeks, far away from Latium, driven by the Fates to wander year after year round all the oceans of the world. So heavy was the cost of founding the Roman race.

The Trojans were in high spirits. They were almost out of sight of Sicily and heading for the open sea with the wind astern and their bronze prows churning the salt sea to foam, as Juno brooded, still nursing the eternal wound deep in her breast: 'Am I to admit defeat and give up my attempt to keep the king of the Trojans away from Italy? So the Fates do not approve! Yet Pallas Athene could fire the fleet and drown my own Argives in the sea because of the guilt of one man, the mad passion of Ajax, son of Oileus. With her own hand she threw the consuming fire of Jupiter from the clouds, shattering his ships and sending winds to churn up the level sea. Then, as he breathed out flame from his breast where the thunderbolt had pierced it, she caught him up in a whirlwind and impaled him on a jagged rock. But here am I, the Queen of the Gods, the sister of Jupiter and his wife, and I have waged war all these years against a whole race of men! Is there no one left who worships the godhead of Juno? Will there be no one in the future to pray to me and lay an offering on my altars?'

These are the thoughts the goddess turned over in her burning heart as she came to Aeolia, the home of the clouds, a place teeming with the raging winds of the south. Here

Aeolus is king and here in a vast cavern he keeps in subjection the brawling winds and howling storms, chained and bridled in their prison. They murmur in loud protest round bolted gates in the mountainside while Aeolus sits in his high citadel, holding his sceptre, soothing their spirits and tempering their angry passions. But for him they would catch up the sea, the earth and the deeps of the sky and sweep them along through space. In fear of this, the All-powerful Father banished them to these black caverns with massive mountains heaped over them, and gave them under a fixed charter a king who knew how to hold them in check or, when ordered, to let them run with free rein. It was to him that Juno made supplication in these words: 'I come to you, Aeolus, because the Father of the Gods and King of Men has given you the power to calm the waves of the sea or raise them by your winds. A race of men hateful to me is sailing the Tyrrhenian sea carrying Ilium to Italy, along with the Penates, their defeated gods. Whip up your winds. Overwhelm their ships and sink them. Drive their fleet in all directions and scatter their bodies over the sea. I have fourteen nymphs of the rarest beauty and the loveliest of them all is Deiopea. I shall make her yours and join you in lawful wedlock. If you do me this service, she shall spend all her years with you and make you the father of beautiful children.'

To this Aeolus made answer: 'Your task, O queen, is to decide your wishes; my duty is to carry out your orders. It is thanks to you that I rule this little kingdom and enjoy this sceptre and the blessing of Jupiter. Through you I have a couch to lie on at the feasts of the gods, and my power over cloud and storm comes from you.'

At these words he struck the side of the hollow mountain with the butt of his spear and the winds seemed to form a column and pour out through an open gate to blow a hurricane over the whole earth. The east wind and the south and the south-west with its squalls all fell upon the sea at once, whipping it up from its bottom-most depths and rolling huge waves towards its shores. Men shouted, ropes screamed, clouds suddenly blotted out the light of the sky from the eyes of the Trojans and black night brooded over the sea as the heavens thundered and lightning flashed again and again across the sky. Wherever the Trojans looked, death stared them in the face. A sudden chill went through Aeneas and his limbs grew weak. Groaning, he lifted his hands palms upward to the stars and cried: 'Those whose fate it was to die beneath the high walls of Troy with their fathers looking down on them were many, many times more fortunate than I. O Diomede, bravest of the Greeks, why could I not have fallen to your right hand and breathed out my life on the plains of Troy, where fierce Hector was killed by the sword of Achilles, where great Sarpedon lies and where the river Simois caught up so many shields and helmets and bodies of brave men and rolled them down its current?'

Even as he threw out these words, a squall came howling from the north, catching his sail full on and raising the waves to the stars. The oars broke, the prow was wrenched round, and as they lay beam on to the seas, there came towering over them a sheer mountain of water. Some of the ships were hanging on the crests of the waves; for others the waters opened and in the troughs could be seen the sea-bed and the seething sand. Three of them were caught by the south wind and driven off course on to a reef hidden in mid-ocean – Italians know it as the Altars – a huge spine of rock just under the surface; three of them the southeaster took and carried helplessly from the high sea on to the sandbanks of the Syrtes, ran them aground and blocked them in with walls of sand; before the very eyes of Aeneas, the ship that carried the faithful Orontes and his Lycians was struck on the stern by a great sea and the helmsman was swept away head first into the water. Three times she spun round on the same spot till the swift whirlpool sucked her down. Here and there men could be seen swimming in the vast ocean, and with them in the waves their armour, spars of wood and the treasures of Troy. One by one the stout ships of Ilioneus and brave Achates, then Abas and old Aletes, succumbed to the storm. The fastenings of the ships' sides were loosened, the deadly water poured in and the timbers sprang.

Neptune, meanwhile, observed the loud disturbance of the ocean, the release of storms, the draining of his deepest pools, and was moved to anger. Rising from the depths, he lifted his head high above the crests of the waves and looked serenely out over the sea at Aeneas' fleet scattered over the face of the waters and the Trojans overwhelmed by the waves and by the rending of the sky. He recognized at once the anger and the cunning of his sister Juno and instantly summoned the east wind and the west and spoke to them in these words: 'Is it your noble birth that has made you so sure of yourselves? Do you winds now dare to move heaven and earth and raise these great masses of water without my divine authority? I could take you now and . . . but first I must still the waves you have stirred up. For any crimes you commit in the future, you will pay a dearer price. Away with you and take this message to your king: "He is not the one who has jurisdiction over the sea or holds the trident that knows no pity. That is my responsibility, given to me by lot. His domain, O Eurus, wind of the east, is the huge crags where you have your home. That is where Aeolus can do his swaggering, confining his rule to the closed walls of the prison of the winds."'

These were his words, and before he had finished speaking, he was calming the swell, dispersing the banked clouds and bringing back the sun. Triton and the sea nymph Cymothoe heaved and strained as they pushed the ships off jagged rocks, while Neptune himself lifted them out of the sandbanks with his trident and opened up the vast Syrtes, restraining the sea as he skimmed along with his chariot wheels touching the crests of the waves. As when disorder arises among the people of a great city and the common mob runs riot, wild passion finds weapons for men's hands and torches and rocks start flying; at such a time if people chance to see a man who has some weight among them for his goodness and his services to the state, they fall silent, standing and listening with all their attention while his words command their passions and soothe their hearts – so did all the crashing of the sea fall silent and Father Neptune, looking out over the waves, drove the horses of his chariot beneath a clear sky and gave them rein to fly before the wind.

Aeneas and his men were exhausted, and making what speed they could for the nearest land, they set course for the coast of Libya. There is a place where a harbour is formed by an island blocking the mouth of a long sound. As the waves come in from the open sea and break on the sides of this island, they are divided into the deep inlets of the bay. Rock cliffs are everywhere. A great pinnacle threatens the sky on either side, and beneath all this the broad water lies still and safe. At the end of the bay there rises a backcloth of shimmering trees, a dark wood with quivering shadows, looming over the water, and there, at the foot of this scene, is a cave of hanging rocks, a home for the nymphs, with fresh spring water inside it and seats in the virgin rock. Here there is no need of chains to moor the weary ships, or of anchors with hooked teeth to hold them fast. This is where Aeneas put in with seven ships gathered from all the Trojan fleet, and great was their longing for the land as they disembarked and stepped at last on to the shore and threw their sea-wasted bodies down on the sand. First of all Achates struck a spark from the flint, caught it in some leaves, fed the flame by putting dry twigs round it and set the fire going with brush-wood. Then weary as they were after all their labours, they laid out their corn, the gift of the goddess Ceres, all tainted with salt, and the goddess's own implements and set themselves to scorch with flame this grain they had saved from the sea and to grind it on stone.

Meanwhile Aeneas climbed a rock to get a view over the whole breadth of the ocean and see if there was any trace of the storm-tossed Antheus or of the double-banked Trojan galleys, Capys perhaps, or Caicus' armour high on the poop. There was not a ship to be seen, but he did see three stags wandering about the shore with all their herd behind them grazing the low ground in a long line. He stopped in his tracks and snatched his bow and swift arrows from the trusty Achates. First he took down the three leaders with their high heads of branching antlers. The whole of the rest of the herd scattered into the leafy cover of the wood, but not before he succeeded in stretching seven huge carcasses on the ground, one for each of the ships. He then made for the harbour and gave them out to all his men. Last of all he shared out the wine the good Acestes with a hero's generosity had poured into casks for them as they left the shores of Sicily. Then, as they mourned, he comforted them, saying: 'My friends, this is not the first trouble we have known. We have suffered worse before, and this too will pass. God will see to it. You have been to Scylla's cave and heard the mad dogs howling in the depths of it. You have even survived rocks thrown by the Cyclops. So summon up your courage once again. This is no time for gloom or fear. The day will come, perhaps, when it will give you pleasure to remember even this. Whatever chance may bring, however many hardships we suffer, we are making for Latium, where the Fates show us our place of rest. There it is the will of God that the kingdom of Troy shall rise again. Your task is to endure and save yourselves for better days.' These were his words, but he was sick with all his cares. He showed them the face of hope and kept his misery deep in his heart.

His men went briskly to work preparing the coming feast.

They flayed the hide off the ribs and exposed the flesh. Some cut it into quivering slices and speared it on spits. Others laid out cauldrons of water on the shore and lit fires. Then at last they ate, and recovered their strength, lying on the grass and taking their fill of old wine and rich venison. When their hunger was satisfied and the remains of the feast removed, they talked at length about their missing comrades, not knowing whether to hope or fear, wondering whether they were still alive or whether at that very moment they were drawing their last breath and beyond all calling. Most of all did Aeneas, who loved his men, mourn to himself the loss of eager Orontes and Amycus and the cruel death of Lycus, then brave Gyas, and brave Cloanthus.

Now the feast was ended and Jupiter was looking down from the height of heaven on the sea flying with sails and the land far beneath him, on the shores of the seas and the far-spread peoples, when suddenly he stopped in his survey at the highest point of the sky and fixed his eyes upon the kingdom of Libya. Even as he was turning over in his mind all the suffering that he saw, his daughter Venus came to him, her shining eyes brimming with tears, and spoke with a sadness greater than his own: 'You who rule the affairs of gods and men with your eternal law and at whose lightning we are all afraid, what great harm has my son Aeneas been able to do to you? What crime have the Trojans committed that they should suffer all this loss of life and the whole world be closed to them for the sake of Italy? Did you not promise that with the rolling years there would come a time when from this stock the Romans would arise? From this blood of Teucer, recalled to Italian soil, there would come leaders of men who would hold power over every land and sea. O father, father, has some argument changed your mind? As for me, I used to console myself with this for the cruel fall and sack of Troy, by weighing one destiny against another. But unrelieved misfortune is now hounding these men from disaster to disaster. O great king, what end do you set to their labours? The Greeks were all around Antenor, but he escaped them, made his way safely into the Illyrian Gulf and the heartlands of the kingdom of the Liburnians, and then went beyond the mouth of the Timavus. From there with a great roar from inside the mountain, a sea of water bursts out of nine mouths and covers the fields with a sounding ocean. But in this place he founded the city of Patavium as a home for his Trojans and gave them a name. There he dedicated the arms with which he fought at Troy and there he now lives in settled peace and quiet. But as for us, your own children to whom you grant a place in the citadel of heaven, we lose our ships. It is unspeakable. We are betrayed and kept far away from the shores of Italy because there is one who hates us. Is this our reward for piety and obedience? Is this how you bring us to our kingdom?'

The Father of Gods and Men, looking at his daughter with the smile that clears the sky and dispels the storms, kissed her lightly on the lips, and said: 'Spare yourself these fears, my lady from Cythera. The destiny of your descendants remains unchanged. You will see the city of Lavinium and its promised walls. You will take great-hearted Aeneas up to the stars of heaven. No argument changes my mind. But now, since you are tormented by this anxiety, I shall tell you more, unrolling for you the secrets of the scroll of the Fates. He will wage a great war in Italy and crush its fierce tribes. He will build walls for his people and establish their way of life, until a third summer has seen him reigning in Latium and a third winter has passed after the subjection of the Rutulians. But the reign of his son Ascanius, who now receives the second name Iulus (it was Ilus while the kingdom of Ilium still stood), shall last while thirty long years revolve, and he shall transfer his kingdom from its seat at Lavinium and build a city with powerful fortifications at Alba Longa. Here the rule of the race of Hector will last for three hundred long years until Ilia the royal priestess, heavy with the seed of Mars, shall give birth to twin sons. Then Romulus shall receive the people, wearing with joy the tawny hide of the wolf which nursed him. The walls he builds will be the walls of Mars and he shall give his own name to his people, the Romans. On them I impose no limits of time or place. I have given them an empire that will know no end. Even angry Juno, who is now wearying sea and land and sky with her terrors, will come to better counsel and join with me in cherishing the people of Rome, the rulers of the world, the race that wears the toga. So it has been decreed. There will come a day, as the years glide by, when the house of Assaracus will reduce Achilles' Pthia and glorious Mycenae to slavery and will conquer and rule the city of Argos. From this noble stock there will be born a Trojan Caesar to bound his empire by Oceanus at the limits of the world, and his fame by the stars. He will be called Julius, a name passed down to him from the great Iulus. In time to come, have no fear, you will receive him in the sky, laden with the spoils of the East. He too will be called upon in prayer. Then wars will be laid aside and the years of bitterness will be over. Silver-haired Truth and Vesta, and Romulus Quirinus with his brother Remus, will sit dispensing justice. The dread Gates of War with their tight fastenings of steel will then be closed, and godless Strife will sit inside them on his murderous armour roaring hideously from bloody mouth, hands shackled behind his back with a hundred bands of bronze.'

So spoke Jupiter, and he sent down Mercury, the son of Maia, to make the lands and the citadel of the new city of Carthage hospitable to the Trojans, in case Dido, in her ignorance of destiny, should bar her country to them. Through the great expanse of air he flew, wielding his wings like oars, and soon alighted on the shores of Libya. There he lost no time in carrying out the commands of Jupiter, and in accordance with the divine will the Carthaginians laid aside their fiery temper. Most of all the queen took into her heart a feeling of quiet and kindness towards the Trojans.

But all that night the dutiful Aeneas was turning many things over in his mind. As soon as life-giving morning came, he decided to go out and explore this new land and bring back to his men a true account of the shores to which the winds had driven him, and the beasts and men who lived there, if there were any men, for he saw no signs of cultivation. So, leaving his ships hidden in the wooded cove under the overhanging rocks, and shut in on every side by trees and quivering shade, he set out alone with Achates, gripping two broad-bladed steel spears in his hand. As he walked through the middle of the wood, his mother came to meet him looking like a Spartan girl out hunting, wearing the dress of a Spartan girl and carrying her weapons, or like the Thracian Harpalyce, as she wearies horses with her running and outstrips the swift current of the river Hebrus. She had a light bow hanging from her shoulders in hunting style, her hair was unbound and streaming in the wind and her flowing dress was caught up above the knee. 'Hey there, soldiers,' she called out to them, 'do you happen to have seen one of my sisters wandering about here or in full cry after the foaming boar? She was wearing a spotted lynx skin and had a quiver hanging from her belt.'

So spoke Venus, and Venus' son so began his reply: 'I have neither seen nor heard any of your sisters. But how am I to address a girl like you? Your face is not the face of a mortal, and you do not speak like a human being. Surely you must be a goddess? Are you Diana, sister of Apollo? Are you one of the sister nymphs? Be gracious to us, whoever you may be, and lighten our distress. Tell us what sky this is we now find ourselves beneath. What shore of the world is this on which we now wander, tossed here by the fury of wind and wave?

We do not know the place. We do not know the people. Tell us and many a victim will fall by my right hand before your altars.'

Venus replied: 'I am sure I deserve no such honour. Tyrian girls all carry the quiver and wear purple boots with this high ankle binding. This is a Phoenician kingdom you are looking at. We are Tyrians. This is the city of the people of Agenor, but the land belongs to the Libyans, a race not easy to handle in war. Dido, who came from the city of Tyre to escape her brother, holds sway here. There was a crime long ago. It is a long and winding story, but I shall trace its outlines for you. Her father had given her in marriage to Sychaeus, the wealthiest of the Phoenicians. They were joined with all the due rites of a first marriage and great was the love the poor queen bore for him. But the kingdom of Tyre was ruled by her brother Pygmalion, the vilest of criminals. A mad passion came between the two men. In blind lust for his gold the godless Pygmalion attacked him without warning, ambushing him at the altar. With no thought for his sister's love he killed Sychaeus and for a long time concealed what he had done. Dido was sick with love and he deceived her with false hopes and empty pretences. But one night there appeared to her in a dream the very ghost of her unburied husband. He lifted up his face, pale with the strange pallor of the dead, and, baring the sword wounds on his breast, he pointed to the altar where he had been killed and revealed the whole horror of the crime that had been hidden in their house. He then urged her to escape with all speed from their native land, and to help her on her wanderings he showed her where to find an ancient treasure buried in the earth, an incalculable weight of silver and gold. This moved Dido to plan her escape and gather followers, men driven by savage hatred or lively fear of the tyrant. They seized some ships which happened to be ready for sea. They loaded them with the gold and sailed away with the wealth Pygmalion had coveted. The woman led the whole undertaking. When they arrived at the place where you will now see the great walls and rising citadel of the new city of Carthage, they bought a piece of land called the "Byrsa", the animal's hide, as large an area as they could include within the hide of a bull. But now tell me, who are you? What country have you sailed from? Where are you making for?'

In reply to her questions Aeneas drew a great sigh from the bottom of his heart and said: 'O goddess, if I were to start at the beginning and retrace our whole story, and if you had the time to listen to the annals of our suffering, before I finish the doors of Olympus would close and the Evening Star would lay the day to rest. We come from the ancient city of Troy, if the name of Troy has ever reached your ears. We have sailed many seas and by the chance of the winds we have been driven ashore here in Libya. I am Aeneas, known for my devotion. I carry with me on my ships the gods of my home, the Penates, wrested from my enemies, and my fame has reached beyond the skies. I am searching for my fatherland in Italy. My descent is from highest Jupiter. With my goddess mother to show the way, I embarked upon the Phrygian sea with twenty ships, following the destiny which had been given to me, and now a bare seven of them remain, and these torn to pieces by wind and wave. I am a helpless stranger, driven out of Europe and out of Asia, tramping the desert wastes of Libya.'

Venus could listen to no more. She broke in on the tale of his sufferings, saying: 'Whoever you are, you breathe the breath of life and you have come to this Tyrian city. I do not believe you are hated by the gods. Go on now from here to the queen's door. I can tell you that your comrades are restored and your fleet returned to you. The winds have veered to the north and blown them safe to shore. All this is true unless my parents have failed in their efforts to teach me to interpret the flight of birds. Look at these twelve swans flying joyfully in formation. The eagle of Jupiter was swooping down on them from the heights of heaven and scattering them over the open sky, but now look at them in their long column. Some are reaching land. Some have already reached it and are looking down on it. Just as they have come to their home and their flock has circled the sky in play, singing as they fly with whirring wings, so your ships and your warriors are either already in port or crossing the bar in full sail. Go on now, and follow where the road takes you.'

When she had finished speaking and was turning away, her neck shone with a rosy light and her hair breathed the divine odour of ambrosia. Her dress flowed free to her feet and as she walked he knew she was truly a goddess. As she hastened away, he recognized her as his mother and called after her: 'Why do you so often mock your own son by taking on these disguises? You too are cruel. Why am I never allowed to take your hand in mine, to hear your true voice and speak to you as you really are?'

With these reproaches he took the road that led to the city, but Venus hedged them about with a thick mist as they walked. The goddess spread a great veil of cloud over them so that no one could see them or touch them or cause any delay or ask the reason for their coming. She herself soared high into the sky and departed for Paphos, returning happily to her beloved home where she has her temple, and a hundred altars steam with the incense of Sheba and breathe the fragrance of fresh-cut flowers.

Meanwhile Aeneas and Achates hurried on their way, following the track, and they were soon climbing the great hill which towered over the city and looked down upon the citadel opposite. Aeneas was amazed by the size of it where recently there had been nothing but shepherds' huts, amazed too by the gates, the paved streets and all the stir. The Tyrians were working with a will: some of them were laying out the line of walls or rolling up great stones for building the citadel; others were choosing sites for building and marking them out with the plough; others were drawing up laws and electing magistrates and a senate whom they could revere; on one side they were excavating a harbour; on the other laying deep foundations for a theatre and quarrying huge columns from the rock to make a handsome backdrop for the stage that was to be. They were like bees at the beginning of summer, busy in the sunshine all through the flowery meadows, bringing out the young of the race, just come of age, or treading the oozing honey and swelling the cells with sweet nectar, or taking the loads as they come in or mounting guard to keep the herds of idle drones out of their farmstead. The hive seethes with activity and the fragrance of honey flavoured with thyme is everywhere. 'How fortunate they are!' cried Aeneas, now looking up at the high tops of the buildings. '*Their* walls are already rising!' and he moved on through the middle of the people, hedged about by the miraculous cloud, and no one saw him.

There was a wooded grove which gave abundant shade in the middle of the city. When first the Phoenicians had been driven there by wind and wave, Juno, the Queen of the Gods, had led them to this spot where they had dug up the head of a spirited stallion. This was a sign that from generation to generation they would be a race glorious in war and would have no difficulty in finding fields to graze. Here Sidonian Dido was building for Juno a huge temple rich with offerings and rich, too, with the presence of the goddess. It was a raised temple, and at the top of its steps the threshold was of bronze, the beams were jointed with bronze and the bronze doors grated as they turned in their sockets. Here in this grove Aeneas saw a strange sight which for the first time allayed his fears. Here for the first time he dared to hope, and despite all the calamities of the past to have better confidence in the future. While waiting for the queen and studying everything there was to see under the roof of this huge temple, as he marvelled at the good fortune of the city, the skill of the workmen and all the works of their hands, he suddenly saw, laid out in order, depictions of the battles fought at Troy. The Trojan War was already famous throughout the world. The two sons of Atreus were there, and Priam, and Achilles who hated both sides. Aeneas stopped, and wept, and said to Achates: 'Is there anywhere now on the face of this earth that is not full of the knowledge of our misfortunes? Look at Priam. Here too there is just reward for merit, there are tears for suffering and men's hearts are touched by what man has to bear. Forget your fears. We are known here. This will give you some hope for the future.'

As he spoke these words, he was feeding his spirit with the empty images and groaning, and rivers of tears washed down his cheeks as he gazed at the fighting round the walls of Troy. On one side Greeks were in flight with Trojan warriors hard on their heels; on the other Trojans were retreating and Achilles with his crested helmet was pursuing them in his chariot. He wept, too, when he recognized the white canvas of the tents of Rhesus nearby. It was the first sleep of the night. The tents had been betrayed, and were being torn down by Diomede, red with the blood of all the men he had slaughtered. He stole the fiery horses and took them back to the Greek camp before they could crop the grass of Troy or drink the water of the Xanthus. In another part of the picture poor Troilus, a mere boy and no match for Achilles, had lost his armour and was in full flight. His horses had run away with the chariot and he was being dragged along helpless on his back behind it, still holding on to the reins. His neck and hair were trailing along the ground and the end of his spear was scoring the dust behind him. The women of Troy, meanwhile, were going in supplication to the temple of Pallas Athene, but the goddess was hostile to them. Their hair was unbound, and they were carrying a robe to offer her, beating their breasts in grief, but her head was turned from them and her eyes were fixed upon the ground. There too was Achilles. He had dragged Hector three times round the walls of Troy, and now was selling his dead body for gold. Aeneas groaned from the depths of his heart to see the armour stripped off him, the chariot, the corpse of his dear friend and Priam stretching out his feeble hands. Aeneas even recognized himself in the confusion of battle, with the leaders of the Greeks all around him. There were the warriors of the East, the armour of Memnon and his dark skin. The Amazons were there in their thousands with crescent shields and their leader Penthesilea in the middle of her army, ablaze with passion for war. There, showing her naked breast supported by a band of gold, was the warrior maiden, daring to clash with men in battle.

While Trojan Aeneas stood gazing, rooted to the spot and lost in amazement at what he saw, queen Dido in all her beauty arrived at the temple with a great crowd of warriors around her. She was like Diana leading the dance on the banks of the Eurotas or along the ridges of Mount Cynthus with a thousand mountain nymphs thronging behind her on either side. She carries her quiver on her shoulder, and as she walks, she is the tallest of all the goddesses. Her mother Latona does not speak, but a great joy stirs her heart at the sight of her. Dido was like Diana, and like Diana she bore herself joyfully among her people, urging on their work for the kingdom that was to be. Then she sat on her high throne under the coffered roof, in the middle of the temple before the doors of the shrine of the goddess. There, as she was giving laws and rules of conduct to her people, and dividing the work that had to be done in equal parts or allocating it by lot, Aeneas suddenly saw a great throng approaching, Antheus, Sergestus, brave Cloanthus and the other Trojans who had been scattered over the sea by the dark storm and swept away to distant shores. He was astounded, and Achates, too, was stunned with joy and fear. They burned with longing to clasp the hands of their comrades, but were at a loss because they did not understand what they saw. They did nothing, but stayed hidden in their cloak of cloud, waiting to learn how Fortune had dealt with their comrades. On what shore had they left their fleet? Why were they here? For these were picked men coming from each of the ships to plead their case, and they were now walking to the temple with shouting all about them.

They came in and were allowed to address the queen. Ilioneus, the oldest of them, made this appeal: 'You are a queen whom Jupiter has allowed to found a new city and curb proud peoples with your justice; we are the unhappy men of Troy, blown by the winds over all the oceans of the world, and we come to you as suppliants. Save our ships from the impious threat of fire. We are god-fearing men. Take pity on us. Look more closely at us – we have not come to Libya to pillage your homes and their gods, to take plunder and drive it down to the shore. Such violence and arrogance are not to be found in the hearts of the defeated.

'There is a place which Greeks know by the name Hesperia. It is an ancient land, strong in war and rich in the fertility of its soil. It was once tilled by Oenotrians, but now we believe their descendants have called themselves Italians after their king Italus. This is where we were steering when suddenly Orion rose in cloud and tempest and drove us on to hidden shallows, the sea overwhelmed us and fierce southerly squalls scattered us far and wide among breakers and uncharted rocks. A few of us drifted ashore here to your land. What manner of men are these? Is this a country of barbarians that allows its people to act in this way? Sailors have a right to the shore and we are refused it. They make war on us and will not let us set foot on land. You may be no respecters of men. You may fear no men's arms, but think of the gods, who see right and wrong and do not forget. Our king was Aeneas. He had no equal for his piety and his care for justice, and no equal in the field of battle. If the Fates still protect him, if he still breathes the air of heaven, if he is not even now laid low among the merciless shades, you would have nothing to fear or to regret by taking the lead in a contest of kindness. In the land of Sicily we have arms and cities and the great Acestes, sprung from Trojan blood. Allow us to draw up our storm-battered ships, to hew timbers in your woods and shape new oars, so that we can make for Italy and Latium with joy in our hearts, if indeed we go to Italy with our comrades and our king; but if they are lost, if you, great Father of the Trojans, are drowned in the sea off Libya, and there are no hopes left in Iulus, then we can at least go back to where we came from across the Sicilian sea, to the place that is prepared for us, and return to king Acestes.' So spoke Ilioneus and all the Trojans to a man murmured in agreement.

Then Dido looked down at them and made a brief answer: 'Have no fear, men of Troy. Put every anxious thought out of your hearts. This is a new kingdom, and it is harsh necessity that forces me to take these precautions and to post guards on all our frontiers. But who could fail to know about the people of Aeneas and his ancestry, or the city of Troy, the valour of its men and the flames of war that engulfed it? We here in Carthage are not so dull in mind as that. The sun does spare a glance for our Tyrian city when he yokes his horses in the morning. Whether you choose to go to great Hesperia and the fields of Saturn, or to the land of Eryx and king Acestes, you will leave here safe under my protection, and I shall give you supplies to help you on your way. Or do you wish to settle here with me on an equal footing, even here in this kingdom of Carthage? The city which I am founding is yours. Draw up your ships on the beach. Trojan and Tyrian shall be as one in my eyes. I wish only that your king Aeneas had been driven by the same south wind, and were here with you now. But what I can, I shall do. I shall send men whom I can trust all along the coast, and order them to cover every furthest corner of Libya, in case he has been shipwrecked and is wandering in any of the woods or cities.'

The brave Achates and Father Aeneas had long been

impatient to break out of the cloud, and at Dido's words their eagerness increased. 'Aeneas,' said Achates, 'son of the goddess, what thoughts are now rising in your heart? You see there is no danger. Our ships are safe. Our comrades are rescued. Only one of them is missing, and we saw him with our own eyes founder in mid-ocean. Everything else is as your mother Venus said it would be.'

He had scarcely finished speaking when the cloud that was all about them suddenly parted and dissolved into the clear sky. Aeneas stood there resplendent in the bright light of day with the head and shoulders of a god. His own mother had breathed upon her son and given beauty to his hair and the sparkle of joy to his eyes, and the glow of youth shone all about him. It was as though skilled hands had added embellishments to ivory or applied gilding to silver or Parian marble. Then suddenly, to the surprise of all, he addressed the queen: 'The man you are looking for is standing before you. I am Aeneas the Trojan, saved from the Libyan sea. And you, Dido, alone have pitied the unspeakable griefs of Troy. We are the remnants left by the Greeks. We have suffered every calamity that land and sea could inflict upon us. We have lost everything. And now you offer to share your city and your home with us. It is not within our power to repay you as you deserve, nor could whatever survives of the Trojan race, scattered as it is over the face of the wide earth. May the gods bring you the reward you deserve, if there are any gods who have regard for goodness, if there is any justice in the world, if their minds have any sense of right. What happy age has brought you to the light of life? What manner of parents have produced such a daughter? While rivers run into the sea, while shadows of mountains move in procession round the curves of valleys, while the sky feeds the stars, your honour, your name, and your praise will remain for ever in every land to which I am called.' As he spoke, he put out his right hand to his friend Ilioneus and his left to Serestus, then greeted the others, brave Gyas, and brave Cloanthus.

Dido of Sidon was amazed at her first sight of him and then at the thought of the ill fortune he had endured. 'What sort of chance is this,' she exclaimed, 'that hounds the son of a goddess through all these dangers? What power has driven you to these wild shores? Are you that Aeneas whom the loving goddess Venus bore to Dardanian Anchises in Phrygia by the river waters of the Simois? I myself remember the Greek Teucer coming to Sidon after being exiled from his native Salamis. He was looking to found a new kingdom, and was helped by my father Belus, who in those days was laying waste the wealth of Cyprus. He had conquered the island and it was under his control. From that day on I knew all the misfortunes of the city of Troy. I knew your name and the names of the Greek kings. Teucer himself, your enemy, held the Teucrians, the people of Troy, in highest respect and claimed descent from an ancient Teucrian family. This is why I now invite your warriors to come into my house. I, too, have known ill fortune like yours and been tossed from one wretchedness to another until at last I have been allowed to settle in this land. Through my own suffering, I am learning to help those who suffer.'

With these words she led Aeneas into her royal palace, and as she went she appointed sacrifices to be offered in the temples of the gods. Nor at that moment did she forget Aeneas' comrades on the shore, but sent down to them twenty bulls, a hundred great bristling hogs' backs and a hundred fat lambs with their mothers, rich gifts to celebrate the day. Meanwhile the inside of her palace was being prepared with all royal luxury and splendour. They were laying out a banquet in the central hall and the draperies were of proud purple, richly worked. The silver was massive on the tables, with the brave deeds of their ancestors embossed in gold, a long tradition of feats of arms traced through many heroes from the ancient origins of the race.

But a father's love allowed Aeneas' mind no rest, and he asked Achates to go quickly ahead to the ships to take the news to Ascanius and bring him back to the city. All his thoughts were on his dear son Ascanius. He also told Achates to bring back with him as gifts for Dido some of the treasures that had been rescued from the ruins of Troy, a cloak stiff with gold-embroidered figures and a dress with a border woven of yellow acanthus flowers. These miracles of workmanship had been given to Helen of Argos by her mother Leda, and she had taken them from Mycenae when she came to Troy for her illicit marriage with Paris. There was also the sceptre which had once been carried by Ilione, the eldest daughter of Priam, a necklace of pearls and a double gold coronet set with jewels. Achates set off for the ships in great haste to carry out his instructions.

Venus meanwhile was turning over new schemes in her mind and devising new plans. She decided to change the form and features of Cupid, and send him in place of the lovely young Ascanius to inflame the heart of the queen, driving her to madness by the gifts and winding the fire of passion round her bones. For Venus was afraid of the treacherous house of Carthage and the double-tongued people of Tyre. The thought of the bitterness of Juno's hatred burned in her heart, and as night began to fall and her anxiety kept returning, she spoke to the winged god of love in these words: 'My dear son, you are the source of my power. You are my great strength. Only you, my son, can laugh at the thunderbolts which my father, highest Jupiter, hurled against the Giant Typhoeus. To you I come for help. I am your suppliant, begging the aid of your divine power. You well know how Juno's bitter hatred is tossing your own brother from shore to shore round all the seas of the world and you have often grieved to see me grieving. Now he is in the hands of the Phoenician Dido, who is delaying him with honeyed words, and I am afraid of Juno's hospitality and what it may bring. She will not stand idle when the gate of the future is turning. That is why I am resolved to act first, taking possession of the queen by a stratagem and surrounding her with fire. No power in heaven will change her. I shall grapple her to myself in love for Aeneas. As for how you are to achieve this, listen now and I shall tell you my mind. Aeneas has sent for his son, whom I so love, and the young prince is preparing to go to the city of Carthage, bringing gifts which have survived the burning of Troy and the hazards of the sea. I shall put him into a deep sleep and hide him in one of my sacred shrines on Mount Idalium or on the heights of Cythera, so that he will not know of my scheme or suddenly arrive to interrupt it. You will have to use your cunning and take on his appearance for just one night. He is a boy like yourself and you know him, so put on his features, and when the royal table is flowing with wine that brings release, and Dido takes you happily on to her lap and gives you sweet kisses, you can then breathe fire and poison into her and she will not know.'

Cupid obeyed his beloved mother. He took off his wings and strutted about copying Iulus' walk and laughing. But the goddess poured quiet and rest into all the limbs of Ascanius, and holding him to the warmth of her breast, she lifted him into the high Idalian woods, where the soft amaracus breathed its fragrant shade and twined its flowers around him.

Now Cupid was obeying his instructions and taking the royal gifts, amused to be escorted by Achates. When he came in, the queen was already sitting under a rich awning on a golden couch in the middle of the palace. Presently Father Aeneas and after him the men of Troy arrived and reclined on purple coverlets. Attendants gave them water for their hands, plied them with bread from baskets and brought them fine woollen napkins with close-cut nap. Inside were fifty serving-women, whose task it was to lay out the food in order in long lines and honour the Penates by tending their fires. There were a hundred other female slaves and a hundred men, all of the same age, to load the tables for the banquet and set out the drinking cups. The Tyrians, too, came thronging through the doors, and the palace was full of joy as they took their appointed places on the embroidered couches. They admired the gifts Aeneas had given. They admired Iulus, the glowing face of the god and his false words, the cloak and the dress embroidered with yellow acanthus flowers. But most of all the unfortunate Dido, doomed to be the victim of a plague that was yet to come, could not have her fill of gazing, and as she gazed, moved by the boy as much as by the gifts, the fire within her grew. After he had embraced Aeneas and hung on his neck to satisfy the great love of his father who was not his father, he went to the queen. She fixed her eyes and her whole heart on him and sometimes dandled him on her knee, without knowing what a great god was sitting there marking her out to suffer. But he was remembering his mother, the goddess of the Acidalian spring, and he began gradually to erase the memory of Sychaeus, trying to turn towards a living love, a heart that had long been at peace and long unused to passion.

As soon as the first pause came in the feasting and the tables were cleared away, they set up great mixing bowls full of wine and garlanded them with flowers. The palace was ringing with noise and their voices swelled through the spacious hall. Lamps were lit and hung from the gold-coffered ceilings and the flame of torches routed the darkness. The queen now asked for a golden bowl heavy with jewels, and filled it with wine unmixed with water. From this bowl Belus had drunk, and all the royal line descended from Belus. They called for silence in the great chamber as Dido spoke: 'Jupiter, to you we pray, since men say that you ordain the laws of hospitality. Grant that this day may be a day of happiness for the Tyrians and the men from Troy, and may our descendants long remember it. Let Bacchus, giver of good cheer, be among us, and kindly Juno, and you, Tyrians, celebrate this gathering with welcome in your hearts.'

At these words she poured a libation of wine on the table to honour the gods, and having poured it, she took it first and just touched it to her lips. She then passed it to Bitias with a smile and a challenge. Nothing loth, he took a great draught from the golden bowl foaming to the brim, and bathed himself in wine. The other leaders of the Carthaginians did the same after him. Long-haired Iopas, the pupil of mighty Atlas, then sang to his gilded lyre of the wanderings of the moon and the labours of the sun, the origin of the human race and of the animals, the causes of rain and of the fires of heaven, of Arcturus, of the Hyades, bringers of rain, of the two Triones, the oxen of the Plough; why the winter suns are so eager to immerse themselves in the ocean, and what it is that slows down the passage of the nights. The Tyrians applauded again and again and the Trojans followed their lead.

So the doomed Dido was drawing out the night with all manner of talk, drinking long draughts of love as she asked question after question about Priam and Hector, what armour Memnon, son of the Dawn, was wearing when he came, what kind of horses did Diomede have, how tall was Achilles. 'But no,' she said, 'come tell your hosts from the beginning about the treachery of the Greeks, the sufferings of your people and your own wanderings, for this is now the seventh summer that has carried you as a wanderer over every land and sea.'

☙ 2 ❧

THE FALL OF TROY

They all fell silent, gazing at Father Aeneas, and he began to speak from his raised couch: 'O Queen, the sorrow you bid me bring to life again is past all words, the destruction by the Greeks of the wealth of Troy and of the kingdom that will be mourned for ever, and all the horrors I have seen, and in which I played a large part. No man could speak of such things and not weep, none of the Myrmidons of Achilles or the Dolopians of Neoptolemus, not even a follower of Ulixes, a man not prone to pity. Besides, the dewy night is already falling fast from the sky and the setting stars are speaking to us of sleep. But if you have such a great desire to know what we suffered, to hear in brief about the last agony of Troy, although my mind recoiled in anguish when you asked and I shudder to remember, I shall begin:

Year after year the leaders of the Greeks had been broken in war and denied by the Fates, until, with the aid of the divine skill of Pallas Athene, they built a horse the size of a mountain, cutting pine trees to weave into it for ribs. They pretended it was a votive offering for their safe return to Greece, and that was the story on men's lips. Then they chose some men by lot from their best warriors and shut them up in the darkness of its belly, filling the vast cavern of its womb with armed soldiers.

Within sight of the mainland is the island of Tenedos,

famous in story. While the kingdom of Priam stood, it was rich and prosperous, but now there is only a bay giving a none too safe anchorage for ships. The Greeks sailed here and took cover on its lonely shore. We thought they had left us and sailed for Mycenae with favouring winds. The whole of Troy then shook itself free of its long sorrow. The gates were thrown open and the people went out rejoicing to see the Greek encampment, the deserted shore and all the places abandoned by the enemy. Here was the Dolopian camp and here fierce Achilles had his tent. This was where the fleet was drawn up. This was where they used to fight their battles. Some gazed at the fatal offering to the virgin goddess Minerva and marvelled at the huge size of the horse. Thymoetes was the first to urge them to drag it inside their walls and set it on their citadel, whether it was treachery that made him speak, or whether the Fates of Troy were already moving towards that end. But Capys, and those of sounder judgement, did not trust this offering. They thought it was some trick of the Greeks and should be thrown into the sea, or set fire to and burned, or that they should bore holes in its hollow belly and probe for hiding places. The people were uncertain and their passions were divided.

Then suddenly at the head of a great throng Laocoon came running down in a blaze of fury from the heights of the citadel, shouting from a distance as he came: 'O you poor fools! Are you out of your minds, you Trojans? Do you seriously believe that your enemies have sailed away? Do you imagine Greeks ever give gifts without some devious purpose? Is this all you know about Ulixes? I tell you there are Greeks hiding in here, shut up in all this wood, or else it is a siege engine designed for use against our walls, to spy on our homes and come down on the city from above, or else there is some other trick we cannot see. Do not trust the horse, Trojans. Whatever it is, I am afraid of Greeks, particularly when they bring gifts.'

With these words he threw a great spear with all his

strength into the beast's side, into the curved timbers of its belly. It stuck there vibrating, the creature's womb quivered and the hollow caverns boomed and groaned. If divine Fate, if the minds of the gods had not been set against us, Laocoon would surely have forced us to tear open the hiding places of the Greeks with our swords, Troy would still be standing and the high citadel of Priam would still be in its place.

While this was going on, there was a sudden outcry, and some Trojan shepherds came before the king, dragging a man with his hands tied behind his back. They knew nothing about him. They had come upon him and he had given himself up. This was all part of his scheme. His purpose was to open Troy to the Greeks. He knew exactly what he wanted to do, and he was ready for either outcome, to spin his web or to meet certain death if he failed. In their eagerness to see the prisoner, Trojan soldiers came running up from all sides, and gathered round to join in jeering at him. Listen now to this story of Greek treachery, and from this one indictment, learn the ways of a whole people. Dishevelled and defenceless, he stood there with every eye upon him, looking all round him at the warriors of Troy, and said with a great sigh: 'There is nowhere for me now on sea or land. There is nothing left for a man like me, who has no place among the Greeks, and now here are my enemies the Trojans, baying for my blood.'

He groaned. We had a change of heart, and all our passions were checked. We fell to asking him what his family was, and what he had come to tell us. We wanted to hear why he had allowed himself to be taken prisoner.

'O king Priam,' he replied, 'I am the sort of man who will confess the whole truth to you, whatever it may be. First of all, I am a Greek from Argos, and I will not deny it. Fortune may have made Sinon an object of pity, but for all her malice, she will never make him a cheat or a liar. You may perhaps have heard tell of the name of Palamedes, son of Belus, and the great glory that was his. Although he was innocent, false information was infamously laid against him. His offence was that he objected to the war, and the Greeks put him to death. They murdered him and now they mourn him. This Palamedes was my comrade and my kinsman. My father was a poor man, and sent me here to the war to be with him from my earliest years. While Palamedes was secure in his kingship and had authority in the council of the kings, we too had some standing and some credit. But after he left the shores of this upper world, the victim of the jealousy of Ulixes and his smooth tongue (you all know about Ulixes), I was prostrate and dragged out my life in darkness and grief, brooding to myself over the downfall of my innocent friend, till, like a madman, I broke my silence and promised that I would miss no chance of revenge if ever I came back in victory to our native Argos. My words roused his bitter hatred. This was my first step on a slippery path. From this moment on, Ulixes kept me in a constant state of fear by one new accusation after another. From this moment on he spread vague rumours about me among the common soldiers. He knew he was guilty and was looking for weapons to use against me. Nor did he rest until with Calchas the priest as his lackey . . . but why do I waste time? Why go over this sordid story to no purpose? If in your eyes all Greeks are the same, and all you have to know is that a man is a Greek, then give me my punishment. It is long overdue. This would please Ulixes, our friend from Ithaca, and Agamemnon and Menelaus would pay you well for it.'

By this time we were burning to ask questions and find out why all this had happened. We had never met villainy on this scale before. We were not familiar with the arts of Greece. He went on with his lies, cringing with fear as he spoke:

'The Greeks have often wanted to make their escape from here and leave Troy far behind them, abandoning this long and weary war. And oh how I wish they had done so! But again and again rough seas here kept them in port or the south wind alarmed them as they were setting sail. And most of all, when this construction of interwoven maple beams, this horse, was at last in position here, the black clouds thundered all round the sky. We were at a loss and sent Eurypylus to consult the oracle of Phoebus Apollo, and this is the grim response he brought back from the shrine: "When you Greeks first came to Troy you killed a virgin and appeased the winds with her blood. With blood you must find a way to return. You must sacrifice a Greek life." When this answer came to people's ears, they did not know where to turn, and the cold fear ran through the marrow of their bones. For whom were they to prepare death? Whom did Apollo want? At this point there was a great uproar, and the Ithacan dragged out the prophet Calchas into the middle of us and demanded to know what was the will of the gods. Many people could detect even then the ruthless hand of the schemer directed against me. They saw what was to come and held their peace. For ten days Calchas gave no answer, concealing himself and refusing to say the word that would betray a man and send him to his death. But at long last, all according to plan, he allowed the clamour raised by the Ithacan to force him to break his silence and mark me out for the altar. They all agreed. They had all been afraid, but now one man was doomed, and this they could endure.

'The day of the abomination was soon upon us. The sacred rites were all prepared for me. The salted meal was sprinkled and the sacrificial ribbons were round my head. I escaped from death, I admit it, I broke my bonds, and lay hidden all night in the reeds of a marsh, waiting for them to set sail, and wondering if they had. I have no hope now of seeing the land which was once my home, or my beloved children, or my father whom I have so often longed for. Perhaps they will be punished for my escape, and wash away this guilt of mine with their own helpless blood. But I beg of you by the gods who know the truth, by any honesty that may survive unsullied between men, pity me in my great suffering. I know in my heart I have not deserved it.'

He wept. We spared him and and even began to pity him. Priam spoke first and ordered him to be freed from the manacles and the ropes that tied him, and spoke these friendly words: 'Whoever you are, from this moment on forget the Greeks whom you have lost. You will be one of us. But now give full and truthful answers to the questions I ask you: why have they set up this huge monster of a horse? Who proposed it? What is the purpose of it? Does it have some supernatural power? Is it an engine of war?'

Sinon was ready with all his Greek arts and stratagems. Raising to the skies the hands we had just freed from their shackles, he cried: 'I call upon you, eternal fires of heaven and your inviolable godhead. I call upon the altars and the impious swords from which I have escaped. I call upon the sacred ribbons which I wore as sacrificial victim. It is no sin for me to break my sacred oaths of allegiance to the Greeks. It is no sin for me to hate these men and bring all their secrets out into the open. I am no longer subject to the laws of my people. Only you must stand by your promises. If I keep Troy safe, Troy must keep its word and save me, if what I say is true, and what I offer is a full and fair exchange.

'All the hopes and confidence of the Greeks in this war they started have always depended upon the help of Pallas Athene. But ever since the impious Diomede and Ulixes, the schemer behind all their crimes, took it upon themselves to tear the fateful Palladium, the image of the goddess, from her own sacred temple in Troy, ever since they slew the guards on the heights of the citadel and dared to touch the sacred bands on the head of the virgin goddess with blood on their hands, from that moment their hopes turned to water and ebbed away from them, their strength was broken and the mind of the goddess was set against them. Tritonian Pallas gave clear signs of this by sending portents that could not be doubted. No sooner had they laid down the image in the Greek camp, than its eyes glared and flashed fire, the salt sweat streamed over its limbs and by some miracle the image of the goddess leapt three times from the ground with her shield and spear quivering. Calchas declared that they had to take to instant flight across the sea, and prophesied that Troy could not be sacked by Argive weapons unless they first took the omens again in Argos, and then brought back to Troy the divine image which they have now carried away across the sea on their curved ships. So now they have set sail for their native Mycenae to rearm and to muster their gods to come with them and they will soon remeasure the ocean and be back here when you least expect them. This is how Calchas interprets the omens, and on his advice they have set up this effigy of a horse to atone for the violation of the Palladium and the divinity of Pallas, and for their deadly sin of sacrilege. But he told them to make it an immense structure of interlaced timbers soaring to the sky, so that it could not be taken through the gates and brought into the city or protect the people should they receive it with their traditional piety. For if your hands violate this offering to Minerva, then total destruction shall fall upon the empire of Priam and the Trojans (and may the gods rather send that on his own head). But if your hands raise it up into your city, Asia shall come unbidden in a mighty war to the walls of Pelops, and that is the fate in store for our descendants.'

The trap was laid. These were the arts of the liar Sinon, and we believed it all. Cunning and false tears had overcome the men who had not been subdued by Diomede, son of Tydeus, nor Achilles of Larisa, not by ten years of siege nor a thousand ships.

And now there came upon this unhappy people another and yet greater sign, which caused them even greater fear. Their hearts were troubled and they could not see what the future held. Laocoon, the chosen priest of Neptune, was sacrificing a huge bull at the holy altar, when suddenly there came over the calm water from Tenedos (I shudder at the memory of it), two serpents leaning into the sea in great coils and making side by side for the shore. Breasting the waves, they held high their blood-stained crests, and the rest of their bodies ploughed the waves behind them, their backs winding, coil upon measureless coil, through the sounding foam of the sea. Now they were on land. Their eyes were blazing and flecked with blood. They hissed as they licked their lips with quivering tongues. We grew pale at the sight and ran in all directions, but they made straight for Laocoon. First the two serpents seized his two young sons, twining round them both and feeding on their helpless limbs. Then, when Laocoon came to the rescue with his sword in his hand, they seized him and bound him in huge spirals, and soon their scaly backs were entwined twice round his body and twice round his throat, their heads and necks high above him as he struggled to prise open their coils, his priestly ribbons befouled by gore and black venom, and all the time he was raising horrible cries to heaven like the bellowing of a wounded bull shaking the ineffectual axe out of its neck as it flees from the altar. But the two snakes escaped, gliding away to the highest temples of the city and making for the citadel of the heartless Pallas, the Tritonian goddess, where they sheltered under her feet and under the circle of her shield.

At that moment a new fear crept into all their trembling hearts. They said that Laocoon had been justly punished for his crime. He had violated the sacred timbers by hurling his sinful spear into the horse's back, and they all shouted together that it should be taken to a proper place and prayers offered up to the goddess. We breached the walls and laid open the buildings of our city. They all buckled to the task, setting wheels to roll beneath the horse's feet and stretching ropes of flax to its neck. The engine of Fate mounted our walls, teeming with armed men. Unmarried girls and boys sang their hymns around it and rejoiced to have a hand on the rope. On it came, gliding smoothly, looking down on the heart of the city. O my native land! O Ilium, home of the gods! O walls of the people of Dardanus, famous in war! Four times it stopped on the very threshold of the gate, and four times the armour clanged in its womb. But we paid no heed and pressed on blindly, madly, and stood the accursed monster on our consecrated citadel. Even at this last moment Cassandra was still opening her lips to foretell the future, but God had willed that these were lips the Trojans would never believe. This was the last day of a doomed people and we spent it adorning the shrines of the gods all through the city with festal garlands.

Meanwhile the sky was turning and night was rushing up from the Ocean to envelop in its great shadow the earth, the sky and the treachery of the Greeks, while the Trojans were lying quiet in their homes, their weary bodies wrapped in sleep. The Greek fleet in full array was already taking the army from Tenedos through the friendly silence of the moon and making for the shore they knew so well, when the royal flagship raised high the fire signal and Sinon, preserved by the cruelty of the divine Fates, stealthily undid the pine bolts of the horse and freed the Greeks from its womb. The wooden horse was open, and the Greeks were pouring gratefully out of its hollow chambers into the fresh air, the commanders Thessandrus and Sthenelus and fierce Ulixes sliding down the rope they had lowered, and with them Acamas, Thoas, Neoptolemus of the line of Peleus, Machaon, who came out first, Menelaus and Epeos himself, the maker of the horse that tricked the Trojans. They moved into a city buried in wine and sleep, slaying the guards and opening the gates to let in all their waiting comrades and join forces as they had planned.

It was the time when rest, the most grateful gift of the gods, was first beginning to creep over suffering mortals, when Hector suddenly appeared before my eyes in my sleep, full of sorrow and streaming with tears. He looked as he did when he had been dragged behind the chariot, black with dust and caked with blood, his feet swollen where they had been pierced for the leather thongs. What a sight he was! How changed from the Hector who had thrown Trojan fire on to the ships of the Greeks or come back clad in the spoils of Achilles. His beard was filthy, his hair matted with blood, and he had on his body all the wounds he had received around the walls of his native city. In my dream I spoke to him first, forcing out my words, and I too was weeping and full of sorrow: 'O light of Troy, best hope and trust of all Trojans, what has kept you so long from us? Long have we waited for you, Hector. From what shores have you come? With what eyes do we look upon you in our weariness after the death of so many of your countrymen, after all the sufferings of your people and your city? What has so shamefully disfigured the face that was once so serene? What wounds are these I see?'

There was no reply. He paid no heed to my futile questions, but heaved a great groan from the depths of his heart and said: 'You must escape, son of the goddess. You must save yourself from these flames. The enemy is master of the walls and Troy is falling from her highest pinnacle. You have given enough to your native land and to Priam. If any right hand could have saved Troy, mine would have saved it. Into your care she now commends her sacraments and her household gods. Take them to share your fate. Look for a great city to establish for them after long wanderings across the sea.' These were his words, and he brought out in his own hands from her inmost shrine the mighty goddess Vesta with the sacred ribbons on her head and her undying flame.

Meanwhile the city was in utter confusion and despair. Although the house of my father Anchises stood apart and was screened by trees, the noise was beginning to be heard and the din of battle was coming closer and closer. I shook the sleep from me and climbed to the top of the highest gable of the roof, and stood there with my ears pricked up like a shepherd when a furious south wind is carrying fire into a field of grain, or a mountain river whirls along in spate, flattening all the fields, the growing crops and all the labour of oxen, carrying great trees headlong down in its floods while the shepherd stands stupefied on the top of the rock, listening to the sound without knowing what it is. Then in that moment I knew the truth. The treacherous scheming of the Greeks was there to see. Soon the great house of Deiphobus yielded to the flames and fell in ruins. Soon his neighbour Ucalegon was burning and the broad waters of the strait of Sigeum reflected the flames. The clamour of men and the clangour of trumpets rose to high heaven. Mindlessly I put on my armour, for reason had little use for armour, but my heart was burning to gather comrades for battle and rush to the citadel with them. Frenzy and anger drove me on and suddenly it seemed a noble thing to die in arms.

I now caught sight of Panthus, just escaped from the weapons of the Greeks, Panthus, son of Othrys, priest of Apollo and of the citadel. He was carrying in his hands the sacraments and the defeated gods from the temple, and dragging his young grandson along behind him in a mad rush to the door of my father's house. 'Where is our strong-point? Where are we rallying?' I had scarcely time to speak before he replied, groaning: 'The last day has come for the people of Dardanus. This is the hour they cannot escape. The Trojans are no more. Ilium has come to an end and with it the great glory of the race of Teucer. Pitiless Jupiter has given everything over to Argos. The Greeks are masters of the burning city. The horse stands high in the heart of it, pouring out its armed men, and Sinon is in triumph, spreading the flames and gloating over us. The great double gates are open and Greeks are there in their thousands, as many as ever came from great Mycenae. Others have blocked the narrow streets with their weapons levelled. Their lines are drawn up and the naked steel is flashing, ready for slaughter. Only the first few guards on the gates are trying to fight and offering blind resistance.'

I went where I was driven by the words of Panthus and the will of the gods, into the fighting and the flames, where the grim Fury of war called me, where I could hear the din of battle and the shouts rising to heaven. I came across Rhipeus in the moonlight and Epytus, huge in his armour, and they threw in their lot with me. Hypanis and Dymas too came to my side, and so did Coroebus, son of Mygdon. He had happened to come to Troy just in these last few days, burning with mad love for Cassandra, and was fighting as son-in-law on the side of Priam and the Trojans. It was his misfortune not to heed the advice his bride had given him in her prophetic frenzy.

When I saw them standing shoulder to shoulder and spoiling for battle, I addressed them in these words: 'You are the bravest of all our warriors, and your bravery is in vain. If your desire is fixed to follow a man who fights to the end, you see how things stand with us. All the gods on whom this empire once depended have left their shrines and their altars. You are rushing to defend a burning city. Let us die. Let us rush into the thick of the fighting. The one safety for the defeated is to have no hope of safety.'

These words added madness to their courage. From that moment, like wolves foraging blindly on a misty night, driven out of their lairs by a ravening hunger that gives them no rest and leaving their young behind to wait for them with their throats all dry, we ran the gauntlet of the enemy to certain death, holding our course through the middle of the city, with the hollow blackness of dark night hanging over us. Who could unfold the horrors of that night? Who could speak of such slaughter? Who could weep tears to match that suffering? It was the fall of an ancient city that had long ruled an empire. The bodies of the dead lay through all its streets and houses and the sacred shrines of its gods. Nor was it only Trojans who paid their debts in blood; sometimes valour came back even to the hearts of the defeated and Greeks were cut down in their hour of triumph. Bitter grief was everywhere. Everywhere there was fear, and death in many forms.

The first of the Greeks to come to meet us was Androgeos, and he had a large contingent of men with him. Not knowing who we were, but thinking we were allies, he called out first to us: 'Move along there, friends! Why are you so slow? What is keeping you back? The citadel is on fire, and everyone else is pillaging and plundering. Have you just arrived from your tall ships?' He spoke, and when no convincing answer came, he instantly realized that he had fallen amongst enemies. He was stupefied and started backwards without another word. He was like a man going through rough briers who steps on a snake with all his weight without seeing it, and starts back in sudden panic as it raises its wrath and puffs up its blue-green neck: that is how Androgeos recoiled in terror at the sight of us. We fell upon them and surrounded them with a wall of weapons. They did not know the ground, and were stricken with fear, so we cut them down wherever we caught them. Fortune gave us a fair wind for our first efforts, and Coroebus, his spirits raised by our success, cried out: 'Come comrades, let us take the first road Fortune shows us to safety, and go where she shows that she approves. Let us change shields with the Greeks and put on their insignia. Is this treachery or is it courage? Who would ask in dealing with an enemy? The Greeks themselves will provide our armour.'

He spoke, and then put on the plumed helmet of Androgeos and his richly blazoned shield, and buckled the Greek sword to his side. Rhipeus cheerfully followed suit, then Dymas himself and the whole band. Every man armed himself with the spoils he had just taken, and, moving through the city, we mingled with the Greeks and fought many battles under gods not our own, clashing blindly in the night, and many a Greek did we send down to Orcus. Some scattered towards their ships, running for the safety of the shore. Some climbed back in abject fear into the huge horse, and hid themselves in its familiar belly.

But no man can put trust in gods who are opposed to him. Suddenly there was Cassandra, the maiden daughter of Priam, being dragged from the temple of Minerva, from her very sanctuary, with hair streaming and her burning eyes raised in vain to heaven, but only her eyes – they had tied her gentle hands. Coroebus could not endure the sight of this, but a wild frenzy took him and he hurled himself into the middle of the enemy to his death. We all went after him and ran upon their spears where they were thickest. First we were attacked by our own men and overwhelmed by their missiles thrown from the high gable of the temple roof, and the sight of our armour and the confusion caused by our Greek crests brought pitiable slaughter on us. Then the Greeks raised furious alarm at the rescue of Cassandra and gathered from every quarter to attack us, Ajax fiercest of them all, the two sons of Atreus and the whole army of the Dolopians. It was as though a whirlwind had burst and opposing winds were clashing, the west, the south, and the east wind glorying in the horses of the morning, with woods wailing and wild Nereus churning up the sea from its depths. Then also appeared all those Greeks who had been routed by our stratagem in the darkness of the night and scattered through the city. They realized that our shields and weapons were not our own and did not accord with the words on our lips. In an instant they overwhelmed us by the sheer weight of their numbers. Coroebus was the first to die. He fell by the right hand of Peneleus and lay there face down on the altar of Minerva, goddess mighty in arms. Rhipeus also fell. Of all the Trojans he was the most righteous, the greatest lover of justice. But the gods made their own judgements. Hypanis and Dymas were cut down by their fellow-Trojans, and as for you, Panthus, you found as you fell that your great devotion and the ribbon you wore as priest of Apollo were no protection. I call to witness the ashes of Troy. I call upon the flames in which my people died. In the hour of your fall I did not flinch from the weapons of the Greeks or from anything they could do. If it had been my fate to fall, my right hand fully earned it.

From here we were swept along in the fighting, Iphitus and Pelias with me. Iphitus was no longer young, and Pelias had been slowed by a wound he had received from Ulixes. The noise of shouting drew us straight to Priam's palace and there we found the fighting so heavy that it seemed there were no battles anywhere else, that this was the only place in the city where men were dying. We saw Mars, the irresistible God of War, Greeks rushing to the palace, men with shields locked over their backs packing the threshold, ladders hooked to the walls and men struggling to climb them right against the very doorposts, thrusting up their shields on their left arms to protect themselves while their right hands gripped the top of the walls. The Trojans for their part were tearing down their towers and the roofs of all their buildings. They saw the end was near, and these were the weapons they were preparing to defend themselves with in the very moment of death, rolling down on the heads of their enemies the gilded beams and richly ornamented ceilings of their ancestors. Down on the ground others were standing shoulder to shoulder with drawn swords blocking the doorway. My spirit was renewed and I rushed to bring relief to the palace of my king, to help its defenders, to put heart into men who were defeated.

There was a forgotten entrance at the rear, a secret doorway entering into a passage which joined the different parts of Priam's palace. While the kingdom of Troy still stood, poor Andromache often used to come this way unattended to visit Hector's parents, taking her son Astyanax to see his grandfather. I slipped through this door and climbed to the highest gable of the roof, from where the doomed Trojans were vainly hurling missiles. There was a tower rising sheer towards the stars from the top of the palace roof, from which we used to look out over the whole of Troy, the Greek fleet and the camp of the Achaeans. We set about this tower and worked round it with iron bars where there was a join we could open up above the top floor of the palace. Having loosened it from its deep bed in the walls, we rocked it and suddenly sent it toppling, spreading instant destruction and crushing great columns of Greeks. But others still came on and the hail of rocks and other missiles never slackened.

In the portico in front of the palace, on the very threshold, Pyrrhus, son of Achilles, whom men also call Neoptolemus, was rampaging and the light flashed on the bronze of his weapons. He was like a snake which has fed on poisonous herbs and hidden all winter in the cold earth, but now it emerges into the light, casts its slough and is renewed. Glistening with youth, it coils its slithering back and lifts its breast high to the sun with its triple tongue flickering from its mouth. Huge Periphas was with him, and Automedon, the charioteer and armour-bearer of Achilles. With him too were all the young warriors of Scyros coming to attack the palace and throwing firebrands on to the roof. Pyrrhus himself at their head seized a double-headed axe and with it smashed the hard stone of the threshold, wrenching the bronze-plated doorposts from their sockets. He then hacked a panel out of the mighty timbers of the door and broke a gaping hole which gave them a view into the house. There before their eyes were the long colonnades and the inner chambers. There before their eyes was the heart of the palace of Priam and the ancient kings. They saw armed men standing in the doorway, but inside all was confusion and lamentation, and deep into the house the hollow chambers rang with the wailing of women, and their cries rose to strike the golden stars. Frightened mothers were wandering through the great palace, clinging to the doorposts and kissing them. But Pyrrhus pressed on with all the violence of his father Achilles, and no bolts or guards could hold him. The door gave way under repeated battering and the posts he had dislodged from their sockets fell to the ground. Brute force made the breach and the Greeks went storming through, butchering the guards who stood in their way and filling the whole house with soldiers. No river foaming in spate was ever like this, bursting its banks and leaving its channel to overwhelm everything in its path with its swirling current, as it bears down furiously on ploughed fields in a great wave, and cattle and their pens are swept all over the plains. I myself saw Neoptolemus in an orgy of killing and both the sons of Atreus on the threshold. I saw Hecuba with a hundred women, her daughters and the wives of her sons. I saw Priam's blood all over the altar, polluting the flame which he himself had sanctified. Down fell the fifty bedchambers with all the hopes for generations yet to come, and down came the proud doorposts with their spoils of barbaric gold. Everything not claimed by fire was now held by Greeks.

Perhaps you may also ask how Priam died. When he saw the capture and fall of his city, the doors of his palace torn down and his enemy in the innermost sanctuary of his home, although he could achieve nothing, the old man buckled his armour long unused on shoulders trembling with age, girt on his feeble sword and made for the thick of the fight, looking for his death. In the middle of the palace, under the naked vault of heaven, there stood a great altar, and nearby an ancient laurel tree leaning over it and enfolding the household gods in its shade. Here, vainly embracing the images of the gods, Hecuba and her daughters were sitting flocked round the altar, like doves driven down in a black storm. When Hecuba saw that Priam had now put on his youthful armour, 'O my poor husband,' she cried, 'this is madness. Why have you put on this armour? Where can you go? This is not the sort of help we need. You are not the defender we are looking for. Not even my Hector, if he were here now . . . Just come here and sit by me. This altar will protect us all, or you will die with us.' As she spoke she took the old man to her and led him to a place by the holy altar.

Suddenly Polites, one of Priam's sons, came in sight. He had escaped death at the hands of Pyrrhus and now, wounded and with enemy weapons on every side, he was running through the long porticos of the palace and across the empty halls with Pyrrhus behind him in full cry, almost within reach, pressing him hard with his spear and poised to strike. As soon as he reached his father and mother, he fell and vomited his life's blood before their eyes. There was no escape for Priam. Death was now upon him, but he did not check himself or spare the anger in his voice. 'As for you,' he cried, 'and for what you have done, if there is any power in heaven that cares for such things, may the gods pay you well. May they give you the reward you have deserved for making me see my own son dying before my eyes, for defiling a father's face with the murder of his son. You pretend that Achilles was your father, but this is not how Achilles treated his enemy Priam. He had respect for my rights as a suppliant and for the trust I placed in him. He gave me back the bloodless body of Hector for burial and allowed me to return to the city where I was king.' With these words the old man feebly threw his harmless spear. It rattled on the bronze of Pyrrhus' shield and hung there useless sticking on the surface of the central boss. Pyrrhus then made his reply. 'In that case you will be my messenger and go to my father, son of Peleus. Let him know about my wicked deeds and do not forget to tell him about the degeneracy of his son Neoptolemus. Now, die.' As he spoke the word, he was dragging Priam to the very altar, his body trembling as it slithered through pools of his son's blood. Winding Priam's hair in his left hand, in his right he raised his sword with a flash of light and buried it to the hilt in Priam's side.

So ended the destiny of Priam. This was the death that fell to his lot. He who had once been the proud ruler over so many lands and peoples of Asia died with Troy ablaze before his eyes and the citadel of Pergamum in ruins. His mighty trunk lay upon the shore, the head hacked from the shoulders, a corpse without a name.

Then for the first time I knew the horror that was all about me. What was I to do? There came into my mind the image of my own dear father, as I looked at the king who was his equal in age breathing out his life with that cruel wound. There came into my mind also my wife Creusa whom I had left behind, the plundering of my home and the fate of young Iulus. I turned to look at the men fighting by my side. Exhausted, they had all deserted me and thrown themselves from the roof or given their suffering bodies to the flames.

Now that I was alone, I caught sight of Helen keeping watch on the doors of the temple of Vesta where she was staying quietly in hiding. The fires gave a bright light and I was gazing all around me wherever I went. This Helen, this Fury sent to be the scourge both of Troy and of her native Greece, was afraid of the Trojans, who hated her for the overthrow of their city. She was afraid the Greeks would punish her and afraid of the wrath of the husband she had deserted, so, hated by all, she had gone into hiding and was sitting there at the altar. The passion flared in my heart and I longed in my anger to avenge my country even as it fell and to exact the penalty for her crimes. 'So this woman will live to set eyes on Sparta and her native Mycenae again, and walk as queen in the triumph she has won? Will she see her husband, her father's home and her children and be attended by women of Troy and Phrygian slaves, while Priam lies dead by the sword, Troy has been put to the flames and the shores of the land of Dardanus have sweated so much blood? This will not be. Although there is no fame worth remembering to be won by punishing a woman and such a victory wins no

praise, nevertheless I *shall* win praise for blotting out this evil
and exacting a punishment which is richly deserved. I shall
also take pleasure in feeding the flames of vengeance and
appeasing the ashes of my people.'

As I ran towards her ranting and raving, my loving mother
suddenly appeared before my eyes. I had never before seen
her so clearly, shining in perfect radiance through the darkness of the night. She revealed herself as a goddess as the
gods in heaven see her, in all her majesty of form and stature.
As she caught my right hand and held me back, she opened
her rosy lips and spoke to me – 'O my son, what bitterness
can have been enough to stir this wild anger in you? Why this
raging passion? Where is all the love you used to have for
me? Will you not first go and see where you have left your
father, crippled with age, and find whether your wife Creusa
is still alive, and your son Ascanius? The whole Greek army
is prowling all around them and they would have been carried
off by the flames or slashed by the swords of the enemy if my
loving care were not defending them. It is not the hated beauty
of the Spartan woman, the daughter of Tyndareus, that is
overthrowing all this wealth and laying low the topmost
towers of Troy, nor is it Paris although you all blame him, it
is the gods, the cruelty of the gods. Look, for I shall tear away
from all around you the dank cloud that veils your eyes and
dulls your mortal vision. You are my son, do not be afraid to
do what I command you, and do not disobey me. Here where
you see shattered masonry, stone torn from stone, and waves
of dust-laden smoke, Neptune has loosened the foundations
with his great trident and is shaking the walls, tearing up
your whole city from the place where it is set. Here too is
Juno, cruellest of all, the first to seize the Scaean Gate, standing
there sword in hand, and furiously calling up the supporting
columns from the ships. Now look behind you, Tritonian
Pallas is already sitting on top of your citadel shining out of
the cloud with her terrible Gorgon, while the Father of the

Gods himself puts heart into the Greeks and gives them strength. It is Jupiter himself who is rousing the gods against the armies of Troy. Escape, my son, escape with all haste. Put an end to your struggle, I shall not leave your side till I see you safely standing on the threshold of your father's door.' She finished speaking and melted into the dense shadows of that night, and there before my eyes I saw the dreadful vision of the gods in all their might, the enemies of Troy.

At that moment I seemed to see the whole of Ilium settling into the flames and Neptune's Troy toppling over from its foundations like an ancient ash tree high in the mountains which farmers have hacked with blow upon blow of their double axes, labouring to fell it; again and again it threatens to fall, its foliage shudders and its head trembles and nods until at last it succumbs to its wounds and breaks with a dying groan, spreading ruin along the ridge. I came down from the roof and with the god to lead me a way opened through fire and sword. The weapons parted and the flames drew back before me.

When at last I had reached the door of my father's house and our ancient home, my first wish was to find my father and take him into the high mountains, but he refused to go on living now that Troy had been levelled to the earth. He would not hear of exile, but cried: 'Those of you with young blood still thick in your veins, those of you whose strength is sound and unimpaired, you are the ones who must busy yourselves with escaping. If the gods in heaven had wished me to go on living, they would have preserved this place for me. I have already seen one sack of the city and survived its capture, and that is more than enough. Here I lie and here I stay. Take your farewells and leave me. My own right hand will earn me my death. The enemy will take pity on me. They will be looking for spoils. I shall have no tomb, but that is an easy loss to bear. For long years, ever since the Father of the

Gods and King of Men blew the wind of his thunderbolt upon me and touched me with its fire, I have been lingering here hated by the gods and useless to men.'

As he said these words he stood there rooted and no power could move him. Streaming with tears, my wife Creusa, Ascanius, all of us begged him not to bring everything down on his own head: when Fate batters a house, the father should not add his weight to the blows. But he still refused. He stood by his decision and stayed where he was. I rushed to take up arms again in complete despair. Death was the only thing I could hope for. What course could I follow? What fate was in store for us? 'Did you think I could run away and leave my father here?' I exclaimed. 'How did such a sacrilege escape my father's lips? If the gods above decree that nothing of this great city is to survive, if your mind is fixed and it is your pleasure to add yourself and those you love to the destruction of the city, the door is open and the deaths you want will come. Pyrrhus will soon be here, soaked in the blood of Priam. He is the one who murders the son before the face of the father, and the father at the altar. O my loving mother, is this why you took me through fire and sword, so that I could see my enemy in the innermost sanctuary of my home, and Ascanius and my father and my wife Creusa with them lying sacrificed in each other's blood? Bring me my armour, comrades. Bring it here. This is the last light we shall see and it is calling the defeated. Give me back to the Greeks. Let me go back and rejoin the battle. Today we die. But not all of us shall die unavenged.'

I buckled on my sword again and was fixing my left arm into the shield. But as I was leaving Creusa suddenly threw herself at my feet in the doorway and held me, stretching out our little son Iulus towards me. 'If you are going to your death,' she cried, 'take us with you to share your fate, whatever it is. But if you have reason to put any hope in arms, your first duty is to guard this house. If you leave us here, what fate is waiting for little Iulus, for your father and for the woman who used to be called your wife?'

Her cries of anguish were filling the whole house, when suddenly there was a great miracle. At the very moment when we were both holding Iulus and he was there between our sorrowing faces, a light began to stream from the top of the pointed cap he was wearing and the flame seemed to lick his soft hair and feed round his forehead without harming him. We took fright and rushed to beat out the flames in his hair and quench the holy fire with water, but Father Anchises, looking joyfully up to the stars of heaven and raising his hands palms upward, lifted his voice in prayer: 'O All-powerful Jupiter, if ever you yield to prayers, look down upon us, that is all we ask, and if we deserve anything for our devotion, give us help at last, Father Jupiter, and confirm this omen.'

Scarcely had he spoken when a sudden peal of thunder rang out on the left and a star fell from the sky, trailing a great torch of light in its course through the darkness. We watched it glide over the topmost pinnacles of the house and bury itself, still bright, in the woods of Mount Ida, leaving its path marked out behind it, a broad furrow of light, and the whole place smoked all around with sulphur. Now at last my father was truly convinced. He rose up and addressed the gods, praying to the sacred star: 'There is now no more delay. Now I follow, O gods of my fathers. Wherever you lead, there am I. Preserve this house. Preserve my grandson. This is your sign. Troy is in your mighty hands. Anchises yields. I am willing to go with you, my son, and be your companion.'

He had spoken. The noise of the fires was growing louder and louder through the city and the tide of flame was rolling nearer. 'Come then, dear father, up on my back. I shall take you on my shoulders. Your weight will be nothing to me. Whatever may come, danger or safety, it will be the same for

both of us. Young Iulus can walk by my side and my wife can
follow in my footsteps at a distance. And you, the slaves of
our house, must pay attention to what I am saying. As you
leave the city there is a mound with a lonely old temple of
Ceres. Near it is an ancient cypress preserved and revered for
many long years by our ancestors. We shall go to that one
place by different routes. You father, take in your arms the
sacraments and the ancestral gods of our home. I am fresh
from all the fighting and killing and it is not right for me to
touch them till I have washed in a running stream.'

When I had finished speaking, I put on a tawny lion's skin
as a covering for my neck and the breadth of my shoulders
and then I bowed down and took up my burden. Little Iulus
twined his fingers in my right hand and kept up with me with
his short steps. Creusa walked behind us and we moved
along, keeping to the shadows. This was the man who had
been unmoved by all the missiles of the Greeks and had long
faced their serried ranks without a tremor, but now every
breath of wind frightened me and I started at every sound, so
anxious was I, so afraid both for the man I carried and for the
child at my side.

I was now coming near the gates and it seemed that our
journey was nearly over and we had escaped, when I suddenly
thought I heard the sound of many marching feet and my
father looking out through the darkness cried: 'Run, my son,
run. They are coming this way. I can see the flames reflected
on their shields and the bronze glinting.' At that moment
some hostile power confused me and robbed me of my wits.
I ran where there was no road, leaving the familiar area of the
streets. Then it was that my wife Creusa was torn from me by
the cruelty of Fate – whether she stopped or lost her way or
sat down exhausted, no one can tell. I never saw her again.
Nor did I look behind me or think of her or realize that she
was lost till we arrived at the mound and the ancient sanctuary
of Ceres. But when at last everyone had gathered there, she

was the only one who was not with us and neither her companions nor her son nor her husband knew how she had been lost. I stormed and raged and blamed every god and man that ever was. This was the cruellest thing I saw in all the sack of the city. Leaving Ascanius, my father and the gods of Troy with my companions and hiding them all away in a winding valley, I put on my flashing armour and went back to the city, resolved to face all its dangers again, to go back through the whole of Troy and once more put my life at peril. First I went back to the walls and the dark gateway by which I had left the city. I found my route and retraced it, gazing all around me through the darkness. Horror was everywhere and the very silence chilled the blood. Then I went on to our house, thinking it was possible, just possible, that she had gone there. The Greeks had come flooding in and were everywhere. Consuming flames, fanned by the winds, were soon rolling to the top of the roof and leaping above it as their hot breath raged at the sky. From there I went on to Priam's palace and the citadel where Phoenix and the terrible Ulixes, who had been chosen to keep watch, were already guarding the loot in the empty porticos of the shrine of Juno. Here Greeks were piling up the treasures of Troy, pillaged from all the burning temples – the tables of the gods, mixing bowls of solid gold and all the robes they had plundered. Children and frightened mothers stood around in long lines. I even dared to call her name into the darkness, filling the streets with my shouts. Grief-stricken I called her name 'Creusa! Creusa!' again and again, but there was no answer. I would not give up the search but was still rushing around the houses of the city when her likeness appeared in sorrow before my eyes, her very ghost, but larger than she was in life. I was paralysed. My hair stood on end. My voice stuck in my throat. Then she spoke to me and comforted my sorrow with these words: 'O husband that I love, why do you choose to give yourself to such wild grief? These things do not happen without the approval of the gods.

It is not their will that Creusa should go with you when you leave this place. The King of High Olympus does not allow it. Before you lies a long exile and a vast expanse of sea to plough before you come to the land of Hesperia where the Lydian river Thybris flows with smooth advance through a rich land of brave warriors. There prosperity is waiting for you, and a kingdom and a royal bride. Wipe away the tears you are shedding for Creusa whom you loved. I shall not have to see the proud palaces of the Myrmidons and Dolopians. I am a daughter of Dardanus and my husband was the son of Venus, and I shall never go to be a slave to any matron of Greece. The Great Mother of the Gods keeps me here in this land of Troy. Now fare you well. Do not fail in your love for our son.'

She spoke and faded into the insubstantial air, leaving me there in tears and longing to reply. Three times I tried to put my arms around her neck. Three times her phantom melted in my arms, as weightless as the wind, as light as the flight of sleep.

By now the night was over. I returned to my comrades without her. Here I found that new companions had streamed in and I was amazed at the numbers of them, men and women, an army collected for exile, a pitiable crowd. They had come from all directions ready to follow me with all their resources and all their hearts to whatever land I should wish to lead them. And now Lucifer was rising above the ridges of Mount Ida and bringing on the day. The Greeks were on guard at the gates and there was no hope of helping the city. I yielded. I lifted up my father and set out for the mountains.

○β 3 ຊ

THE WANDERINGS

When the gods had seen fit to lay low the power of Asia and
the innocent people of Priam, when proud Ilium had fallen
and all Neptune's Troy lay smoking on the ground, we were
driven by signs from heaven into distant exile to look for a
home in some deserted land. There, hard by Antandros under
the Phrygian mountain range of Ida, we were mustering men
and building a fleet without knowing where the Fates were
leading us or where we would be allowed to settle. The
summer had barely started and Father Anchises was bidding
us hoist sail and put ourselves in the hands of the Fates. I
wept as I left the shores of my native land and her harbours
and the plains where once had stood the city of Troy. I was
an exile taking to the high seas with my comrades and my
son, with the gods of our house and the great gods of our
people.

At some distance from Troy lay the land of Mars, a land of
vast plains farmed by Thracians, once ruled by the savage
Lycurgus. This people had ancient ties with Troy, while the
fortunes of Troy remained, and our household gods were
linked in alliance. Here I sailed, and using the name Aeneadae,
formed after my own, I laid out my first walls on the curved
shore. But the Fates frowned on these beginnings. I was worshipping my mother Venus, the daughter of Dione, and the
gods who preside over new undertakings, and sacrificing a
gleaming white bull to the Most High King of the Heavenly

54

Gods. Close by there happened to be a mound on top of which there grew a thicket bristling with spears of cornel and myrtle wood. I had gone there and was beginning to pull green shoots out of the ground to cover the altar with leafy branches, when I saw a strange and horrible sight. As soon as I broke the roots of a tree and was pulling it out of the ground, dark gouts of blood dripped from it and stained the earth with gore. The horror of it chilled me to the bone, I trembled and my blood congealed with fear.

I went on, pulling up more tough shoots from another tree, searching for the cause, however deep it might lie, and the dark blood flowed from the bark of this second tree. With my mind in turmoil I began to pray to the country nymphs and to Father Mars Gradivus who rules over the fields of the Getae, begging them to turn what I was seeing to good and to make the omen blessed, but after I had set about the spear-like shoots of a third shrub with greater vigour and was on my knees struggling to free it from the sandy soil (shall I speak? Or shall I be silent?) I heard a heart-rending groan emerge from deep in the mound and a voice rose into the air: 'Why do you tear my poor flesh, Aeneas?' it cried. 'Take pity now on the man who is buried here and do not pollute your righteous hands. I am no stranger to you. It was Troy that bore me and this is no tree that is oozing blood. Escape, I beg you, from these cruel shores, from this land of greed. It is Polydorus that speaks. This is where I was struck down and an iron crop of weapons covered my body. Their sharp points have rooted and grown in my flesh.' At this, fear and doubt oppressed me. My hair stood on end with horror and the voice stuck in my throat.

This was the Polydorus the doomed Priam had once sent in secret with a great mass of gold, to be brought up by the king of Thrace, when at last he was losing faith in the arms of Troy and saw his city surrounded by besiegers. When Fortune deserted the Trojans and their wealth was in ruins, the king went over to the side of the victors and joined the armies of Agamemnon. Breaking all the laws of God, he murdered Polydorus and seized the gold. Greed for gold is a curse. There is nothing to which it does not drive the minds of men. When the fear had left my bones, I told the chosen leaders of the people and first of all my father about this portent sent by the gods and asked what should be done. They were of one mind. We must leave this accursed land where the laws of hospitality had been violated and let our ships run before the wind. So we gave Polydorus a second burial, heaping the earth high in a mound and raising to his shade an altar dark with funeral wreaths and black cypress, while the women of Troy stood all around with their hair unbound in mourning. With offerings of foaming cups of warm milk and bowls of sacrificial blood we committed his soul to the grave and lifted up our voices to call his name for the last time.

Then as soon as we could trust ourselves to the waves, when the winds had calmed the swell and a gentle breeze was rattling the rigging to call us out to sea, my comrades drew the ships down to the water and crowded the shore. We sailed out of the harbour, and the land and its cities soon fell away behind us. In the middle of the ocean lies a beautiful island dear to Aegean Neptune and the mother of the Nereids. It used to float from shore to shore until in gratitude the Archer God Apollo moored it to Gyaros and high Myconos, allowing it to stand firm and be inhabited and mock the winds. Here I sailed, and in this peaceful haven of Delos we came safe to land, weary from the sea. We went ashore and were admiring Apollo's city when its king Anius, king of men and priest of the god, came to meet us, his forehead garlanded with ribbons and the sacred laurel. Recognizing Anchises as an old friend, he gave us his hand in hospitality and we entered his house.

There I gazed in reverence at the god's temple built high of ancient stone and made this prayer to Apollo: 'O god of Thymbra, grant us a home of our own. We are weary. Grant us walls and descendants and a city that will endure. Preserve these remnants that have escaped the Greeks and pitiless Achilles, to be a second citadel for Troy. Whom are we to follow? Where do you bid us go? Where are we to settle? Send us a sign, O Father, and steal into our hearts.'

I had scarcely spoken when everything seemed to begin to tremble. The threshold of the doors of the god, his laurel tree, and all the mountain round about were shaken. The sanctuary opened and a bellowing came from the bowl on the sacred tripod. We threw ourselves to the ground and these were the words that came to our ears: 'O much-enduring sons of Dardanus, the land which first bore you from your parents' stock will be the land that will take you back to her rich breast. Seek out your ancient mother. For that is where the house of Aeneas and his sons' sons and their sons after them will rule over the whole earth.'

So spoke Phoebus Apollo, and a great joy and tumult arose among us, all asking what city this was, where Apollo was directing us in our wanderings, what this land was to which we were to return. Then spoke my father Anchises who had been turning over in his mind what he had heard from the men of old: 'Listen,' he said, 'you leaders of Troy, and learn what you have to hope for. In the middle of the ocean lies Crete, the island of great Jupiter, where there is a Mount Ida, the cradle of our race, and where the Cretans live in a hundred great cities, the richest of kingdoms. If I remember rightly what I have heard, our first father Teucer sailed from there to Asia, landing at Cape Rhoeteum, and chose that place to found his kingdom. Troy was not yet standing, nor was the citadel of Pergamum, and they lived low down in the valleys. This is the origin of the Great Mother of Mount Cybele, the bronze cymbals of the Corybants, our grove of Ida, the inviolate silence of our worship and the yoked lions that draw the chariot of the mighty goddess. Come then, let us follow where we are led by the bidding of the gods. Let us appease the winds and set forth for the kingdoms of Cnossus. It is not far to sail. If only Jupiter is with us, the third day will see our ships on the shores of Crete.' So he spoke, and made due sacrifice on the altars, a bull to Neptune and a bull to fair Apollo, a black lamb to the storms and a white lamb to favouring breezes.

Rumour as she flew told the tale of the great Idomeneus, how he had been forced to leave his father's kingdom and how the shores of Crete were now deserted. Here was a place empty of our enemies, their homes abandoned, waiting for us. We left the harbour of Ortygia and flew over the sea to Naxos where Bacchants dance on the mountain ridges and to green Donusa, to Olearos, to Paros marble-white and the Cyclades scattered on the face of the sea, skimming over an ocean churned up by the coasts of a hundred islands. The sailors raised all manner of shouts as they vied with one another in their rowing and my comrades kept urging me to make for Crete and go back to the home of their ancestors. The wind rising astern sped us on our way and we came to shore at last on the ancient land of the Curetes. Impatiently I set to work on walls for the city we all longed for. I called it Pergamea and the people rejoiced in the name. I urged them to love their hearths and homes and raise a citadel to protect them.

Our ships were soon drawn up on dry land, our young men were busy with marrying and putting new land under plough and I was giving them homes and laws to live by, when suddenly from a polluted quarter of the sky there came a cruel, suppurating plague upon our bodies and upon the trees and crops. It was a time of death. Men were losing the lives they loved or dragging around their sickly bodies. The Dogstar burned the fields and made them barren, the grass dried, the crops were infected and gave us no food. My father bade me retrace our course back across the sea to Phoebus Apollo and his oracle at Ortygia, to pray for his gracious favour and ask when he would put an end to our toil, where we were to look for help in our adversity and what course we were to steer.

It was night and sleep held in its grasp all living things upon the earth. There as I lay, the holy images of the gods, the Phrygian Penates whom I had rescued from the thick of the flames of the burning city of Troy, seemed to be standing bathed in clear light before my eyes, where the full moon streamed in through the unshuttered windows. At last they spoke to me and comforted my sorrow with these words: 'Apollo here speaks the prophecy he will give you if you sail back to Ortygia. By his own will he has sent us here and we stand at your door. We followed you and your arms when Troy was burned to ashes. With you to lead us we have sailed across unmeasured tracts of swelling seas, and in time to come we shall raise your sons to the stars and give dominion to your city. Your task is to build great walls to guard this great inheritance. You must never flag in the long toil of exile, and you must leave this place. Delian Apollo did not send you to these shores. Crete is not where he commanded you to settle. There is a place – Greeks call it Hesperia – an ancient land, strong in arms and in the richness of her soil. The Oenotrians lived there, but the descendants of that race are now said to have taken the name of their king Italus and call themselves Italians. This is our true home. This is where Dardanus sprang from and his father Iasius from whom our race took its beginning. Rise then with cheerful heart and pass on these words to Anchises your father, and let him be in no doubt. He must look for Corythus and the lands of Ausonia. Jupiter forbids you the Dictaean fields of Crete.'

I was astounded by this vision and by the words of the gods. This was no sleep. I seemed to be face to face with them and to recognize their features and the garlands on their heads, and at the sight my whole body was bathed in cold sweat. Leaping from my bed, I raised my hands palms upward to the sky and lifted up my voice in prayer, making pure offerings at the hearth. Having performed these rites, I went with joyful heart to Anchises and told him everything in order. He remembered that our race had two founders, Dardanus and Teucer, a double ancestry. He realized that he had fallen into a new mistake about these ancient places. 'O my son,' he said, 'you who have been so tested by the Fates of Troy, only Cassandra made such a prophecy to me. Now I remember how she used to foretell that this is what Fate had in store for us and she kept talking about Hesperia and about the kingdoms of Italy. But who would have believed that Trojans would land on the shores of Hesperia? Who in those days would have believed the prophecies of Cassandra? Let us yield to Phoebus Apollo. We have been advised. Let us follow the better course.' We all accepted his command with cries of joy and abandoned this second settlement, leaving only a few of our number behind, and set sail upon our hollow ships to run before the wind over the vast ocean.

When we were out at sea and no longer in sight of land, and all around was sky and all around was sea, I saw a dark cloud come over our heads bringing storm and black night, and the waves shivered in the darkness. The wind soon whipped up a great swell and the storm rose and scattered us all over the ocean. A pall of cloud obscured the light, rain fell from a sky we could not see, and lightning tore the clouds, flash upon flash. We were thrown off course and drifted blindly in the waves. Under that sky even Palinurus said he had lost his bearings in mid-ocean and could not tell day from night. For three long days, if days they were, of darkness, and three starless nights we ran before the storm, until at last on the fourth day we saw the first land rising before us and there opened a clear view of distant mountains and curling smoke. Down came the sails and we sprang to the oars. The sailors were not slow to sweep the blue sea and churn it into foam. I was saved from the ocean and the shores of the Strophades were the first to receive me.

This is the Greek name for islands in the great Ionian sea. This is where the deadly Celaeno and the other Harpies have lived ever since the house of Phineus was barred to them and they were frightened away from the tables where they used to feed. These are the vilest of all monsters. No plague or visitation of the gods sent up from the waves of the river Styx has ever been worse than these. They are birds with the faces of girls, with filth oozing from their bellies, with hooked claws for hands and faces pale with a hunger that is never satisfied.

As soon as we reached the Strophades and entered the harbour, there we saw on every side rich herds of cattle on the level ground and flocks of goats unguarded on the grass. We drew our swords and rushed upon them, calling on the gods and on Jupiter himself to share our plunder. Then we raised couches along the shore of the bay and were feasting on this rich fare when suddenly the Harpies were among us swooping down from the mountains with a fearful clangour of their wings, tearing the food to pieces and polluting everything with their foul contagion. The stench was rank, and through all this we heard their hideous screeching. Once again, in a sheltered spot far back under an overhanging rock, we relaid our tables and relit the altar fires. Once again the noisy flock came from some hidden roost in a different quarter of the sky and fluttered round their prey, clutching it in their hooked claws and fouling it in their mouths. Then it was I ordered my men to arm themselves to make war against this fearsome tribe. They did as ordered, hiding swords and shields here and there in the grass. And so when Misenus in his high lookout heard the sound of them swooping down along the whole curved shore of the bay, he raised the alarm by blowing on the hollow bronze of his trumpet and my comrades attacked. This was a new kind of battle – swords against filthy sea birds. But these were feathers that felt no violence and backs that could receive no wounds. They soared in swift flight up towards the stars, leaving behind them the half-eaten food and their filthy droppings, all but one who remained, perched high on a pinnacle of rock (Celaeno was her name), and from her breast there burst this dire prophecy: 'Is it war you offer us now, sons of Laomedon, for the slaughter of our bullocks and the felling of our oxen? Is it your plan to make war against the innocent Harpies and drive us from the kingdom of our ancestors? Listen to what I have to say and fix it in your minds. These words were spoken by the Almighty Father of the Gods to Phoebus Apollo, and Phoebus Apollo spoke them to me, and now I, the greatest of the Furies, speak them to you. You are calling upon the winds and trying to sail to Italy. To Italy you will go and you will be allowed to enter its harbours, but you will not be given a city, and you will not be allowed to build walls around it before a deadly famine has come upon you, and the guilt of our blood drives you to gnaw round the edges of your tables, to put them between your teeth and eat them.'

With these words she rose on her wings and flew into the forest. In that instant the blood of my comrades was congealed with fear. Their spirits fell and they lost all stomach for fight, telling me to plead and pray to the creatures for peace, whether they were goddesses or foul and deadly birds. Then Father Anchises stood on the shore and raised his hands palms upward to heaven, calling upon the great gods and pledging to pay them all the honours that were their due. 'O you gods,' he cried, 'let not this threat be fulfilled. O gods, turn away this fate from us and graciously preserve your devoted people.' He then gave orders to pull in the cables, undo the sail-ropes and let them run. The south wind filled the canvas, and wind and helmsman each set the same course for us as we flew over the foaming waves. Soon there appeared in mid-ocean the woods of Zacynthus, and Dulichium, Same and the stone cliffs of Neritos. We raced away from the rocks of Ithaca, the kingdom of Laertes, and cursed the land that had nurtured the villain Ulixes. In no time there rose before us the cloudy cap of Mount Leucas and Apollo's temple, the terror of sailors. Being weary we set course for it and came to land at the little city. The anchors ran out from the prows and our ships stood to the shore.

So at last our feet were on dry land again – more than we had dared to hope for. We performed rites of purification to Jupiter and lit altar fires in fulfilment of our vows, crowding the shores of Actium with our Trojan games. My comrades stripped and made their bodies slippery with oil and wrestled in the style of their fathers, as we celebrated our escape and safe voyage past so many Greek cities, right through the middle of our enemies.

In due course the sun rolled on round the great circle of the year. Icy winter came and the north winds were roughening the seas. I then took a concave shield of bronze, the armour once carried by great Abas, and nailed it on the doors of the temple where all could see, proclaiming the dedication of it with this inscription:

AENEAS DEDICATES THESE ARMS
TAKEN FROM THE CONQUERING GREEKS

Then I gave orders to leave port and told the rowers to sit to their benches. They vied with one another to strike the sea and sweep the surface of it with their oars. We had soon put the cloud-capped citadels of Phaeacia down below the horizon and we coasted along Epirus until we entered the harbour of Chaonia and then walked up to the lofty city of Buthrotum.

Here there came to our ears a story almost beyond belief, that Helenus, a son of Priam, was king over these Greek cities of Epirus, having succeeded to the throne and the bed of Pyrrhus, son of Achilles and descendant of Aeacus. Andromache, once wife of Hector, had for a second time taken a husband from her own people. I was astounded and the heart within me burned with love for the man and longing to meet him and find out about these great events. I was walking away from the harbour leaving ships and shore behind me when I caught sight of Andromache, offering a ritual meal and performing rites to the dead in a grove in front of a city on the banks of a river Simois, but not the true Simois of Troy. She was pouring a libation to the ashes of her husband Hector, calling on his shade to come to the empty tomb, a mound of green grass on which she had consecrated two altars. There she used to go and weep. When she saw me approaching with armed Trojans all about me, she was beside herself, numb with fear the moment she saw this great miracle, and the warmth of life went out of her bones. She fainted, and only after a long time was she at last able to speak to me: 'Is this a true vision? Is it a true messenger that comes to me, son of the goddess? Are you alive? If the light of life has left you, why are you here? Where is Hector?' As she spoke she burst into tears and her cries filled all the grove. I could hardly find an answer to these wild words, but stammered a few broken phrases. 'I am indeed alive. After all that has happened I still go on living. Do not doubt it. What you see is true. But tell me, what fate has overtaken you since you were deprived of such a husband? What has fallen to the lot of Hector's Andromache? Are you still the wife of Pyrrhus?'

She answered, and her voice was low and her eyes downcast: 'The happiest of all Trojan women was the virgin daughter of Priam who was made to die by the tomb of her enemy Achilles under the high walls of Troy. Polyxena did not have to endure the casting of lots or live to be the slave of a conqueror and lie in a master's bed! But we saw our home burned and sailed over many seas. We submitted to the arrogance of the house of Achilles and the insolence of his son and bore him a child in slavery. In due course he turned his attention to marrying a Spartan, Hermione, granddaughter of

Leda, giving his slave Andromache over to his slave Helenus.
But Orestes loved Hermione and had hoped to marry her.
Incensed at losing her and driven on by the madness brought
upon him by his own crimes, he caught Pyrrhus where
Pyrrhus least expected him and slaughtered him on the altar
he had raised to his father Achilles. At his death some of
the kingdom he had ruled over came into the possession of
Helenus, who then called the plains the Chaonian plains and
the whole district Chaonia after Chaon of Troy. He then built
a Pergamum, this Trojan citadel on the ridge. But what winds
and what fates have given you passage here? Is it some god
that has driven you to these shores that you did not know
were ours? What about your boy Ascanius? Is he alive and
breathing the air? If he were with you now in Troy ... But
does he ever think of the mother he has lost? Does the old
courage and manliness ever rise in him at the thought of his
father Aeneas and his uncle Hector?'

She was weeping her useless tears and sobbing bitterly as
these words poured from her when the hero Helenus, son of
Priam, arrived from the walls of the city with a great escort.
He recognized his own people and took us gladly to his home.
He too was weeping and could speak only a few broken words
to us between his tears. As I walked I recognized a little Troy,
a citadel modelled on great Pergamum and a dried-up stream
they called the Xanthus. There was the Scaean Gate and I
embraced it. Nor were my Trojans slow to enjoy this Trojan
city with me. The king received them in a broad colonnade
and in the middle of the courtyard they poured libations of
the wine of Bacchus and fed off golden dishes and every man
had a goblet in his hand.

Day after day wore on with breezes tempting our sails and
the canvas filling and swelling in the south wind, until I went
to the prophet Helenus with this request: 'You are Trojan
born. You can read the signs sent by the gods. You understand
the will of Phoebus Apollo of Claros, his tripods and his

laurels. You know the meaning of the stars, the cries of birds and the omens of their flight. Come tell me – for every sign I have received from heaven has spoken in favour of this journey, and I am persuaded by all the divine powers to set course for Italy and try to find that distant land. Only the Harpy Celaeno has prophesied a strange and monstrous portent, threatening us with her deadly anger and all the horrors of famine – come tell me now, what dangers am I to avoid as I start upon this journey? And as it goes on, what must I do to overcome such adversities?'

Before replying Helenus first performed a ritual slaughter of bullocks and asked for the blessing of the gods. He then loosened the ribbons from his consecrated head, and taking my hand, he led me in anxious expectation into the mighty presence of the god. In due course he spoke as priest and this was the prophecy that came from his hallowed lips. 'O son of the goddess, the proof is full and clear that the highest auspices favour your voyage. This is the fate allotted to you by the King of the Gods. This is how your fortune rolls and this is the order of its turning. My words will tell you a small part of all there is to know so that you may trust yourself more safely to cross the seas that are waiting to receive you, and come to harbour in Ausonia. The Fates do not allow Helenus to know the rest and Saturnian Juno forbids it to be spoken. First, you are wrong to imagine that it is a short voyage to Italy and that there are harbours close at hand for you to enter. Far and pathless are the ways that lie between you and that far distant land. You must first bend the oar in the waves of Sicilian seas, then cross the ocean of Ausonia and the lakes of the underworld, and pass Aeaea, the island of Circe, before you can come to the land which will be safe for the founding of your city. I shall give you a sign and you must keep it deep within your heart: when in an hour of perplexity by the flowing waters of a lonely river you find under some holm-oaks on the shore a great sow with the litter of thirty piglets she has farrowed, lying there on her side all white, with her young all white around her udders, that will be the place for your city. There you will find the rest ordained for all your labours. Nor is there any need for you to shudder at the thought of eating your tables. The Fates will find a way. Call upon Apollo and he will come. But you must quickly leave this land of ours and keep well clear of the shore of Italy that lies nearest us bathed by the tide of our sea, for hostile Greeks live in all these cities. Here Locrians from Narycum have built their walls and the army of the Cretan Idomeneus of Lyctos has seized the Sallentine plains in Calabria. Here too is the little town of Petelia perching on the wall built for it by Philoctetes, leader of the Meliboeans. And when you have passed all these and your ships are moored across the sea, when you have raised altars on the shore to fulfil your vows, do not forget to veil your head in purple cloth so that when the altar fires are burning to honour the gods, no enemy presence can intrude and spoil the omens. Your comrades and you yourself must keep this mode of sacrifice and your descendants must maintain this purity of worship for ever.

'But when you sail on and the wind carries you near the shore of Sicily, and the close-set barriers of Pelorus open before you, make for the land to the south and the sea to the south, taking the long way round Sicily and keeping well clear of the breakers on the coast to starboard. Men say these lands were originally one but were long ago convulsed by some great upheaval and torn apart. Such changes can occur in the long ageing of time. The waves of the sea burst in between them and cut Sicily loose from the flank of the land of Hesperia, putting coastlines between their fields and cities and flowing in between them in a narrow tide. On your right waits Scylla in ambush and on your left the insatiable Charybdis. Three times a day with the deep vortex of her whirlpool Charybdis sucks great waves into the abyss and then throws them upwards again to lash the stars. But Scylla lurks in the dark recesses of her cave and shoots out her mouths to seize ships and drag them on to the rocks. She has a human face and as far as the groin she is a girl with lovely breasts, but below she is a monstrous sea creature, her womb full of wolves, each with a dolphin's tail. It is better to lose time by taking the long course round Cape Pachynus rather than set eyes on the hideous Scylla deep in her cave or see those rocks loud with the barking of dogs as blue as the sea.

'One thing more: if the prophet Helenus has any insight into the future, if there is any reason to believe what I say, if Apollo fills my mind with the truth, there is one prophecy I shall make to you above all others, one counsel I shall repeat to you again and again – worship the godhead of great Juno first and foremost in your prayers, of your own free will submit your vows to Juno and win over the mighty Queen of Heaven with your offerings as you pray. If you do this you will at last leave Sicily behind you and succeed in reaching the shores of Italy. When you have landed and come to the city of Cumae and the sacred lakes of Avernus among their sounding forests, there deep in a cave in the rock you will see a virgin priestess foretelling the future in prophetic frenzy by writing signs and names on leaves. After she has written her prophecies on these leaves she seals them all up in her cave where they stay in their appointed order. But the leaves are so light that when the door turns in its sockets the slightest breath of wind dislodges them. The draught from the door throws them into confusion and the priestess never makes it her concern to catch them as they flutter round her rocky cave and put them back in order or join up the prophecies. So men depart without receiving advice and are disappointed in the house of the Sibyl. No matter how impatient your comrades, no matter how the winds may cry out to your sails to take to sea, though you know that you could fill the canvas with favouring breezes, you must not begrudge the time but must stay to visit the priestess. Approach her oracle with prayers and beg her by her own gracious will to prophesy to you herself, opening her lips and speaking to you in her own voice. She will tell you of the peoples of Italy and the wars that are to come, and how you are to escape or endure all the labours that lie before you. If you do her reverence she will give you a prosperous voyage. This is as much as my voice may utter to give you guidance. Now go forward and by your actions raise the greatness of Troy to the skies.'

After the prophet Helenus had told us these things in the friendliness of his heart, he then ordered his people to carry gifts of solid gold and carved ivory down to our ships and stowed a great quantity of silver in their hulls with cauldrons from Jupiter's temple at Dodona, a breastplate of chain mail interwoven with triple threads of gold and a noble helmet with crest and streaming plumes once worn by Neoptolemus. There were other gifts for my father, and he also gave us horses and leaders of men, rowers to make up the crews and arms for my comrades.

Meanwhile Anchises was ordering us to fit out the ships with their sails and not lose the following winds when the priest of Apollo addressed him in deep respect: 'Anchises, the gods love you. You have been thought worthy of the highest of all honours, the love of Venus. You have been twice rescued from the ruins of Troy, and now before you, look, the land of Ausonia. Sail there and take possession of it. But you must sail past the opposite coast. The part of Ausonia which Apollo reveals to you is far from here. Go then, Anchises, fortunate in the devotion of your son. There is no more to say. Why do I keep you talking when the wind is rising?'

Andromache also grieved at this parting that was to be our last and brought us robes embroidered with gold thread and a Phrygian cloak for Ascanius. She was as generous as Helenus had been, heaping the gifts of her weaving upon him and saying: 'Take these too, my boy, and I hope the work of my hands may remind you of Andromache, wife of Hector, and be a token of my long-enduring love for you. Accept them. They are the last gifts you will receive from your own people. You are the only image left to me of my own son Astyanax. He had just those eyes, and just those hands. His face was just like yours. He would have been growing up now, the same age as yourself.'

The tears were starting to my eyes as I was leaving them, and I spoke these words. 'Live on and enjoy the blessing of heaven. Your destiny has been accomplished. But we are called from fate to fate. Your rest is won. You do not need to plough tracts of ocean searching for the ever-receding Ausonian fields. You have before your eyes an image of the river Xanthus and a Troy made by your own hands, more fortunate, I pray, than the Troy that was, and less of a stumbling-block to the Greeks. If ever I reach the river Thybris and the fields through which the Thybris flows and see my people with their own city walls, we shall in some future age unite our cities and the peoples of Hesperia and Epirus, for we are kith and kin, the same Dardanus is our founder and the same destiny attends us. We shall make them both one Troy in spirit. Let that be a duty for our descendants.'

Down the coast we sailed near the Ceraunian rocks where the crossing to Italy is shortest, and as we sailed the sun set and shadow darkened the mountains. At last we lay down by the waves of the sea in the lap of earth, and after allotting the next day's order of rowing, we took our ease all along the dry beach and sleep washed into our weary limbs.

Night in its chariot drawn by the Hours was not yet coming up to the middle of the sky, but there was no more sleep for Palinurus. He rose from his bed and studied all the winds, pricking up his ears to test the air and marking the path of every star gliding in the silent sky, Arcturus and the rainy Hyades and the two Triones, the oxen of the Plough, and he looked round to the south at Orion armed in gold, and saw that the whole sky was serene and settled. Clear came his signal from the high stern. We broke camp, started our voyage and spread the wings of our sails.

The stars had been put to flight and dawn was reddening in the sky when we sighted in the far distance the dim hills and plains of Italy. 'Italy!' – the first shout was from Achates – and 'Italy!' – the men took up the cry in cheerful salute. Then Father Anchises, standing on the high stern, garlanded a great mixing bowl, filled it with unwatered wine and called upon the gods: 'O you who rule sea, land and storm, give us an easy wind for our voyage. Blow kindly upon us.'

His prayer was answered. The breeze freshened and a harbour opened up before us growing nearer and nearer till we could see the temple of Minerva on the citadel. My comrades furled their sails and pointed their prows to the shore. The harbour was shaped like a bow, curving away from the swell which came in from the east. The rocks at the mouth were foaming with salt spray but the harbour lay tucked away behind. Towering rocks on either side stretched down their arms to form a double wall and the temple stood well back from the shore. The first omen I saw here was four horses white as snow cropping the grass on a broad plain and my father Anchises interpreted it: 'This land that receives us is promising us war! Men arm horses for war and so this troop of horses means threat of war. Yet at other times they are harnessed to chariots and accept reins under the yoke in harmony. There is hope of peace also.'

At that moment we prayed to the sacred godhead of Pallas, clasher of arms, the first goddess to welcome us in this hour of our joy. Standing at the altar we veiled our heads with Phrygian cloth, and in accordance with the instructions which Helenus had told us to follow before all others, duly paid the prescribed honour to Juno of Argos with our burnt offerings.

We did not linger there but as soon as we had performed the rites in due order we raised our sails, swung the yards round and left behind us this home of Greeks, this land we could not trust. Next we saw the bay of Tarentum, the city of Hercules if the story is true, and over against it rose the temple of the goddess Juno at Lacinium, the citadel of Caulon and the bay of Scylaceum, that great breaker of ships. Then from far out at sea we sighted Mount Etna in Sicily and heard a loud moaning of waters and grinding of rocks and the voice of breakers beating on the shore, as the sea began to rise and swirl the sand in its surge. Father Anchises cried out: 'This must be the deadly Charybdis. These are the cliffs Helenus warned us against. These are the terrible rocks. Use all your strength to save yourselves, comrades. Keep well in time and rise to the oar.' They did as they were bidden. Palinurus was the first to wrench his ship to port and out to sea with a loud creaking of the bow, and the whole fleet with every sail and oar steered to port with him. A great arching wave came and lifted us to the sky and a moment later as the wave was sucked down we plunged into the abyss of hell. Three times the cliffs roared between their hollow rocks. Three times we saw the foam shoot up and spatter the stars. Meanwhile the sun had set, the wind had fallen and we were weary and lost, drifting towards the shore of the Cyclopes.

The harbour there is out of the wind. It is still and spacious but close by Mount Etna thunders and hurls down its deadly debris. Sometimes, it shoots a pitch-black cloud of swirling smoke and glowing ashes into the sky and tosses up balls of flame to lick the stars. Sometimes it belches boulders, tearing out the bowels of the mountain and throwing molten rock up into the air, seething and groaning in its very depths. The story goes that the body of Enceladus, half-consumed by the fire of the thunderbolt, is crushed under this great mass. Mighty Etna lies on top of him breathing fire from its shattered furnaces and every time he turns over from one weary flank to another the whole of Sicily trembles and murmurs and wreathes the sky with smoke. We hid in the woods and lived through a night of horror, not seeing what was making these monstrous sounds. The fire of the stars was quenched and the dark bowl of heaven was denied their radiance. Clouds darkened the sky and unbroken night obscured the moon.

At last the Morning Star appeared and the next day was beginning to rise. The Goddess of the Dawn had dispersed the dank mists from the sky when suddenly we saw a strange sight coming out of the woods. It was a man we did not know, in pitiable plight and half-dead with hunger, coming towards us on the shore with his hands stretched out in supplication. We stared at him. The filth on his body was indescribable. He had a straggling beard and the rags he wore were pinned together by thorns, but for all that he was a Greek, one of those who had been sent to Troy bearing the arms of his country. When still at a distance he saw our Trojan clothes and Trojan armour, he checked his stride and stood in terror at the sight of us. But he soon rushed down to the shore weeping and pleading: 'I beg you, Trojans, by all the stars, by the gods above, by the bright air of heaven which we breathe, take me aboard your ships. Take me anywhere. That is all I ask. I know I was one of those who sailed with the Greek fleet. I admit I made war against the gods of your homes in Troy. If that offence is so great, tear me limb from limb, scatter the pieces on the waves and let them sink into the vastness of the sea. If I am to die, I shall be pleased to die at the hands of men.'

When he had spoken he clasped our knees, he grovelled on his knees, and would not rise. We urged him to explain who he was, what family he came from and what misfortune was driving him to this. Father Anchises himself was not slow to offer his right hand and that assurance gave him courage. He laid aside his fear and told his story: 'My native land is Ithaca. I am a comrade of the unfortunate Ulixes. My name is Achaemenides. My father Adamastus being poor, I went to Troy – cursed be the day! My comrades, distraught with fear, forgot me and left me here in the vast cave of the Cyclops when they crossed that cruel threshold to safety. This huge cavern was his home, deep and dark and filthy with the gore of his feasts. He himself was so tall that his head knocked against the stars – O you gods, relieve the earth of all such monsters. No one dared to look at him or speak to him. He fed on the flesh of his victims and drank the black blood. I have seen him with my own eyes lolling in the middle of his cave with two of our men in one huge hand, bashing their bodies on the rock till the threshold was swimming with blood. I have seen him chewing arms and legs with black gore oozing from them and the warm limbs twitching between his teeth. But he met his punishment. The man from Ithaca did not submit to this. Whatever happened Ulixes was always Ulixes. As soon as the Cyclops had his fill and was sunk in a drunken stupor, lying there with his head back and his neck exposed, sprawling all over the cave and belching blood and wine and pieces of flesh as he slept, we prayed to the great gods and after casting lots spread ourselves out all round him. Then, taking a sharp weapon we drilled the one huge eye that lay, like an Argive shield or the lamp of Apollo's sun, deep set in that dreadful forehead. That was how in the end we took sweet revenge for the death of our comrades. But you are in danger. You must escape and escape now. Cut your moorings and put to sea. You know what Polyphemus is and how huge he is, keeping his woolly sheep penned there in his hollow cave and squeezing the milk from their udders, but there are a hundred other horrible Cyclopes living together near this shore and roving the high mountains. This is now the third time I have seen the horns of the moon filling with light as I have dragged out my existence in the woods alone among the dens and lairs of wild beasts, climbing rocks to keep watch on the giant Cyclopes and trembling at the sound of their voices and the tread of their feet. My food is miserable. The trees yield me some berries and the fruit of the cornel, hard as stone, and I tear up herbs by the root and eat them. I have kept constant watch but this is the first time I have seen ships coming near this shore. I have put myself in your hands, and would have done so whoever you had been. It is enough for me to escape from this unspeakable people. You can take this life of mine by whatever means you please.'

Scarcely had he finished speaking when we saw the shepherd Polyphemus himself high up on the mountain among his sheep, heaving his vast bulk down towards the shore he knew so well. He was a terrifying sight, huge, hideous, blinded in his one eye and using the trunk of a pine tree to guide his hand and give him a firm footing. His woolly sheep were coming with him. They were the only pleasure he had left, his sole consolation in distress. As soon as he felt the waves deepening and reached the level ocean, he washed away with sea water the blood that was still trickling from his gouged-out eye, grinding his teeth and moaning, and as he strode now in mid-ocean, the waves still did not wet his towering flanks.

We were terrified and lost no time in taking the fugitive aboard – he had suffered enough – and making our escape. Keeping silence as we cut the cables we churned the surface of the sea, leaning forward and straining at the oars. He heard us, and whirled round in the direction of our voices, but he had no chance of laying a hand on us or keeping up with the current of the Ionian sea, so he raised a great clamour which set the ocean and all its waves shivering. The whole land of Italy trembled with fear and the bellowing boomed in the hollow caverns of Mount Etna. The tribe of Cyclopes was roused and came rushing down from their woods and high mountains to the harbour and filled the shore. We saw the brotherhood of Etna standing there helpless, each with his one eye glaring and head held high in the sky, a fearsome gathering, standing like high-topped mountain oaks or cone-bearing cypresses in Jupiter's soaring forest or the grove of Diana. With terror driving us along we let the sheets full out

and filled our sails with whatever wind was blowing. This is
what Helenus had told us not to do. He had advised us that
it was a narrow passage between Scylla and Charybdis with
death on either side if I did not hold a steady course. I resolved
to turn about, and sure enough the north wind came to our
rescue and blew down the narrow strait from Cape Pelorus. I
sailed south past the mouth of the river Pantagias with its
harbour of natural rock, past the bay of Megara and low-lying
Thapsus. Achaemenides pointed out such places to us as we
took him back along the shores he had once sailed as the
comrade of the unfortunate Ulixes.

At the entrance to the bay of Syracuse, opposite the wave-
beaten headland of Plemyrium, there stands an island which
men of old called Ortygia. The story goes that the river-god
Alpheus of Elis forced his way here by hidden passages under
the sea and now mingles with Sicilian waters at the mouth
of Arethusa's fountain. Obeying the instructions we had
received, we worshipped the great gods of the place and I
then sailed on leaving behind the rich lands around the
marshy river Helorus. From here we rounded Cape Pachynus,
keeping close in to its jutting cliffs of rock, and Camerina
came into view in the distance, the place the Fates forbade to
move, and then the Geloan plains and Gela itself, called after
its turbulent river. Then in the far distance appeared the great
walls of Acragas on its crag, once famous for the breeding of
high-mettled horses. Next the winds carried me past Selinus,
named after the parsley it gave to crown the victors in Greek
games, and I steered past the dangerous shoals and hidden
rocks of Lilybaeum.

I then put into port at Drepanum, but had little joy of that
shore. This was the place where weary as I was with all these
batterings of sea and storm, to my great grief I lost my father
Anchises who had been my support in every difficulty and
disaster. This is where you left me, O best of fathers, whom I
rescued from so many dangers and all to no purpose. Neither

Helenus for all his fearsome predictions nor the Harpy Celaeno gave me any warning of this sorrow. This was the last of my labours. With this my long course was run. From here I sailed, and God drove me upon your shores.

In these words did Father Aeneas recount his wanderings and the fates the gods had sent him, and they all listened. At last he was silent. Here he made an end and was at peace.

ᛋ 4 ᛞ

D I D O

But the queen had long since been suffering from love's deadly wound, feeding it with her blood and being consumed by its hidden fire. Again and again there rushed into her mind thoughts of the great valour of the man and the high glories of his line. His features and the words he had spoken had pierced her heart and love gave her body no peace or rest. The next day's dawn was beginning to traverse the earth with the lamp of Phoebus' sunlight and had moved the dank shadow of night from the sky when she spoke these words from the depths of her affliction to her loved and loving sister: 'O Anna, what fearful dreams I have as I lie there between sleeping and waking! What a man is this who has just come as a stranger into our house! What a look on his face! What courage in his heart! What a warrior! I do believe, and I am sure it is true, he is descended from the gods. If there is any baseness in a man, it shows as cowardice. Oh how cruelly he has been hounded by the Fates! And did you hear him tell what a bitter cup of war he has had to drain? If my mind had not been set and immovably fixed against joining any man in the bonds of marriage ever since death cheated me of my first love, if I were not so utterly opposed to the marriage torch and bed, this is the one temptation to which I could possibly have succumbed. I will admit it, Anna, ever since the death of my poor husband Sychaeus, since my own brother spilt his blood and polluted the gods of our home, this is the only man who has stirred my feelings and moved my mind to waver: I sense the return of the old fires. But I would pray that the earth open to its depths and swallow me or that the All-powerful Father of the Gods blast me with his thunderbolt and hurl me down to the pale shades of Erebus and its bottomless night before I go against my conscience and rescind its laws. The man who first joined himself to me has carried away all my love. He shall keep it for himself, safe in his grave.'

The tears came when she had finished speaking, and streamed down upon her breast. But Anna replied: 'O sister, dearer to me than the light of life, are you going to waste away, living alone and in mourning all the days of your youth, without knowing the delight of children and the rewards of love? Do you believe this is what the dead care about when they are buried in the grave? Since your great sadness you have paid no heed to any man in Libya, or before that in Tyre. You have rejected Iarbas and other chiefs bred in Africa, this rich home of triumphant warriors. Will you now resist even a love your heart accepts? Have you forgotten what sort of people these are in whose land you have settled? On the one side you are beset by invincible Gaetulians, by Numidians, a race not partial to the bridle, and the inhospitable Syrtes; on the other, waterless desert and fierce raiders from Barca. I do not need to tell you about the war being raised against you in Tyre and your brother's threats. I for my part believe that it is with the blessing of the gods and the favour of Juno that the Trojan ships have held course here through the winds. Just think, O my sister, what a city and what a kingdom you will see rising here if you are married to such a man! To what a pinnacle of glory will Carthage be raised if Trojans are marching at our side! You need only ask the blessing of the gods and prevail upon them with sacrifices. Indulge your guest. Stitch together some reasons to keep him here while stormy seas and the downpours of Orion are exhausting their fury, while his ships are in pieces and it is no sky to sail under.'

With these words Anna lit a fire of wild love in her sister's breast. Where there had been doubt she gave hope and Dido's conscience was overcome. First they approached the shrines and went round the altars asking the blessing of the gods. They picked out yearling sheep, as ritual prescribed, and sacrificed them to Ceres the Lawgiver, to Phoebus Apollo, to Bacchus the Releaser and above all to Juno, the guardian of the marriage bond. Dido in all her beauty would hold a sacred dish in her right hand and would pour wine from it between the horns of a white cow or she would walk in state to richly smoking altars before the faces of the gods, renewing her offerings all day long, and when the bellies of the victims were opened she would stare into their breathing entrails to read the signs. But priests, as we know, are ignorant. What use are prayers and shrines to a passionate woman? The flame was eating the soft marrow of her bones and the wound lived quietly under her breast. Dido was on fire with love and wandered all over the city in her misery and madness like a wounded deer which a shepherd hunting in the woods of Crete has caught off guard, striking her from long range with steel-tipped shaft; the arrow flies and is left in her body without his knowing it; she runs away over all the wooded slopes of Mount Dicte, and sticking in her side is the arrow that will bring her death.

Sometimes she would take Aeneas through the middle of Carthage, showing him the wealth of Sidon and the city waiting for him, and she would be on the point of speaking her mind to him but checked the words on her lips. Sometimes, as the day was ending, she would call for more feasting and ask in her infatuation to hear once more about the sufferings of Troy and once more she would hang on his lips as he told the story. Then, after they had parted, when the fading moon was dimming her light and the setting stars seemed to speak of sleep, alone and wretched in her empty house she would cling to the couch Aeneas had left. There she would lie long after he had gone and she would see him and hear him when he was not there for her to see or hear. Or she would keep back Ascanius and take him on her knee, overcome by the likeness to his father, trying to beguile the love she could not declare. The towers she was building ceased to rise. Her men gave up the exercise of war and were no longer busy at the harbours and fortifications making them safe from attack. All the work that had been started, the threatening ramparts of the great walls and the cranes soaring to the sky, all stood idle.

As soon as Saturnian Juno, the dear wife of Jupiter, realized that Dido was infected by this sickness and that passion was sweeping away all thought for her reputation, she went and spoke to Venus: 'You are covering yourselves with glory. These are the supreme spoils you are bringing home, you and that boy of yours – and what a noble and notable specimen of the divine he is – one woman has been overthrown by the arts of two gods! I do not fail to see that you have long been afraid of our walls and looked askance at the homes of lofty Carthage. But how is this going to end? Where is all this rivalry going to lead us now? Why do we not instead agree to arrange a marriage and live at peace for ever? You have achieved what you have set your whole heart on: Dido is passionately in love and the madness is working through her bones. So let us make one people of them and share authority equally over them. Let us allow her to become the slave of a Phrygian husband and to hand over her Tyrians to you as a dowry!'

Venus realized this was all pretence in order to divert the empire of Italy to the shores of Libya, and made this response to the Queen of Heaven: 'Who would be so insane as to reject such an offer and choose instead to contend with you in war? If only a happy outcome could attend the plan you describe! But I am at the mercy of the Fates and do not know whether Jupiter would wish there to be one city for the Tyrians and those who have come from Troy or whether he would approve the merging of their peoples and the making of alliances. You are his wife. It could not be wrong for you to approach him with prayers and test his purpose. You proceed and I shall follow.'

'That will be my task,' replied Juno. 'But now listen and I shall explain in a few words how the first part of the plan may be carried out. Aeneas and poor Dido are preparing to go hunting together in the forest as soon as tomorrow's sun first rises and the rays of the Titan unveil the world. When the beaters are scurrying about and putting nets round copses, I shall pour down a dark storm of rain and hail on them and shake the whole sky with thunder. Their companions will run away and be lost to sight in a pall of darkness. Dido and the leader of the Trojans will both take refuge in the same cave. I shall be there, and if your settled will is with me in this, I shall join them in lasting marriage and make her his. This will be their wedding.' This was what Juno asked and Venus of Cythera did not refuse her but nodded in assent. She saw through the deception and laughed.

Meanwhile Aurora rose from the ocean and when her light came up into the sky, a picked band of men left the gates of Carthage carrying nets, wide-meshed and fine-meshed, and broad-bladed hunting spears, and with them came Massylian horsemen at the gallop and packs of keen scented hounds. The queen was lingering in her chamber and the Carthaginian leaders waited at her door. There, resplendent in its purple and gold, stood her loud-hoofed, high-mettled horse champing its foaming bit. She came at last with a great entourage thronging round her. She was wearing a Sidonian cloak with an embroidered hem. Her quiver was of gold. Gold was the clasp that gathered up her hair and her purple tunic was fastened with a golden brooch. Nor was the Trojan company slow to move forward, Ascanius with them in high glee. Aeneas himself marched at their head, the most splendid of them all, as he brought his men to join the queen's. He was like Apollo leaving his winter home in Lycia and the waters of the river Xanthus to visit his mother at Delos, there to start the dancing again, while all around the altars gather noisy throngs of Cretans and Dryopes and painted Agathyrsians; the god himself strides the ridges of Mount Cynthus, his streaming hair caught up and shaped into a soft garland of green and twined round a band of gold, and the arrows sound on his shoulders – with no less vigour moved Aeneas and his face shone with equal radiance and grace. When they had climbed high into the mountains above the tracks of men where the animals make their lairs, suddenly some wild goats were disturbed on the top of a crag and came running down from the ridge. Then on the other side there were deer running across the open plain. They had gathered into a herd and were raising the dust as they left the high ground far behind them. Down in the middle of the valley young Ascanius was riding a lively horse and revelling in it, galloping past the deer and the goats and praying that among these flocks of feeble creatures he could come across a foaming boar or that a tawny lion would come down from the mountains.

While all this was happening a great rumble of thunder began to stir in the sky. Down came the rain and the hail, and Tyrian huntsmen, men of Troy and Ascanius of the line of Dardanus and grandson of Venus, scattered in fright all over the fields, making for shelter as rivers of water came rushing down the mountains. Dido and the leader of the Trojans took refuge together in the same cave. The sign was first given by Earth and by Juno as matron of honour. Fires flashed and the heavens were witness to the marriage while nymphs wailed on the mountain tops. This day was the beginning of her death, the first cause of all her sufferings. From now on Dido gave no thought to appearance or her good name and no longer kept her love as a secret in her own heart, but called it marriage, using the word to cover her guilt.

Rumour did not take long to go through the great cities of Libya. Of all the ills there are, Rumour is the swiftest. She thrives on movement and gathers strength as she goes. From small and timorous beginnings she soon lifts herself up into the air, her feet still on the ground and her head hidden in the clouds. They say she is the last daughter of Mother Earth who bore her in rage against the gods, a sister for Coeus and Enceladus. Rumour is quick of foot and swift on the wing, a huge and horrible monster, and under every feather of her body, strange to tell, there lies an eye that never sleeps, a mouth and a tongue that are never silent and an ear always pricked. By night she flies between earth and sky, squawking through the darkness, and never lowers her eyelids in sweet sleep. By day she keeps watch perched on the tops of gables or on high towers and causes fear in great cities, holding fast to her lies and distortions as often as she tells the truth. At that time she was taking delight in plying the tribes with all manner of stories, fact and fiction mixed in equal parts: how Aeneas the Trojan had come to Carthage and the lovely Dido had thought fit to take him as her husband; how they were even now indulging themselves and keeping each other warm the whole winter through, forgetting about their kingdoms and becoming the slaves of lust. When the foul goddess had spread this gossip all around on the lips of men, she then steered her course to king Iarbas to set his mind alight and fuel his anger.

Jupiter had ravished a Garamantian nymph and Iarbas was his son. Over his broad realm he had erected a hundred huge temples to the god and set up a hundred altars on which he had consecrated ever-burning fires to keep undying holy vigil, enriching the earth with the blood of slaughtered victims and draping the doors with garlands of all kinds of flowers. Iarbas, they say, was driven out of his mind with anger when he heard this bitter news. Coming into the presence of the gods before their altars in a passion of rage, he offered up prayer upon prayer to Jupiter, raising his hands palms upward in supplication: 'Jupiter All-powerful, who now receives libations of wine from the Moorish people feasting on their embroidered couches, do you see all this? Or are we fools to be afraid of you, Father, when you hurl your thunderbolts? Are they unaimed, these fires in the clouds that cow our spirits? Is there no meaning in the murmur of your thunder? This woman was wandering about our land and we allowed her at a price to found her little city. We gave her a piece of shore to plough and laid down the laws of the place for her and she has spurned our offer of marriage and taken Aeneas into her kingdom as lord and master, and now this second Paris, with eunuchs in attendance and hair dripping with perfume and Maeonian bonnet tied under his chin, is enjoying what he has stolen while we bring gifts to temples we think are yours and keep warm with our worship the reputation of a useless god.'

As Iarbas prayed these prayers with his hand on the altar, the All-powerful god heard him and turned his eyes towards the royal city and the lovers who had lost all recollection of their good name. Then he spoke to Mercury and gave him these instructions: 'Up with you, my son. Call for the Zephyrs, glide down on your wings and speak to the Trojan leader who now lingers in Tyrian Carthage without a thought for the cities granted him by the Fates. Take these words of mine down to him through the swift winds and tell him that this is not the man promised us by his mother, the loveliest of the goddesses. It was not for this that she twice rescued him from the swords of the Greeks. She told us he would be the man to rule an Italy pregnant with empire and clamouring for war, passing the high blood of Teucer down to his descendants and subduing the whole world under his laws. If the glory of such a destiny does not fire his heart, if he does not strive to win fame for himself, ask him if he grudges the citadel of Rome to his son Ascanius. What does he have in mind? What does he hope to achieve dallying among a hostile people and sparing not a thought for the Lavinian fields and his descendants yet to be born in Ausonia? He must sail. That is all there is to say. Let that be our message.'

Jupiter had finished speaking and Mercury prepared to obey the command of his mighty father. First of all he fastened on his feet the golden sandals whose wings carry him high above land and sea as swiftly as the wind. Then, taking the rod which summons pale spirits out of Orcus or sends them down to gloomy Tartarus, which gives sleep and takes it away and opens the eyes of men in death, he drove the winds before him and floated through the turbulent clouds till in his flight he saw the crest and steep flanks of Atlas whose rocky head props up the sky. This is the Atlas whose head, covered in pine trees and beaten by wind and rain, never loses its dark cap of cloud. The snow falls upon his shoulders and lies there, then rivers of water roll down the old man's chin and his bristling beard is stiff with ice. This is where Mercury the god of Mount Cyllene first landed, fanning out his wings to check his flight. From here he let his weight take him plummeting to the wave tops, like a bird skimming the sea as it flies along the shore, among the rocks where it finds the fish. So flew the Cyllenian god between earth and sky to the sandy beaches of Libya, cleaving the winds as he swooped down from the mountain that had fathered his own mother, Maia.

As soon as his winged feet touched the roof of a Carthaginian hut, he caught sight of Aeneas laying the foundations of the citadel and putting up buildings. His sword was studded with yellow stars of jasper, and glowing with Tyrian purple there hung from his shoulders a rich cloak given him by Dido into which she had woven a fine cross-thread of gold. Mercury wasted no time: 'So now you are laying foundations for the high towers of Carthage and building a splendid city to please your wife? Have you entirely forgotten your own kingdom and your own destiny? The ruler of the gods himself,

BOOK FOUR

by whose divine will the heavens and the earth revolve, sends me down from bright Olympus and bids me bring these commands to you through the swift winds. What do you have in mind? What do you hope to achieve by idling your time away in the land of Libya? If the glory of such a destiny does not fire your heart, spare a thought for Ascanius as he grows to manhood, for the hopes of this Iulus who is your heir. You owe him the land of Rome and the kingdom of Italy.'

No sooner had these words passed the lips of the Cyllenian god than he disappeared from mortal view and faded far into the insubstantial air. But the sight of him left Aeneas dumb and senseless. His hair stood on end with horror and the voice stuck in his throat. He longed to be away and leave behind him this land he had found so sweet. The warning, the command from the gods, had struck him like a thunderbolt. But what, oh what, was he to do? What words dare he use to approach the queen in all her passion? How could he begin to speak to her? His thoughts moved swiftly now here, now there, darting in every possible direction and turning to every possible event, and as he pondered, this seemed to him a better course of action: he called Mnestheus, Sergestus and brave Serestus and ordered them to fit out the fleet and tell no one, to muster the men on the shore with their equipment at the ready, and keep secret the reason for the change of plan. In the meantime, since the good queen knew nothing and the last thing she expected was the shattering of such a great love, he himself would try to make approaches to her and find the kindest time to speak and the best way to handle the matter. They were delighted to receive their orders and carried them out immediately.

But the queen – who can deceive a lover? – knew in advance some scheme was afoot. Afraid where there was nothing to fear, she was the first to catch wind of their plans to leave, and while she was already in a frenzy, that same wicked Rumour brought word that the Trojans were fitting out their fleet and preparing to sail away. Driven to distraction and burning with passion, she raged and raved round the whole city like a Bacchant stirred by the shaking of the sacred emblems and roused to frenzy when she hears the name of Bacchus at the biennial orgy and the shouting on Mount Cithaeron calls to her in the night. At last she went to Aeneas, and before he could speak, she cried: 'You traitor, did you imagine you could do this and keep it secret? Did you think you could slip away from this land of mine and say nothing? Does our love have no claim on you? Or the pledge your right hand once gave me? Or the prospect of Dido dying a cruel death? Why must you move your fleet in these winter storms and rush across the high seas into the teeth of the north wind? You are heartless. Even if it were not other people's fields and some home unknown you were going to, if old Troy were still standing, would any fleet set sail even for Troy in such stormy seas? Is it me you are running away from? I beg you, by these tears, by the pledge you gave me with your own right hand – I have nothing else left me now in my misery – I beg you by our union, by the marriage we have begun – if I have deserved any kindness from you, if you have ever loved anything about me, pity my house that is falling around me, and I implore you, if it is not too late for prayers, give up this plan of yours. I am hated because of you by the peoples of Libya and the Numidian kings. My own Tyrians are against me. Because of you I have lost all conscience and self-respect and have thrown away the good name I once had, my only hope of reaching the stars. My guest is leaving me to my fate and I shall die. "Guest" is the only name I can now give the man who used to be my husband. What am I waiting for? For my brother Pygmalion to come and raze my city to the ground? For the Gaetulian Iarbas to drag me off in chains? Oh if only you had given me a child before you abandoned me! If only there were a little Aeneas to play in my palace! In spite of everything his face would remind me of yours and I would not feel utterly betrayed and desolate.'

She had finished speaking. Remembering the warnings of Jupiter, Aeneas did not move his eyes and struggled to fight down the anguish in his heart. At last he spoke these few words: 'I know, O queen, you can list a multitude of kindnesses you have done me. I shall never deny them and never be sorry to remember Dido while I remember myself, while my spirit still governs this body. Much could be said. I shall say only a little. It never was my intention to be deceitful or run away without your knowing, and do not pretend that it was. Nor have I ever offered you marriage or entered into that contract with you. If the Fates were leaving me free to live my own life and settle all my cares according to my own wishes, my first concern would be to tend the city of Troy and my dear ones who are still alive. The lofty palace of Priam would still be standing and with my own hands I would have built a new citadel at Pergamum for those who have been defeated. But now Apollo of Gryneum has commanded me to claim the great land of Italy and "Italy" is the word on the lots cast at his Lycian oracle. That is my love, and that is my homeland. You are a Phoenician from Asia and you care for the citadel of Carthage and love the very sight of this city in Libya; what objection can there be to Trojans settling in the land of Ausonia? How can it be a sin if we too look for distant kingdoms. Every night when the earth is covered in mist and darkness, every time the burning stars rise in the sky, I see in my dreams the troubled spirit of my father Anchises coming to me with warnings and I am afraid. I see my son Ascanius and think of the wrong I am doing him, cheating him of his kingdom in Hesperia and the lands the Fates have decreed for him. And now even the messenger of the gods has come down through the swift winds – I swear it by the lives of both of us – and brought commands from Jupiter himself. With my own eyes I have seen the god in the clear light of day coming within the walls of your city. With my own ears I have listened to his voice. Do not go on causing distress to yourself and to me by these complaints. It is not by my own will that I still search for Italy.'

All the time he had been speaking she was turned away from him, but looking at him, speechless and rolling her eyes, taking in every part of him. At last she replied on a blaze of passion: 'You are a traitor. You are not the son of a goddess and Dardanus was not the first founder of your family. It was the Caucasus that fathered you on its hard rocks and Hyrcanian tigers offered you their udders. Why should I keep up a pretence? Why should I keep myself in check in order to endure greater suffering in the future? He did not sigh when he saw me weep. He did not even turn to look at me. Was he overcome and brought to tears? Had he any pity for the woman who loves him? Where can I begin when there is so much to say? Now, after all this, can mighty Juno and the son of Saturn, the father of all, can they now look at this with the eyes of justice? Is there nothing we can trust in this life? He was thrown helpless on my shores and I took him in and like a fool settled him as partner in my kingdom. He had lost his fleet and I found it and brought his companions back from the dead. It drives me to madness to think of it. And now we hear about the augur Apollo and lots cast in Lycia and now to crown all the messenger of the gods is bringing terrifying commands down through the winds from Jupiter himself, as though that is work for the gods in heaven, as though that is an anxiety that disturbs their tranquillity. I do not hold you or bandy words with you. Away you go. Keep on searching for your Italy with the winds to help you. Look for your kingdom over the waves. But my hope is that if the just gods have any power, you will drain a bitter cup among the ocean rocks, calling the name of Dido again and again, and I shall follow you not in the flesh but in the black fires of death and when its cold hand takes the breath from my body, my shade shall be with you wherever you may be. You will receive the punishment you deserve, and the news of it will reach me deep among the dead.'

At these words she broke off and rushed indoors in utter despair, leaving Aeneas with much to say and much to fear. Her attendants caught her as she fainted and carried her to her bed in her marble chamber. But Aeneas was faithful to his duty. Much as he longed to soothe her and console her sorrow, to talk to her and take away her pain, with many a groan and with a heart shaken by his great love, he nevertheless carried out the commands of the gods and went back to his ships.

By then the Trojans were hard at work. All along the shore they were hauling the tall ships down to the sea. They set the well-caulked hulls afloat and in their eagerness to be away they were carrying down from the woods unworked timber and green branches for oars. You could see them pouring out of every part of the city, like ants plundering a huge heap of wheat and storing it away in their home against the winter, and their black column advances over the plain as they gather in their booty along a narrow path through the grass, some putting their shoulders to huge grains and pushing them along, others keeping the column together and whipping in the stragglers, and the whole track seethes with activity. What were your feelings, Dido, as you looked at this? Did you not moan as you gazed out from the top of your citadel and saw the broad shore seething before your eyes and confusion and shouting all over the sea? Love is a cruel master. There are no lengths to which it does not force the human heart. Once again she had recourse to tears, once again she was driven to try to move his heart with prayers, becoming a suppliant and making her pride submit to her love, in case she should die in vain, leaving some avenue unexplored. 'You see, Anna, the bustle all over the shore. They are all gathered there, the canvas is calling for the winds, the sailors are delighted and have set garlands on the ships' sterns. I was able to imagine that this grief might come; I shall be able to endure it. But Anna, do this one service for your poor sister. You are the only one the traitor respected. To you he entrusted his very deepest feelings. You are the only one who knew the right time to approach him and the right words to use. Go to him, sister. Kneel before our proud enemy and tell him I was not at Aulis and made no compact with the Greeks to wipe out the people of Troy. I sent no fleet to Pergamum. I did not tear up the ashes of his dead father Anchises. Why are his cruel ears closed to what I am saying? Where is he rushing away to? Ask him to do this last favour to the unhappy woman who loves him and wait till there is a following wind and his escape is easy. I am no longer begging for the marriage which we once had and which he has now betrayed. I am not pleading with him to do without his precious Latium and abandon his kingdom. What I am asking for is some time, nothing more, an interval, a respite for my anguish, so that fortune can teach me to grieve and to endure defeat. This is the last favour I shall beg. O Anna, pity your sister. I shall repay it in good measure at my death.'

These were Dido's pleas. These were the griefs her unhappy sister brought and brought again. But no griefs moved Aeneas. He heard but did not heed her words. The Fates forbade it and God blocked his ears to all appeals. Just as the north winds off the Alps vie with one another to uproot the mighty oak whose timber has hardened over long years of life, blowing upon it from this side and from that and howling through it; the trunk feels the shock and the foliage from its head covers the ground, but it holds on to the rocks with roots plunged as deep into the world below as its crown soars towards the winds of heaven – just so the hero Aeneas was buffeted by all this pleading on this side and on that, and felt the pain deep in his mighty heart but his mind remained unmoved and the tears rolled in vain.

Then it was that unhappy Dido prayed for death. She had seen her destiny and was afraid. She could bear no longer to look up to the bowl of heaven, and her resolve to leave the light was strengthened when she was laying offerings on the incense-breathing altars and saw to her horror the consecrated milk go black and the wine, as she poured it, turn to filthy gore. No one else saw it and she did not tell even her sister. There was more. She had in her palace a marble shrine dedicated to Sychaeus, who had been her husband. This she used to honour above all things, hanging it with white fleeces and sacred branches. When the darkness of night covered the earth, she thought she heard, coming from this shrine, the voice of her husband and the words he uttered as he called to her, and all the while the lonely owl kept up its long dirge upon the roof, drawing out its doleful song of death. And there was more. She kept remembering the predictions of ancient prophets that terrified her with their dreadful warnings, and as she slept Aeneas himself would drive her relentlessly in her madness, and she was always alone and desolate, always going on a long road without companions, looking for her Tyrians in an empty land. She would be like Pentheus in his frenzy when he was seeing columns of Furies and a double sun and two cities of Thebes; or like Orestes, son of Agamemnon, driven in flight across the stage by his own mother armed with her torches and black snakes, while the avenging Furies sat at the door.

And so Dido was overwhelmed by grief and possessed by madness. She decided to die and planned in her mind the time and the means. She went and spoke to her sorrowing sister with her face composed to conceal her plan and her brow bright with hope. 'My dear Anna, rejoice with your sister. I have found a way to bring him back to me in love or else to free me from him. Near Oceanus and the setting of the sun is the home of the Ethiopians, the most distant part of our earth, where mightiest Atlas turns on his shoulders the axis of the sky, studded with its burning stars. From here, they say, there comes a Massylian priestess who was the guardian of the temple of the Hesperides. She used to keep watch over the branches of the sacred tree and bring rich foods for the serpent, spreading the oozing honey and sprinkling the sleep-bringing seeds of the poppy. She undertakes to free by her spells the mind of anyone she wishes and to send cruel cares to others, to stop the flow of rivers and turn stars back in their courses. At night she raises the spirits of the dead and you will see the ash trees coming down from the mountains and hear the earth bellow beneath your feet. I call the gods and your own sweet self to witness, O my dearest sister, that it is not by my own will that I have recourse to magic arts. Go now, telling no one, and build up a pyre under the open sky in the inner courtyard of the palace and lay on it the armour this traitor has left hanging on the walls of my room, every-thing there is of his remaining, and the marriage bed on which I was destroyed. I want to wipe out everything that can remind me of such a man and that is what the priestess advises.'

She spoke, and spoke no more. Her face grew pale, but Anna did not understand that these strange rites were a pretence and that her sister meant to die. She had no inkling that such madness had seized Dido, no reason to fear that she would suffer more than she had at the death of Sychaeus. She did what she was asked.

But the queen knew what the future held. As soon as the pine torches and the holm-oak were hewn and the huge pyre raised under the open sky in the very heart of the palace, she hung the place with garlands and crowned the pyre with funeral branches. Then she laid on a bed an effigy of Aeneas with his sword and everything of his he had left behind. There were altars all around and the priestess with hair streaming called with a voice of thunder upon three hundred gods, Erebus, Chaos, triple Hecate and virgin Diana of the three faces. She had also sprinkled water to represent the spring of

Lake Avernus. She also sought out potent herbs with a milk of black poison in their rich stems and harvested them by moonlight with a bronze sickle. She found, too, a love charm, torn from the forehead of a new-born foal before the mare could bite it off. Dido herself took meal in her hands and worshipped, standing by the altars with one foot freed from all fastenings and her dress unbound, calling before she died to gods and stars to be witnesses to her fate and praying to whatever just and mindful power there is that watches over lovers who have been betrayed.

It was night and weary living things were peacefully taking their rest upon the earth. The woods and wild waves of ocean had been stilled. The stars were rolling on in mid-course. Silence reigned over field and flock and all the gaily coloured birds were laid to sleep in the quiet of night, those that haunt broad lakes and those that crowd the thickets dotted over the countryside. But not Dido. Her heart was broken and she found no relief in sleep. Her eyes and mind would not accept the night, but her torment redoubled and her raging love came again and again in great surging tides of anger. These are the thoughts she dwelt upon, this is what she kept turning over in her heart: 'So then, what am I to do? Shall I go back to those who once wooed me and see if they will have me? I would be a laughing stock. Shall I beg a husband from the Numidians after I have so often scorned their offers of marriage? Shall I then go with the Trojan fleet and do whatever the Trojans ask? I suppose they would be delighted to take me after all the help I have given them! They are sure to remember what I have done and be properly grateful! No: even if I were willing to go with them, they will never allow a woman they hate to come aboard their proud ships. There is nothing left for you, Dido. Do you not know, have you not yet noticed, the treacheries of the race of Laomedon? But if they did agree to take me, what then? Shall I go alone into exile with a fleet of jubilant sailors? Or shall I go in force with all my Tyrian bands crowding at my side? It was not easy for me to uproot them from their homes in the city of Sidon. How can I make them take to the sea again and order them to hoist sail into the winds? No, you must die. That is what you have deserved. Let the sword be the cure for your suffering. You could not bear, Anna, to see your sister weeping. When the madness was taking me, you were the first to lay this load upon my back and put me at the mercy of my enemy. I was not allowed to live my life without marriage, in innocence, like a wild creature, and be untouched by such anguish as this – I have not kept faith with the ashes of Sychaeus.'

While these words of grief were bursting from Dido's heart, Aeneas was now resolved to leave and was taking his rest on the high stern of his ship with everything ready for sailing. There, as he slept, appeared before him the shape of the god, coming to him with the same features as before and once again giving advice, in every way like Mercury, the voice, the radiance, the golden hair, the youthful beauty of his body: 'Son of the goddess, how can you lie there sleeping at a time like this? Do you not see danger all around you at this moment? Have you lost your wits? Do you not hear the west wind blowing off the shore? Having decided to die, she is turning her schemes over in her mind and planning some desperate act, stirring up the storm tides of her anger. Why do you not go now with all speed while speed you may? If morning comes and finds you loitering here, you will soon see her ships churning the sea and deadly torches blazing and the shore seething with flames. Come then! No more delay! Women are unstable creatures, always changing.'

When he had spoken he melted into the blackness of night and Aeneas was immediately awake, terrified by the sudden apparition. There was no more rest for his men, as he roused them to instant action: 'Wake up and sit to your benches,' he shouted. 'Let out the sails and quick about it. A god has been sent down again from the heights of heaven – I have just seen

him – spurring us on to cut our plaited ropes and run from
here. We are following you, O blessed god, whoever you are.
Once again we obey your commands and rejoice. Stand beside
us and graciously help us. Put favouring stars in the sky for
us.'

As he spoke he drew his sword from its scabbard like a
flash of lightning and struck the mooring cables with the
naked steel. In that instant they were all seized by the same
ardour and set to, hauling and hustling. The shore was emp-
tied. The sea could not be seen for ships. Bending to the oars
they whipped up the foam and swept the blue surface of the
sea.

Aurora was soon leaving the saffron bed of Tithonus and
beginning to sprinkle new light upon the earth. The queen
saw from her high tower the first light whitening and the fleet
moving out to sea with its sails square to the following winds.
She saw the deserted shore and harbour and not an oarsman
in sight. Three times and more she beat her lovely breasts and
tore her golden hair, crying 'O Jupiter! Will this intruder just
go, and make a mockery of our kingdom? Why are they not
running to arms and coming from all over the city to pursue
him? And others should be rushing ships out of the docks.
Move! Bring fire and quick about it! Give out the weapons!
Heave on the oars! – What am I saying? Where am I? What
madness is this that changes my resolve? Poor Dido, you have
done wrong and it is only now coming home to you. You
should have thought of this when you were offering him your
sceptre. So much for his right hand! So much for his pledge,
the man who is supposed to be carrying with him the gods of
his native land and to have lifted his weary old father up on
to his shoulders! Could I not have taken him and torn him
limb from limb and scattered the pieces in the sea? Could I
not have put his men to the sword, and Ascanius, too, and
served his flesh at his father's table? I know the outcome of a
battle would have been in doubt. So it would have been in

doubt! Was I, who am about to die, afraid of anyone? I would have taken torches to his camp and filled the decks of his ships with fire, destroying the son and the father and the whole Trojan people before throwing myself on the flames. O heavenly Sun whose fires pass in review all the works of this earth, and you, Juno, who have been witness and party to all the anguish of this love, and Hecate whose name is heard in nightly howling at crossroads all over our cities, and the avenging Furies and you, the gods of dying Dido, listen to these words, give a hearing to my sufferings, for they are great, and heed my prayers. If that monster of wickedness must reach harbour, if he must come to shore and that is what the Fates of Jupiter demand, if the boundary stone is set and may not be moved, then let him be harried in war by a people bold in arms; may he be driven from his own land and torn from the embrace of Iulus; may he have to beg for help and see his innocent people dying. Then, after he has submitted to the terms of an unjust peace, let him not enjoy the kingdom he longs for or the life he longs to lead, but let him fall before his time and lie unburied on the broad sand. This is my prayer. With these last words I pour out my life's blood. As for you, my Tyrians, you must pursue with hatred the whole line of his descendants in time to come. Make that your offering to my shade. Let there be no love between our peoples and no treaties. Arise from my dead bones, O my unknown avenger, and harry the race of Dardanus with fire and sword wherever they may settle, now and in the future, whenever our strength allows it. I pray that we may stand opposed, shore against shore, sea against sea and sword against sword. Let there be war between the nations and between their sons for ever.'

Even as she spoke Dido was casting about in her mind how she could most quickly put an end to the life she hated. She then addressed these few words to Sychaeus' nurse, Barce, for the black ashes of her own now lay far away in her ancient homeland: 'My dear nurse, send my sister Anna quickly to me, telling her to sprinkle her body with river water and take with her the animals and the other offerings as instructed. That is how she is to come, and your own forehead must be veiled with a sacred ribbon. I have prepared with due care offerings to Jupiter of the Styx and I am now of a mind to complete them and put an end to the pain of love by giving the pyre of this Trojan to the flames.'

The old woman bustled away leaving Dido full of wild fears at the thought of what she was about to do. Her cheeks trembling and flecked with red, her bloodshot eyes rolling, she was pale with the pallor of approaching death. Rushing through the door into the inner courtyard, she climbed the high pyre in a frenzy and unsheathed the Trojan sword for which she had asked – though not for this purpose. Then her eyes lit on the Trojan clothes and the bed she knew so well, and pausing for a moment to weep and to remember, she lay down on the bed and spoke these last words: 'These are the possessions of Aeneas which I so loved while God and the Fates allowed it. Let them receive my spirit and free me from this anguish. I have lived my life and completed the course that Fortune has set before me, and now my great spirit will go beneath the earth. I have founded a glorious city and lived to see the building of my own walls. I have avenged my husband and punished his enemy who was my brother. I would have been happy, more than happy, if only Trojan keels had never grounded on our shores.' She then buried her face for a moment in the bed and cried: 'We shall die unavenged. But let us die. This, this, is how it pleases me to go down among the shades. Let the Trojan who knows no pity gaze his fill upon this fire from the high seas and take with him the omen of my death.'

So she spoke and while speaking fell upon the sword. Her attendants saw her fall. They saw the blood foaming on the blade and staining her hands, and filled the high walls of the palace with their screaming. Rumour ran raving like a

Bacchant through the stricken city. The palace rang with
lamentation and groaning and the wailing of women and the
heavens gave back the sound of mourning. It was as though
the enemy were within the gates and the whole of Carthage
or old Tyre were falling with flames raging and rolling over
the roofs of men and gods. Anna heard and was beside herself.
She came rushing in terror through the middle of the crowd,
tearing her face and beating her breast, calling out her sister's
name as she lay dying: 'So this is what it meant? It was all to
deceive your sister! This was the purpose of the pyre and the
flames and the altars! You have abandoned me. I do not know
how to begin to reproach you. Did you not want your sister's
company when you were dying? You could have called me
to share your fate and we would both have died in the same
moment of the same grief. To think it was my hands that built
the pyre, and my voice that called upon the gods of our
fathers, so that you could be so cruel as to lay yourself down
here to die without me. It is not only yourself you have
destroyed, but also your sister and your people, their leaders
who came with you from Sidon and the city you have built.
Give me water. I shall wash her wounds and catch any last
lingering breath with my lips.'

Saying these words, she had climbed to the top of the pyre
and was now holding her dying sister to her breast and
cherishing her, sobbing as she dried the dark blood with her
own dress. Once more Dido tried to raise her heavy eyes, but
failed. The wound hissed round the sword beneath her breast.
Three times she raised herself on her elbow. Three times she
fell back on the bed. With wavering eyes she looked for light
in the heights of heaven and groaned when she found it.

All-powerful Juno then took pity on her long anguish and
difficult death and sent Iris down from Olympus to free her
struggling spirit and loosen the fastenings of her limbs. For
since she was dying not by the decree of Fate or by her own
deserts but pitiably and before her time, in a sudden blaze of

madness, Proserpina had not yet taken a lock of her golden hair or consigned her to Stygian Orcus. So Iris, bathed in dew, flew down on her saffron wings, trailing all her colours across the sky opposite the sun, and hovered over Dido's head to say: 'I am commanded to take this lock of hair as a solemn offering to Dis, and now I free you from your body.'

With these words she raised her hand and cut the hair, and as she cut, all warmth went out of Dido's body and her life passed into the winds.

ᴄꙶ 5 ᴃꙶ

FUNERAL GAMES

Meanwhile Aeneas, without slackening in his resolve, kept his fleet on course well out at sea, cutting through waves darkened by the north wind and looking back at the walls of Carthage, glowing now in the flames of poor Dido's pyre. No one understood what had lit such a blaze, but since they all knew what bitter suffering is caused when a great love is desecrated and what a woman is capable of when driven to madness, the minds of the Trojans were filled with dark foreboding. The ships were now in mid-ocean, with no land in sight. All around was sky and all around was sea, when there came a cloud like lead and stood over Aeneas bringing storm and black night and the waves shivered in the darkness. Even Palinurus himself called out from the high stern: 'What can be the meaning of these great clouds filling the sky? What have you in mind for us, Father Neptune?' Not till then did he give orders to shorten sail and bend to the stout oars. Then, setting the canvas aslant to the winds, he turned to Aeneas and said: 'Great-hearted Aeneas, even if Jupiter himself gave me his guarantee, I would not expect to reach Italy under a sky like this. The wind has changed and is freshening, howling across us from the west where the sky is dark. We cannot struggle against it or make any real headway. Since Fortune is too strong for us to resist, let us follow her. Let us change course and go where she calls. I do not think we are far from the safety of the shores of your brother Eryx and the harbours

of Sicily, if only my memory serves me right, and I can plot
our course back by the stars I observed on the way out.'

The good Aeneas then replied: 'That is what the wind
wants. I have seen it myself for some time and watched you
fighting it to no effect. Change course then and adjust the
sails. There is no land that would please me more, nowhere I
would rather put in with our weary ships, than the place that
gives a home to the Trojan Acestes and holds the bones of my
father Anchises in the lap of earth.' As soon as this was said
they set course for harbour and the wind blew from astern
and stretched their sails. The fleet raced over the sea and the
sailors were delighted to have their prows pointing at last
towards a beach they knew.

Far away, on the top of a high mountain, Acestes saw his
friends' ships arriving and was amazed. He came down to
meet them bristling with javelins and the shaggy fur of a
Libyan she-bear. Acestes had been born of a Trojan mother to
the river-god Crinisus and he had not forgotten his ancestry,
but welcomed the returning Trojans and gladly received them
with all the treasures of the countryside, comforting their
weariness with his loving care.

As soon as the next day had risen bright in the east and put
the stars to flight, Aeneas called his men from all along the
shore to a council and addressed them from a raised mound:
'Great sons of Dardanus, who draw your high blood from
the gods, the months have passed and the cycle of the year
is now complete since we laid in the ground the bones that
were all that remained of my divine father and consecrated
an altar of mourning. This is now the day, if I am right, which
I shall always find bitter and always hold in honour, for so
the gods have willed. If I were spending this day as an exile
in the Syrtes among the Gaetulians, or if I had been caught in
Greek waters and were a prisoner in the city of Mycenae, I
would still offer up these annual vows, perform these processions in ritual order and lay due offerings on altars. Today

we find ourselves near the very place where the bones and ashes of my father lie (I for one do not believe this is without the wish and will of the gods), and the sea has taken us into this friendly harbour. Come then, let us all celebrate these rites with joy. Let us ask for favouring winds and may it be his will that we found a city and offer him this worship in it every year in temples dedicated to his name. Trojan-born Acestes is giving you two head of oxen for each ship. Call to your feast the Penates, the gods of your ancestral home, and those of your host Acestes. After all this, when in nine days the dawn, god willing, lifts up her life-giving light among men and the round earth is revealed in her rays, I shall hold games for the Trojans, first a race for the ships, then for those who are fleet of foot, and a contest for those who take the arena in the boldness of their strength to compete with the javelin or the flying arrow, for those too who dare to do battle in rawhide gauntlets. Let them all come and see who wins the prizes of victory. Keep holy silence, all of you, and crown your heads with shoots of living green.'

When he had spoken he shaded his temples with a garland of his mother's myrtle. So did Helymus. So did old Acestes. So did the boy Ascanius and all the men, while Aeneas, and many thousands with him, left the council and walked to the tomb in the middle of this great escort. Here he offered a libation, duly pouring two goblets of unmixed wine upon the ground with two of fresh milk and two of sacrificial blood. Then, scattering red flowers, he spoke these words: 'Once more I greet you, my divine father. I come to greet your sacred ashes, the spirit and the shade of a father rescued in vain. Without you I must search for the land of Italy, for the fields decreed by Fate and for the Thybris of Ausonia, whatever that may be.'

When he had finished speaking, a snake slithered from under the shrine. Moving gently forward in seven great curves and seven great coils, it glided between the altars and twined itself round the tomb, its back flecked with blue and its scales flashing mottled gold like the thousand different colours cast by a rainbow on the clouds opposite the sun. Aeneas was struck dumb at the sight. At last it dragged its long length among the polished bowls and goblets and tasted the offerings, then, harming no one, it left the altars where it had fed and went back under the tomb. Encouraged by this, Aeneas renewed the rites he had begun for his father, not knowing whether to think of the snake as the genius of the place or as his father's attendant spirit. He slew a pair of yearling sheep as ritual prescribed, two swine, and as many black-backed bullocks, pouring wine from bowls and calling repeatedly upon the spirit of great Anchises and his shade released from Acheron. His comrades, too, each brought what gifts he could and gladly offered them. They heaped the altars and slaughtered bullocks while others laid out bronze vessels in due order, and all over the grass there was lighting of fires under spits and roasting of flesh.

The long-awaited day had come and the horses of Phaethon were now drawing the ninth dawn through a cloudless sky. Rumour and the famous name of Acestes had brought out all the surrounding peoples and a joyful crowd had filled the shore, some coming only to see Aeneas and his men, some also to compete. First the prizes were displayed before their eyes in the middle of the arena, sacred tripods, crowns of green, palm leaves for the victors, arms, purple-dyed garments and talents of silver and gold. The trumpet gave the signal from a mound of earth in the middle. The games had started.

The first event was for four heavy-oared ships of the same class picked out of the fleet. The *Pristis* was a fast ship with a keen crew commanded by Mnestheus. He was soon to become the Italian Mnestheus, from whom the family of the Memmii take their name. The huge *Chimaera* was a great hulk of a ship the size of a city, commanded by Gyas, and to drive her through the water the Trojans sat in three tiers and plied three banks of oars one above the other. Sergestus sailed the great *Centaur* (he it was who gave his name to the Sergii), and Cloanthus, the founder of the Roman Cluentii, was in the blue-green *Scylla*.

Well out to sea off a wave-beaten shore there stands a rock which in winter, when the north-westerly winds are darkening the stars, is often submerged and battered by the swell. But in calm weather all is quiet and the level top of it stands up from a glassy sea and gulls love to bask on it. Here Father Aeneas set up a green branch of holm-oak as a mark round which the sailors would know they had to turn to begin the long row home. They then drew lots for their starting positions, and the captains stood on the high sterns gleaming in the splendour of purple and gold. The crews wore garlands of poplar leaves and the oil they had poured on their shoulders glistened on the naked skin. There they sat at the thwarts, straining their arms at the oars and their ears to hear the starting signal. They were shuddering with fear and their hearts were leaping and pumping the blood for the sheer love of glory. When the shrill trumpet sounded, in that one instant the ships all surged forward from the line and the shouting of the sailors rose and struck the heavens. Their arms drew the oars back and the water was churned to foam. Side by side they ploughed their furrows and tore open the whole sea to its depths with their oars and triple beaks, like two-horse chariots streaming full-pelt from the starting gates and racing over the ground, or like charioteers at full gallop cracking the rippling reins on their horses' backs and hanging forward over them with the whip. All the woods resounded with the din and cheers and roars of encouragement. The echo of the shouting rolled round the curve of the shore and bounced back off the hills.

In all this noise and excitement Gyas shot out in front and took the lead over the first stretch of water. Cloanthus was next. His rowers were better but he was slowed down by the weight of his ship. Behind them the *Pristis* and the *Centaur* were contesting third place. Now the *Pristis* has it. Now the huge *Centaur* moves into the lead, and now they are level, bow by bow, ploughing the salt sea with their long keels. They were soon getting near the rock, almost at the turning point, when Gyas, still in the lead at this half-way stage, called out to his helmsman: 'Where are you going, Menoetes? Who told you to steer to starboard? Your line is over here, to port! Hug the shore. The oars on the port side should be scraping the rocks. Leave the deep water to the others!' These were his orders, but Menoetes was afraid of hidden rocks and pulled the bows round to the open sea. 'You're off course!' shouted Gyas, correcting his line. 'Where do you think you're going? Make for the rocks, Menoetes!' and even as he was shouting, he saw Cloanthus close behind him and cutting in, just scraping past on the port side between Gyas' ship and the roaring rocks. He was past in a moment, safe in clear water and sailing away from the mark. Young Gyas was incensed. The rage burned in his bones and tears ran down his cheeks. Without a thought for his own dignity or the safety of his crew he took the sluggard Menoetes and threw him off the high stern head first into the sea. He then took over the tiller himself and became his own helmsman, urging on the rowers and pulling the rudder round to make for the shore. Menoetes was no lightweight and was no longer young. He went straight to the bottom and it was some time before he surfaced. At last he climbed to the top of the dry rock and sat there with the water streaming out of his clothes. The Trojans had laughed as he fell and as he swam and they laughed as he spewed up waves of salt water from his stomach.

Sergestus and Mnestheus in the last two boats were both delighted that Gyas was losing time and both saw a hope of overtaking the flying Gyas. Sergestus took the lead as they came up to the rock, but not by a whole ship's length. His

bow was out in front but the *Pristis* was pressing him hard
and her beak was ahead of his stern. Her captain Mnestheus
was pacing the gangway between the rowers, urging them on
on either side: 'Now is the time!' he cried. 'Now you must rise
to your oars. You are the men who stood with Hector. You
are the men I chose as comrades in the last hours of Troy.
Now let us see the courage and the heart you showed off
Gaetulia in the shoals of the Syrtes and in the Ionian sea when
the waves were driving us on to Cape Malea. I am no longer
hoping to be first. It is not victory that Mnestheus is fighting
for, though who knows? . . . But let victory go to whom Neptune has given it. The disgrace would be to be last. Prevent
that shame, my fellow-Trojans, and that will be our victory.'
At this they bent to the oars and strove with all their might.
The bronzed ship shuddered at their great thrusts and the
surface of the water sped away beneath them. Their breathing
quickened, chests heaved, mouths dried and the sweat poured
off their bodies in rivers. It was pure chance that brought
them the honour they longed for. Sergestus was desperately
forcing the bow of his ship close to the rocks and cutting
inside into dangerous water when all ended in disaster as he
ran aground on a projecting reef. The rock quivered at the
impact, the flailing oars grated on its jagged edges and the
shattered prow was left hanging in mid-air. The crew leapt
up and stood there shouting. Some busied themselves with
iron-tipped poles and their pointed boat-hooks. Some were
salvaging broken oars from the surf. Mnestheus was exultant
and success only made him more determined. The oars pulled
fast and true. He called upon the winds and as he set course
for the homeward stretch and ran shoreward over the open
sea, he was like a dove startled out of the cave where it has its
home and its beloved nestlings in the secret honeycombs of
the rock; it flies off in terror to the fields with a great explosion
of wings inside the cave, but it soon swoops down through
the quiet air and glides along in the bright light; its wings are

swift but they scarcely move – just so was Mnestheus. Just so was the *Pristis* as she cut through the last stretch of water. Just so did she fly along under her own impetus.

First Mnestheus left Sergestus struggling behind him, stuck on his rock high out of the water. There he was in the shallows, shouting in vain for help and learning how to row with broken oars. Next Mnestheus went after Gyas and the huge *Chimaera* which soon fell behind for lack of its helmsman. Now, at the very end of the race, only Cloanthus was in front of him. He took up the pursuit and pressed him hard, straining every nerve.

The shouting grew twice as loud. They all cheered him on as he gave chase and the heavens rang with the noise. Cloanthus and his men on the *Scylla* saw the honour as theirs by right. They had already won the victory and had no intention of giving it up. They would rather have lost their lives than lose the glory. Mnestheus and his men on the *Pristis* were feeding on success. They could win because they thought they could. They drew level and would perhaps have taken the prize if Cloanthus had not stretched out his arms to the sea, pouring out his prayers and calling on the gods to witness his vows: 'O you gods who rule the sea and over whose waters I now race, this is my vow and gladly will I keep it: I shall come to your altars on this shore with a gleaming white bull. On the salt waves of the sea I shall scatter its entrails and pour streams of wine.' He spoke and was heard by the sea nymph Panopaea and all the dancing bands of the Nereids and of Phorcys. As he sailed on, Father Portunus pushed the ship with his own great hand and it flew landward swifter than the wind from the south or the flight of an arrow, till it arrived safe in the deep waters of the harbour.

Then the son of Anchises called them all together in due order and bade the herald loudly proclaim Cloanthus the victor, and veiled his head with the green leaves of the laurel. For each ship there was a gift of wine, three bullocks of their choice and a great talent of silver. In addition the captains were singled out for special honours. The victor received a cloak embroidered with gold round which there ran a broad double meander of Meliboean purple, and woven into it was the royal prince running with his javelin and wearying the swift stags on the leafy slopes of Mount Ida. There he was, eager and breathless, so it seemed, and down from Ida plunged the bird that carries the thunderbolt of Jupiter and carried him off in its hooked talons high into the heavens while the old men who were there as his guards stretched their hands in vain towards the stars and the dogs barked furiously up into the air. To Mnestheus, whose courage had in the end won him second place, Aeneas gave a breastplate interwoven with burnished mail and triple threads of gold, which he had stripped with his own hands from the defeated Demoleos on the banks of the swift Simois under the high walls of Troy. For Mnestheus this was to be a proud possession and his protection in battle. His attendants Phegeus and Sagaris hoisted it up on to their shoulders, all the many layers of it, but they could hardly carry it away, yet Demoleos used to wear it while running all over the battlefield in pursuit of Trojans. The third prize was a pair of bronze drinking cauldrons and some embossed drinking cups of solid silver.

At last they had all received rich gifts and were glorying in them as they walked, their foreheads bound with purple ribbons, when Sergestus appeared, taking in the boat that was the object of all their laughter and had missed all the honours. He had prised her off the cruel rock with great difficulty and no mean skill, but she had lost oars and was limping in with only one bank of them. Like a snake caught crossing a raised road, as they often are, and run over by a bronze wheel or battered by a traveller with a heavy stone and left mangled and half-dead, it tries in vain to escape by twisting its body into long curves, part of it still fierce, the blazing eyes, the hissing, high-uplifted head, but the wounded part holds it back as it writhes and coils and twines itself into knots – this is how the *Centaur* moved, rowing slowly along. But she put up sails and came into the harbour mouth under full canvas. Aeneas, delighted that Sergestus had saved his ship and brought his men to port, gave him a prize, as promised, the Cretan slave woman Pholoe, good with her hands and with two sons at the breast.

After the boat race, dutiful Aeneas strode to a piece of grassy level ground. All around it stood wooded hills and in the middle of the valley there was a circle for a theatre. When he reached this place – and many thousands went with him – Aeneas sat down on a raised platform in the middle of the concourse. Here he offered prizes for any men who might wish to take part in a foot race, whetting their ambition with rewards, and Trojans and Sicanians flocked in from all sides. Nisus and Euryalus were first, Euryalus standing out for the bloom of his youthful beauty and Nisus for the loving care he showed to him. Then came Diores, a prince of the noble line of Priam, and after him Salius and Patron together, one an Acarnanian, the other an Arcadian of Tegean stock. Then came two young Sicilians, Helymus and Panopes, men of the woods, attendants of old Acestes, and many more whose names are buried in oblivion. When they had gathered, Aeneas spoke in the middle of them: 'Give your minds to what I have to say. Mark it well and be of good cheer. No man of you will leave without winning a prize from my hand. Two Cretan arrows I shall give, their steel tips burnished and gleaming, and a two-headed axe embossed with silver. These rewards will be the same for all of you, but there will be other prizes for the first three in the race and crowns woven of golden olive for their heads. The winner will have a horse with splendid trappings, the second an Amazonian quiver full of Thracian arrows, slung on a belt with a broad gold band and the clasp that fastens it is a polished jewel. The third can leave the field content with an Argive helmet.'

When he had finished speaking, they took their places, the signal sounded and they were off, streaming away from the starting-point in one great cloud. But as soon as they came in sight of the finish, Nisus shot out a long way in front of all of them, swifter than the wind and the wings of the lightning. Second, but a long way behind, was Salius. Then, after a gap, came Euryalus in third place. Behind him was Helymus, then, immediately behind him and hard on his heels, was Diores leaning over his shoulder, and if there had been more course to run, he would have overtaken and passed him or they would have run a dead heat.

They were soon almost at the end of the course and tiring as they came up to the line, when the unlucky Nisus slid and fell on a slippery patch of blood that had been spilt where they had killed bullocks and wet the earth and the green grass that grew upon it. Here, as he pounded the track exulting in the very moment of victory, he lost his footing and fell on his face in the filthy dung and blood from the sacrifice. But he was not the man to forget Euryalus and the love he bore him. He rose from the slime and threw himself in the path of Salius and knocked him head over heels, sprawling on the hard-packed sand. Euryalus flashed past. Thanks to his friend he was in the lead and speeding along to loud applause and cheers, Helymus behind him with Diores now winning the third prize. But Salius stood up before the faces of the fathers in the front rows and filled the whole bowl of the huge assembly with loud clamour, demanding the honour of which he had been cheated. On the side of Euryalus were the favour in which he was held, his beauty as he stood there weeping and the manly spirit growing in that lovely body. On his side too was Diores, protesting at the top of his voice. He had come in third but there would be no third prize for him if the first were to be given to Salius. Father Aeneas then spoke: 'You young men will all keep your prizes. The awards have been made and no one changes that. Let it be my task to offer consolation to our friend for the downfall he did nothing to deserve.' With these words he gave Salius the hide of a huge Gaetulian lion, weighed down with gilded claws and mane. This was too much for Nisus, who burst out: 'If losers win prizes like this and you take pity on people who fall, what gift will be enough to give to Nisus? I would have won the victor's crown of glory and deserved it if the same bad luck as brought down Salius had not disposed of me,' and as he spoke he pointed to the filthy wet dung on his face and body. Good Father Aeneas laughed and ordered them to bring out a shield made by the hand of Didymaon which had been dedicated to Neptune and taken down from the doorposts of his temple by Greeks, and he gave this superb gift to the noble young Nisus.

The race was over and the prizes finally awarded. Then spoke Aeneas: 'If there is any courage here, any man with a heart in his breast, now is the time for him to come forward with gloves on his hands and his guard up,' and he set out two prizes for the fight, for the victor a bullock with its head shadowed by ribbons and its horns plated with gold, and a sword and splendid helmet as a consolation prize for the loser. Dares did not hesitate. Immediately that great face of his appeared and all his mighty strength, and the people murmured as he hoisted himself to his feet. He had been the only man who used to stand against Paris. He was the man who had felled the huge Butes and stretched him out to die on the yellow sand by the mound where great Hector lay, when Butes came as champion from the Bebrycian race of Amycus. This was the Dares who stood there with his head held high to begin the battle, flexing his shoulders, throwing lefts and rights and thrashing the air. They looked around for an opponent, but no one in all that company dared go near him or put on the gloves. Thinking that no one was challenging him for the prize, he went straight up to Aeneas and stood there in front of him. Without more ado he took one of the bull's horns in his left hand and said: 'Son of the goddess, if no one dares trust himself to battle, how long are we going to stand here? What is the point of keeping me waiting? Tell them I can take away my prize,' and all the Trojans to a man murmured and told Aeneas to award the prize as promised.

At this Acestes had hard words for Entellus, sitting next him on a bank of green turf. 'Entellus,' he said, 'I have seen the day when you were the bravest of the heroes. Is it all in the past? Are you going to sit there meekly when a prize like this is lifted and no opposition offered? Tell me, where is Eryx now, the god they say was once your teacher? Has all that come to nothing? What about that reputation of yours that used to ring round the whole island of Sicily? And what about the great trophies hanging in your house?' 'I am not afraid,' replied Entellus. 'I have still my pride and my love of honour. But old age is slowing me down. The blood is cold and sluggish. My strength is gone and my body is worn out. But if I were what I once was, if I had the youth that makes that puppy so full of himself, prancing about there, I would not have needed the reward of a pretty bullock to bring me to my feet. I am not interested in prizes.' At these last words he threw into the middle the pair of prodigiously heavy gauntlets in which Eryx used to raise his guard, carrying them into battle with the hard leather stretched over his forearms. They were amazed. The hides of seven huge oxen were there, stiffened by lead and iron sewn into them. Dares was more amazed than anyone and stood well back at the sight of them, but the great-hearted son of Anchises picked them up and felt their weight, turning over the great folds of the jointed hides from one hand to another. Then spoke old Entellus, his voice deep in his chest: 'What would you have thought, any of you, if you had seen the gauntlets that were the armour of Hercules himself and the cruel battle these two fought on this very shore? This, Aeneas, is the armour your brother Eryx used to wear. You see it is still caked with blood and spattered brains.

With these he stood that day against great Hercules. With these I used to fight while there was still good blood in me to give me strength, before old age came to tangle with me and sprinkled both my temples with grey. But if Trojan Dares recoils from this armour of ours, and if good Aeneas is satisfied and my patron Acestes approves, let us level the odds. There's nothing to be afraid of, Dares. For you I give up the boxing leathers of Eryx, and you take off your Trojan gauntlets,' and as he spoke he threw the double cloak off his shoulders and stripped to show the great joints of his limbs, the great bones and muscles on his arms, and stood there a giant in the middle of the arena.

Then the son of Anchises took out two matching pairs of gauntlets, and tied armour of equal weight on the hands of both men. There was no more delay. Each man took up his stance, poised on his toes, stretching to his full height, guard held high in the air and no sign of fear. They kept their towering heads well back from the punches and fist struck fist as they warmed to their work. Dares had youth on his side and speed of foot. Entellus had the reach and the weight, but his knees were going. He was slow and shaky and his whole huge body heaved with the agony of breathing. Blow upon blow they threw at each other and missed. Blow upon blow drummed on the hollow rib cage, boomed on the chest and showered round the head and ears, and the cheekbones rattled with the weight of the punches. Entellus, being the heavier man, held firm in his stance, keeping watchful eyes on his opponent and swaying away from the bombardment. For Dares it was like attacking some massive high-built city or besieging a mountain fortress. This way and that he tried, covering all the ground in his manoeuvres, pressing hard with all manner of assaults and all to no avail. Then Entellus drew himself up and showed his right hand raised for the blow, but Dares was quick to see it coming down and backed away smartly. Entellus' full force was in the blow and it met the empty air. Great was his weight and great was the fall of that huge body. He fell as a hollow pine tree falls, torn up by the roots on great Mount Ida or on Erymanthus. Trojans and Sicilians leapt to their feet as one man in their excitement and the shouting rose to high heaven. Acestes was the first to run to comfort his old friend and help him from the ground. But the hero Entellus did not slow down or lose heart because of a fall. He returned to the fray with his ferocity renewed and anger rousing him to new heights of violence. His strength was kindled by shame at his fall and pride in his prowess, and in a white heat of fury he drove Dares before him all over the arena, hammering him with rights and lefts and allowing him no rest or respite. Like hailstones from a dark cloud rattling down on roofs, Entellus battered Dares with a shower of blows from both hands and sent him spinning.

At this point Father Aeneas did not allow the anger of Entellus to go any further but checked his savage passion and put an end to the fight. As he rescued the exhausted Dares he comforted him with these words: 'Unlucky Dares, what madness is this that has taken possession of you? Do you not see that your strength is not as his and the divine will has turned against you? Yield to God.' He spoke and his voice parted the combatants, and Dares was led back to the ships by his faithful comrades, dragging his weary legs, shaking his head from side to side and spitting out a mixture of gore and teeth. His men were then called and given the helmet and the sword, leaving the palm of victory and the bull to Entellus. Then spoke the victor in all his pride of spirit, glorying in the bull he had won: 'Son of the goddess, know this, and you too, men of Troy: this is the strength there used to be in my body when I was in my prime and this is the death from which you have rescued Dares.' With these words he took up his stance in front of the bullock's head as it stood there as the prize of battle, then, drawing back his right hand and rising to his full height, he swung the brutal gauntlet straight down between its horns, shattering the brains and grinding them into the bone. The ox fell and lay full out on the ground, dead and twitching, and these are the words Entellus spoke and spoke them from the heart: 'The life of this ox is worth more than the life of Dares, and with it, Eryx, I pay my debt to you in full, and here and now in the moment of victory, I lay down my gauntlets and my art.'

Aeneas immediately summoned all those who wished to take part in the archery contest and announced the prizes. With his great hand he set up the mast taken from Serestus' ship and put a cord round a fluttering dove to hang it from the top of the mast as a target for the steel-tipped arrows. The contestants gathered. Lots were thrown into a bronze helmet, and the first to leap out, to loud acclaim, gave the first place to Hippocoon, son of Hyrtacus. Next came Mnestheus, fresh from his triumph in the boat race, Mnestheus with the green olive binding his hair. Third was Eurytion, brother of the famous Pandarus who in days long past had been ordered to break the truce, and had been the first to shoot an arrow into the middle of the Greeks. Last of all, at the bottom of the helmet, was Acestes. He too dared to try his hand at the test of warriors. Soon they were bending their bows with all their strength and taking the arrows out of their quivers. A string twanged and the first arrow, from young Hippocoon, cut through the breezes of heaven to strike home full in the wood of the mast. The mast quivered, there was a flash of wings from the frightened bird and all around rang out the loud applause. Next the eager Mnestheus took his stand and drew, aiming high, straining both eye and bow, but to his dismay he failed to hit the bird, cutting the knot in the linen cords which bound her feet as she hung there at the top of the mast. She made off, flying south towards some dark clouds. Eurytion lost no time (his bow had long been bent and his arrow at the ready), but called upon his brother Pandarus as he prayed, and took aim at the dove now glorying in the freedom of the sky. As she beat her wings just beneath the black cloud, the arrow struck her and she fell dead, leaving her life among the stars of heaven and bringing back as she fell the arrow that had pierced her.

Father Acestes alone remained and the victor's palm was lost to him, but he aimed an arrow high into the breezes of the air to display his old skill and let the sound of his bow be heard. At this a sudden miracle appeared before their eyes, a mighty sign of what the future held in store. In times to come was the great fulfilment revealed and awesome prophets interpreted the omens to future ages. As it flew through the vaporous clouds, the arrow burst into flames and marked its path with fire till it was consumed and faded into thin air, like those stars that leave their appointed places and race across the sky trailing their blazing hair behind them as they fly. Sicilians and Trojans stood stock still in amazement, praying to the gods above, but the mighty Aeneas welcomed the omen and embraced the exultant Acestes, heaping great gifts on him and saying these words: 'Accept these, Father Acestes, for the Great King of Olympus has shown by this sign that he has willed you to receive honours beyond the lot of other men. Here is a gift from my old father Anchises himself, a mixing bowl engraved with figures which he once received as a great tribute from Thracian Cisseus to be a memorial and pledge of his love.' With these words he put a wreath of green laurel round Acestes' temples and declared him first victor above all the others. Nor did good Eurytion grudge him the highest honour although he alone had brought down the dove from the heights of heaven. Next in order for the prizes came the archer who had cut the cord, and last the one who had pierced the mast with his flying arrow.

But before the end of the archery contest Father Aeneas was already calling to his side Epytides, the trusty comrade and guardian of young Iulus, to speak a word in his ear: 'Go now, and if Ascanius has with him his troop of boys all ready and the horses drawn up and prepared to move, tell him to lead on his squadrons in honour of his grandfather and show himself in arms.' The people had all flooded into the circus, so Aeneas ordered them to clear the whole long track and leave the level ground free. Then came the boys, riding in perfect order on their bridled mounts, resplendent in full view of their parents, and all the men of Sicily and of Troy murmured in admiration as they rode. They wore their hair close bound in trimmed garlands in ceremonial style and each carried a pair of cornel-wood spears tipped with steel. Some of them had polished quivers hanging from their shoulders with circlets of twisted gold round neck and chest. They spread out into three separate squadrons of horse, each with its own leader at the head of a dozen boys in two separate files of six, each squadron with its own trainer, all of them gleaming in the sunlight. The first of these three squadrons of young warriors was led in triumph by a little Priam, the noble son of Polites who bore the name of his grandfather and was destined to give increase to the Italian race. His horse was a piebald Thracian with white above its hooves and a white forehead carried high. The second squadron was led by Atys, the founder of the Atii of Latium. Young Atys was a dear friend of the boy Iulus, and Iulus was last and comeliest of them all, riding on a Sidonian horse given to him by the lovely Dido as a memorial and pledge of her love. The other youngsters rode Sicilian mounts presented by old Acestes. They were daunted by the praise they received as the Trojans feasted their eyes upon them, tracing in their features the features of their distant ancestors.

After they had paraded happily on horseback round the whole gathering and shown themselves to their loved ones, when they were all ready, Epytides, standing at a distance, gave the signal with a loud call and a crack of his whip and the warriors wheeled apart into two separate sections, each of the three troops dividing its ranks equally. At a second command the two new formations turned and advanced on each other with spears at the level. All over the arena they charged and turned and charged again, winding in circles now in one direction now in the other, fighting out in full armour the very image of a battle, now exposing their backs in flight, now turning to point their spears at the enemy and now when peace is made riding along side by side. They say there was a labyrinth once in the hills of Crete where the way weaved between blind walls and lost itself in a thousand treacherous paths; there was no following of tracks in this maze, no finding of a way and no retracing of steps – such was the pattern woven by the paths of the sons of the Trojans as they wound their movements of mock battle and retreat, like dolphins swimming in the waters of the sea, cleaving the waves off Carpathos or Libya. The tradition of these manoeuvres and battles was first renewed by Ascanius, who taught the native Latins to celebrate it as he was building his walls round Alba Longa. The Albans taught their sons to do as Ascanius himself and the Trojans had done with him when they were boys. In due course great Rome itself received this tradition from Alba and preserved it. The boys are now called 'Troy' and their troop is called 'the Trojan Troop'. Here ended the games held in honour of the divine father of Aeneas.

At this moment Fortune first changed and turned against them. While they were paying to the tomb the solemn tribute of all these games, Saturnian Juno sent Iris down from the sky to the Trojan fleet and breathed favouring winds upon her as she went. Juno had many schemes in her mind and her ancient bitterness remained unsatisfied. Unseen by human eye the virgin goddess ran her swift course down her bow of a thousand colours till she came within sight of the great assembly. She then passed along the shore and saw the empty harbour and unattended ships. But there, far apart on the deserted beach, were the women of Troy, weeping for the loss of Anchises and weeping, all of them, as they looked out over the unfathomable sea. How weary they were, how numberless the breakers and how vast the sea that still remained for them to cross! These were the words on all their lips. What they were praying for was a city – they were heart sick of toiling with the sea. Iris knew how to cause mischief. She rushed into the middle of them, laying aside her divine form and dress and appearing as Beroe, the aged wife of Doryclus of Tmaros, a woman of good birth, who had borne sons and been held in high regard. In this guise she mingled with the mothers of Troy and spoke these words: 'Our sadness is that Greek hands did not drag us off to our deaths in war under the walls of our native city. O my unhappy people, for what manner of destruction is Fortune preserving you? This is the seventh summer since the fall of Troy that we have been driven by the winds and have measured every sea and land, every inhospitable rock and every angry star, rolling for ever on the waves as we search the mighty ocean for an Italy that ever recedes. Here we are in the land of our brother Eryx and Acestes is our host. Who is to prevent us from laying down the foundations of walls and giving a city to our people? I call upon our native land and household gods snatched from the hands of our enemies to no purpose, tell us, will there never again be walls that will be called the walls of Troy? Shall I never see a place with the rivers that Hector knew, the Xanthus and the Simois? It is too much to endure. Come with me now and set fire to these accursed ships and destroy them. I have seen in a dream the image of the priestess Cassandra putting blazing torches in my hands and saying: "This is your home. This is where you must find your Troy." Now is the time to act. Portents like these brook no delay. Look at these four altars of Neptune. The god himself is giving us the fire and the courage.' While still speaking she took the lead and snatched up the deadly fire, brandished it in her right hand and threw it with all her force. The minds of the women of Troy were roused and their hearts were bewildered, but one

of the many, the oldest of them all, Pyrgo, who had been royal
nurse to all the sons of Priam, called out: 'This is not Beroe
speaking to you, women of Troy. This is not the wife of
Doryclus from Rhoeteum. Look at the marks of divine beauty,
the blazing eyes. Look at her proud bearing, her features, the
sound of her voice, her walk. I have just left Beroe sick and
fretting because she was the only one who could not come
to this ceremony and would not be paying due honour to
Anchises.'

These were the words of Pyrgo and at first the women were
at a loss looking at the ships with loathing in their eyes, torn
between their pitiable desire to stay where they were on land,
and the kingdom to which destiny was calling them, when
the goddess soared through the heavens on poised wings,
cutting in her flight a great rainbow beneath the clouds. This
portent overwhelmed them. Driven at last to madness they
began to scream and snatch flames from the innermost hearths
of the encampment or rob the altar fires, hurling blazing
branches and brushwood and torches. The God of Fire raged
with unbridled fury over oars and benches and the fir wood
of the painted sterns.

It was Eumelus who brought the news to the Trojans while
they were still in the wedge-shaped blocks of seats in the
theatre near the tomb of Anchises, and they could see for
themselves the dark ash flying in clouds of smoke. Ascanius
was happily leading the cavalry manoeuvres, so he made off
to the troubled camp at full gallop although the breathless
trainers tried in vain to hold him back. 'What strange madness
is this?' he cried. 'Where, oh where is this leading you, you
unhappy women of Troy? This is not the camp of your Greek
enemies. What you are burning is your own hopes for the
future! Look at me! I am your own Ascanius!' He had been
wearing a helmet as he stirred the images of war in the mock
battle and now he took it off and threw it on the ground at his
feet. At this moment Aeneas came rushing up and columns

of Trojans with him, but the women took to flight and scattered all over the shore making for the woods and caves in the rocks, wherever they could hide. They were ashamed of what they had done and ashamed to look upon the light of day. Their wits were restored now and they recognized their own people. Juno was cast out of their hearts.

But that did not cause the fire and flame to abate their unquenchable fury. The pitch was still smouldering beneath the wet timbers, oozing slow smoke, and a consuming heat was creeping along the hulls. The canker was sinking deep into the bodies of the ships and all the exertions of men and the pouring on of water were achieving nothing. This was when the devout Aeneas tore the cloak off his shoulders and called upon the gods for help, stretching out his hands and praying: 'All-powerful Jupiter, if you do not yet abhor the whole race of Trojans, if your loving-kindness still looks as of old on the labours of men, grant now, O Father, that our fleet escape the flames. Save from destruction what little remains to the Trojans, or else with your own angry thunder cast the remnants of us down to death and, if that is what I deserve, overwhelm us here with your own right hand.' Scarcely had he spoken, when a black deluge of torrential rain came lashing down, mountain peak and plain trembled at the thunder and from the whole sky streamed the wild tempest of rain, dark with the cloud-bearing winds of the south. It poured down and filled the ships and soaked the charred timbers till all the fire was quenched and, except for four that were lost, all the ships were saved from destruction.

But this was a bitter blow for Aeneas, and his heart was heavy as he turned his thoughts this way and that, wondering whether he should forget about his destiny and settle in the fields of Sicily, or whether he ought to make for the shores of Italy. Then spoke old Nautes. He was the one man Tritonian Pallas had chosen to instruct and make pre-eminent in his art, providing him with responses to explain what the great anger of the gods portended and what the settled order of the Fates demanded. These were the words of comfort he now began to address to Aeneas: 'Son of the goddess, let us follow the Fates, whether they lead us on or lead us back. Whatever fortune may be ours, we must at all times rise above it by enduring it. Acestes is by your side and he is a Trojan, off-spring of the gods. Take him into your counsels. Be one with him. He is willing. Hand over into his care the people from the ships that are lost and those who are heart-weary of your great enterprise and destiny. Choose the old men, the women who are worn out by the sea, all of your company who are frail and have no stomach for danger, and weary as they are, here in this land let them have their city. Acestes will give them his name and they will call it Acesta.'

Aeneas was fired by these words from his old friend, but his heart was divided between all his cares as never before. Dark night had risen in her chariot to command the vault of heaven, when suddenly there appeared the form of his father Anchises gliding down from the sky and these were the words that came pouring from him: 'O my son, dearer to me than life itself in the days when life remained to me, O my son, who has been tested by the Fates of Troy, I come here in fulfilment of the command of Jupiter. He it was who drove the fire from your ships and has at last looked down from the sky and pitied you. Follow now this most wise advice which old Nautes is giving you and choose warriors from your people, the bravest hearts among them, to take to Italy. There in Latium is a wild and hardy people whom you have to overcome in war. But first you must come to the home of Dis in the underworld and go through the depths of hell to seek a meeting with me. I am not confined in the grim shades of impious Tartarus but live in Elysium in the radiant councils of the just. A chaste Sibyl will lead you to this place, shedding the blood of many black cattle in sacrifice. Then you will learn about all the descendants who will come after you and the city walls you are to be given. But now farewell. The dewy night is turning her chariot in mid-course. The cruel sun is beginning to rise in the east and I have felt the breath of his panting horses.' As he finished speaking he fled into thin air like smoke dissolving. 'Where are you going in such haste? Who are you escaping from? Who is there to keep you from my arms?' So cried Aeneas, and he stirred the smouldering ashes of the fire to worship the Lar of Pergamum and the shrine of white-haired Vesta with a ritual offering of coarse meal and incense from a full censer.

Immediately then he called his allies, Acestes first of all, and explained the command of Jupiter, the instructions of his own dear father and the resolve now firm in his own mind. There was no time lost in words and no dissent from Acestes. They transferred the mothers to the city and put ashore those who wished it, those spirits that felt no need for glory, while they themselves repaired the rowing benches, replaced the charred timbers and fitted out the ships with oars and ropes. They were a small band but their hearts were high for war. Meanwhile, Aeneas was ploughing the city bounds and allotting homes to his people. This was to be Ilium, and this was to be Troy. Trojan Acestes was delighting in his kingdom, choosing a site for his forum, summoning a senate and laying down a code of laws. Then they founded a temple to Venus of Ida, soaring to the stars on the peak of Mount Eryx, and appointed a priest to tend the tomb of Anchises, consecrating to his name a great grove all around it.

And now the whole people had feasted for nine days and performed their rites at the altars. A gentle breeze had calmed the waves and the breath of a steady south wind was calling them again to sea. Loud was the weeping along the curved shore of the bay as they lingered for a night and a day in their last embraces. Even the women, even the men who had been shuddering at the sight of the sea and unable to face its god, were now eager to sail and endure to the end the whole agony of exile, but good Aeneas comforted them with words of love and wept as he entrusted them to their kinsman Acestes. At last came the command to sacrifice three calves to Eryx and a lamb to the Storms and to cast off their moorings in due order. There stood Aeneas alone on the prow, his head bound with a wreath of trimmed olive leaves and holding a goblet in his hands as he scattered the sacrificial entrails and poured the streaming wine into the salt sea. His men vied with one another to strike the waves, sweeping them with their oars as a freshening wind from astern helped them on their way.

But Venus, never resting all this time from her cares, went to Neptune and poured out to him these words of complaint from her heart: 'It is the deadly anger of Juno, her implacable fury, that forces me to use every prayer I can. No man's piety can soften her, nor does the long passage of time. Her will is not broken by the Fates nor by the command of Jupiter and she knows no rest. In black hatred she has eaten the city of the Phrygians out of the heart of their race and dragged the Trojans who survive through every form of suffering, but she is still not satisfied. She is still persecuting the dead bones and ashes of the city she has destroyed. She alone can understand her reasons for this terrible rage. You yourself, I know, were a witness of the turmoil she has just created in the waves of the Libyan ocean, stirring up sea and sky to no avail with the help of Aeolus' winds. To think she took all this upon herself in your kingdom! And now this! Look how she has driven the mothers of the Trojans to wrong-doing. It is her cruelty that has burned out their ships, lost them their fleet and forced them to abandon their own dear ones in a strange land. As for what is to come, if what I am asking is readily conceded, if the Fates are giving them a city in that land, I beg of you to allow them a safe crossing and let them reach the Laurentine Thybris.'

Then Neptune, son of Saturn and master of the ocean depths, answered in these words: 'O Venus of Cythera, it is wholly right that you should put your trust in the sea, which is my kingdom, for you are born from it. I also have deserved your trust, for I have often checked the wild fury of the sea and sky and my care for your Aeneas has been no less on land – I call the rivers Xanthus and Simois to testify to this. During Achilles' pursuit of the broken army of Troy, when he was driving them against their own walls and killing them in their thousands, when the rivers were choked and groaning with corpses and Xanthus could find no way to roll down to the sea, there was Aeneas standing against the might of Achilles, his strength not equal to it and the gods opposed, and it was I who caught him up in a hollow cloud, although my own desire was to take these walls that I had built with my own hands for the treacherous Trojans and turn them over from top to bottom. As my mind was then, so is it even now. Put away your fears. He will arrive safely where you wish, at the harbour of Avernus. One only will be lost. One only will you look for in vain upon the sea, and that one life will be given for many.' When these words had soothed and gladdened the heart of the goddess, Father Neptune put a golden yoke on the necks of his horses and bits between their wild and foaming jaws and gave them full rein. As his blue-green chariot skimmed the surface of the sea, the waves were stilled, the swell subsided beneath his thundering axle and the rain clouds fled from the vast vault of heaven. Then all his retinue appeared, the huge sea beasts, Glaucus and his band of ageing dancers, Palaemon, son of Ino, the swift Tritons and all the ranks of Phorcys' army, while there on the left was Thetis with Melite and the maiden Panopaea, Nisaee and Spio, Thalia and Cymodoce.

Now all indecision was past and it was the turn of glad joy to capture the heart of Aeneas. Instantly he ordered all masts to be put up and canvas stretched from the yard-arms. As one man they all set their sails, letting them out in time, first to port and then to starboard. As one man they swung round the high ends of the yard-arms and swung them round again as fair winds carried the fleet on its way. They were sailing close, in line ahead with Palinurus in the lead, and their orders were to make all speed and take their course from him.

The dank night was near the mid-point of the sky. The sailors were taking their rest in peace and quiet, stretched out under their oars along the hard benches, when the God of Sleep, parting the dark and misty air, came gliding lightly down from the stars of heaven. He was coming to you, Palinurus, bringing deadly dreams you did not deserve. The god took the shape of Phorbas and sat on the high poop pouring these soft words into the ears of Palinurus: 'Son of Iasius, the sea is carrying the ships along itself. The breeze is gentle and steady. This is an hour for sleep. Put down your head and steal a little time from your labours to rest your tired eyes. I'll take over a short watch for you myself.'

Scarcely lifting his eyes, Palinurus replied: 'Are you asking me to forget what I know about the calm face of the sea and quiet waters? There is a strange power in the sea and I would never rely on it. Winds are liars and believe me, I would never trust them with Aeneas, I who have so often been betrayed by a clear sky.' This was his answer, and he stood by the tiller, gripping it with no intention of letting it go or taking his eyes off the stars. But look! The god takes a branch dripping with the water of Lethe for forgetfulness and the water of Styx for sleep. He shakes it over Palinurus, first one temple, then the other, and for all his struggles it closes his swimming eyes. As soon as this sudden sleep came upon him and his limbs began to relax, the god leaned over him, broke off a part of the poop, tiller and all, and threw him with it into the waves of the sea. Down fell Palinurus, calling again and again on his comrades, but they did not hear. The god then rose on his wings and flew off into the airy breezes, while the ships sped on their way none the worse, sailing safely on in accordance with the promises of Father Neptune.

They were soon coming near the Sirens' rocks, once a difficult coast and white with the bones of drowned men, and at that moment sounding far with the endless grinding of breaker upon rock, when Father Aeneas sensed that he was adrift without a helmsman. In mid-ocean in the dead of night he took control of the ship himself, and grieving to the heart at the loss of his friend, he cried out: 'You trusted too much, Palinurus, to a clear sky and a calm sea, and your body will lie naked on an unknown shore.'

CS 6 SO

THE UNDERWORLD

So spoke Aeneas, weeping, and gave the ships their head and at long last they glided to land at the Euboean colony of Cumae. The prows were turned out to sea, the teeth of the anchors held and they moored with their curved sterns fringing the shore. Gleaming in the sun, an eager band of warriors rushed out on to the shore of the land of Hesperia, some searching for the seeds of flame hidden in the veins of flint, some raiding the dense woods, the haunts of wild beasts, and pointing the way to rivers they had found. But the devout Aeneas made for the citadel where Apollo sits throned on high and for the vast cave standing there apart, the retreat of the awesome Sibyl, into whom Delian Apollo, the God of Prophecy, breathes mind and spirit as he reveals to her the future. They were soon coming up into the grove of Diana Trivia and Apollo's golden shrine.

They say that when Daedalus was fleeing from the kingdom of Minos, he dared to trust his life to the sky, floating off on swiftly driving wings towards the cold stars of the north, the Greater and Lesser Bears, by a route no man had ever gone before, until at last he was hovering lightly in the air above the citadel of Chalcidian Cumae. Here he first returned to earth, dedicating to Phoebus Apollo the wings that had oared him through the sky, and founding a huge temple. On its doors were depicted the death of Androgeos, son of Minos, and then the Athenians, the descendants of Cecrops, ordered to pay a cruel penalty and yield up each year the living bodies of seven of their sons. The lots are drawn and there stands the urn. Answering this on the other door are Cnossus and the land of Crete rising from the sea. Here can be seen the loving of the savage bull and Pasiphae laid out to receive it and deceive her husband Minos. Here too is the hybrid offspring, the Minotaur, half-man and half-animal, the memorial to a perverted love, and here is its home, built with such great labour, the inextricable Labyrinth. But Daedalus takes pity on the great love of the princess Ariadne and unravels the winding paths of his own baffling maze, guiding the blind steps of Theseus with a thread. You too, Icarus, would have taken no small place in this great work had the grief of Daedalus allowed it. Twice your father tried to shape your fall in gold and twice his hands fell helpless. The Trojans would have gone on gazing and read the whole story through, but Achates, who had been sent ahead, now returned bringing with him Deiphobe, the daughter of Glaucus, priestess of Phoebus and Trivia, who spoke these words to the king: 'This is no time for you to be looking at sights like these. Rather at this moment you should be sacrificing seven bullocks from a herd the yoke has never touched and seven yearling sheep as ritual prescribes.' So she addressed Aeneas. Nor were the Trojans slow to obey, and when the sacrifices were performed she called them into the lofty temple.

This rocky citadel had been colonized by Chalcidians from Euboea, and one side of it had been hollowed out to form a vast cavern into which led a hundred broad shafts, a hundred mouths, from which streamed as many voices giving the responses of the Sibyl. They had reached the threshold of the cavern when the virgin priestess cried: 'Now is the time to ask your destinies. It is the god. The god is here.' At that moment, as she spoke in front of the doors, her face was transfigured, her colour changed, her hair fell in disorder about her head and she stood there with heaving breast and her wild heart bursting in ecstasy. She seemed to grow in stature and speak as no mortal had ever spoken when the god came to her in his power and breathed upon her. 'Why are you hesitating, Trojan Aeneas?' she cried. 'Why are you so slow to offer your vows and prayers? Until you have prayed the great mouths of my house are dumb and will not open.' She spake and said no more. A cold shiver ran through the very bones of the Trojans and their king poured out the prayers from the depths of his heart: 'Phoebus Apollo, you have always pitied the cruel sufferings of the Trojans. You guided the hands of Trojan Paris and the arrow he sent into the body of Achilles. You were my leader as I set out upon all the oceans that lap the great lands of the earth and reached the far-flung peoples of Massylia and the fields that lie out to sea in front of the Syrtes. Now at long last we lay hold upon the shores of Italy that have so often receded before us. I pray that from this moment the fortunes of Troy may follow us no further. You too, you gods and goddesses who could not endure Troy and the great glory of the race of Dardanus, it is now right that you should have mercy upon the people of Pergamum. And you, O most holy priestess, you who know in advance what is to be, grant my prayer, for the kingdom I ask for is no more than what is owed me by the Fates, and allow the Trojans and their homeless and harried gods to settle in Latium. Then I shall found a temple of solid marble to Phoebus and Trivia, and holy days in the name of Phoebus. And for you too there will be a great shrine in our kingdom. Here I shall establish your oracle and the riddling prophecies you have given my people and I shall dedicate chosen priests to your gracious service, only do not consign your prophecies to leaves to be confused and mocked by every wind that blows. Sing them in your own voice, I beg of you.' He said no more.

But the priestess was still in wild frenzy in her cave and still resisting Apollo. The more she tried to shake her body free of the great god the harder he strained upon her foaming mouth, taming that wild heart and moulding her by his pressure. And now the hundred huge doors of her house opened of their own accord and gave her answer to the winds: 'At long last you have done with the perils of the ocean, but worse things remain for you to bear on land. The sons of Dardanus shall come into their kingdom in Lavinium (put that fear out of your mind), but it is a coming they will wish they had never known. I see wars, deadly wars, I see the Thybris foaming with torrents of blood. There you will find a Simois and a Xanthus. There, too, will be a Greek camp. A second Achilles is already born in Latium, and he too is the son of a goddess. Juno too is part of Trojan destiny and will never be far away when you are a suppliant begging in dire need among all the peoples and all the cities of Italy. Once again the cause of all this Trojan suffering will be a foreign bride, another marriage with a stranger. You must not give way to these adversities but must face them all the more boldly wherever your fortune allows it. Your road to safety, strange as it may seem, will start from a Greek city.'

With these words from her shrine the Sibyl of Cumae sang her fearful riddling prophecies, her voice booming in the cave as she wrapped the truth in darkness, while Apollo shook the reins upon her in her frenzy and dug the spurs into her flanks. The madness passed. The wild words died upon her lips, and the hero Aeneas began to speak: 'O virgin priestess, suffering cannot come to me in any new or unforeseen form. I have already known it. Deep in my heart I have lived it all before. One prayer I have. Since they say the gate of the king of the underworld is here and here too is the black swamp which the tide of Acheron floods, I pray to be allowed to go and look upon the face of my dear father. Show me the way and open the sacred doors for me. On these shoulders I carried him away through the flames and a hail of weapons and rescued him from the middle of his enemies. He went on my journey with me over all the oceans and endured all the threats of sea and sky, feeble as he was but finding a strength beyond his years. Besides, it was my father himself who begged and commanded me to come to you as a suppliant and approach your doors. Pity the father, O gracious one, and pity the son, I beg of you. All things are within your power and Hecate had her purpose in giving you charge of the grove of Avernus. Was not Orpheus allowed to summon the shade of his wife with the sound of the strings of his Thracian lyre? And when Pollux was allowed to redeem his brother by sharing his death, did he not often travel that road and often return? Do I need to speak of Theseus? Or of great Hercules? I too am descended from highest Jupiter.'

While he was still speaking these words of prayer with his hand upon the altar, the prophetess began her answer: 'Trojan, son of Anchises, sprung from the blood of the gods, it is easy to go down to the underworld. The door of black Dis stands open night and day. But to retrace your steps and escape to the upper air, that is the task, that is the labour. Some few have succeeded, sons of the gods, loved and favoured by Jupiter or raised to the heavens by the flame of their own virtue. The middle of that world is filled with woods and the river Cocytus glides round them, holding them in its dark embrace. But if your desire is so great, if you have so much longing to sail twice upon the pools of Styx and twice to see black Tartarus, if it is your pleasure to indulge this labour of madness, listen to what must first be done. Hidden in a dark tree, there is a golden bough. Golden are its leaves and its pliant stem and it is sacred to Proserpina, the Juno of the underworld. A whole grove conceals it and the shades of a dark, encircling valley close it in. But no man may enter the hidden places of the earth before plucking the golden foliage and fruit from this tree. The beautiful Proserpina has ordained that this is the offering that must be brought to her. When one golden branch has been torn from that tree, another comes to take its place and the stem puts forth leaves of the same metal. So then, lift up your eyes and look for it, and when in due time you find it, take it in your hand and pluck it. If you are a man called by the Fates, it will come easily of its own accord. But if not, no strength will prevail against it and hard steel will not be able to hack it off. Besides, you have a friend lying dead. Of this you know nothing, but his body is polluting the whole fleet while you linger here at our door asking for oracles. First you must carry him to his place of rest and lay him in a tomb. Then you must bring black cattle to begin the purification. When all this is done, you will be able to see the groves of Styx and the kingdom where no living man may set his foot.' So she spoke and no other word would cross her lips.

With downcast eyes and sorrowing face Aeneas walked from the cave, revolving in his mind the fulfilment of these dark prophecies. With him stride for stride went the faithful Achates, and his heart was no less heavy. Long did they talk and many different thoughts they shared. Who was this dead comrade of whom the priestess spoke? Whose body was this that had to be buried? And when they came to the shore, there above the tide line they found the body of Misenus, who had died a death he had not deserved. Misenus, son of Aeolus, who had no equal at summoning the troops with his trumpet and kindling the God of War with his music, had been the comrade of great Hector, and by Hector's side had borne the brunt of battle, excelling not only with the trumpet but also with the spear. But after Achilles had defeated Hector and taken his life, the brave Misenus had found no less a hero to follow by joining Aeneas of the stock of Dardanus. Then one day in his folly he happened to be blowing into a sea shell, sending the sound ringing over the waves, and challenged the gods to play as well as he. At this his rival Triton, if the tale is to be believed, had caught him up and drowned him in the surf among the rocks. So then they raised around his body a loud noise of lamentation, not least the dutiful Aeneas. Without delay they hastened, still weeping, to obey the commands of the Sibyl, gathering trees to build an altar which would be his tomb and striving to raise it to the skies. Into the ancient forest they went among the deep lairs of wild beasts. Down came the pines. The ilex rang under the axe. Beams of ash and oak were split along the grain with wedges, and they rolled great manna ashes down from the mountains.

Aeneas took the lead in all this work, urging on his comrades and carrying at his side the same tools as they, but he was always gloomily turning one thought over in his mind as he looked at the measureless forest and he chanced to utter it in this prayer: 'If only that golden bough would now show itself to us in this great grove, since everything the priestess said about Misenus has proved only too true.' No sooner had he spoken than two doves chanced to come flying out of the sky and settle there on the grass in front of him. Then the great Aeneas knew they were his mother's birds and he was glad. 'Be my guides,' he prayed, 'if there is a way, and direct your swift flight through the air into the grove where the rich branch shades the fertile soil. And you, goddess, my mother, do not fail me in my time of uncertainty.' So he spoke and waited to see what signs they would give and in what direction they would move. They flew and fed and flew again, always keeping in sight of those who followed. Then, when they came to the evil-smelling throat of Avernus, first they soared and then they swooped down through the clear air and settled where Aeneas had prayed they would settle, on the top of the tree that was two trees, from whose green there gleamed the breath of gold along the branch. Just as the mistletoe, not sown by the tree on which it grows, puts out fresh foliage in the woods in the cold of winter and twines its yellow fruit round slender tree trunks, so shone the golden foliage on the dark ilex, so rustled the golden foil in the gentle breeze. Aeneas seized the branch instantly. It resisted, but he broke it off impatiently and carried it into the house of the priestess, the Sibyl.

All this time the Trojans on the shore did not cease to weep for Misenus and pay their last tributes to his ungrateful ashes. First they built a huge pyre with rich pine torches and oak logs, and wove dark-leaved branches into its sides, setting up funeral cypresses in front of it and crowning it with his shining armour. Some prepared hot water in cauldrons and when it was seething over the flames, they washed and anointed the cold body and raised their lament. When they had wept their fill, they placed him on the bier and draped him in his familiar purple robes. Others then performed their sad duty of carrying the bier and held their torches to the bottom of the pyre with averted faces, after the practice of their ancestors. Then all the heaped-up offerings burned – the incense, the sacrificial food, the bowls filled with oil. After the embers had collapsed and the flames died down, they washed with wine the thirsty ashes that were all that remained of him and Corynaeus collected his bones and sealed them in a bronze casket. Three times he carried them in solemn ritual round the comrades of Misenus and sprinkled the heroes lightly with pure water from the branch of a fruitful olive tree, uttering words of farewell as he performed the lustration. But dutiful Aeneas raised a great mound as a tomb and set on it the hero's arms, the oars he rowed with and the trumpet he had blown, there near the airy top of Mount Misenus which bears his name now and for ever through all years to come.

As soon as this was done he hastened to carry out the commands of the Sibyl. There was a huge, deep cave with jagged pebbles underfoot and a gaping mouth guarded by dark woods and the black waters of a lake. No bird could wing its flight over this cave and live, so deadly was the breath that streamed out of that black throat and up into the vault of heaven. Hence the Greek name, 'Aornos', 'the place without birds'. Here first of all the priestess stood four black-backed bullocks and poured wine upon their foreheads. She then plucked the bristles from the peak of their foreheads between their horns to lay upon the altar fires as a first offering and lifted up her voice to call on Hecate, mighty in the sky and mighty in Erebus. Attendants put the knife to the throat and caught the warm blood in bowls. Aeneas himself took his sword and sacrificed a black-fleeced lamb to Night, the mother of the Furies and her sister Earth, and to Proserpina a barren cow. Then he set up a night altar for the worship of the Stygian king and laid whole carcasses of bulls on its flames and poured rich oil on the burning entrails. Then suddenly, just before the sun had crossed his threshold in the sky and begun to rise, the earth bellowed underfoot, the wooded ridges quaked and dogs could be heard howling in the darkness. It was the arrival of the goddess. 'Stand apart, all you who are unsancti-fied,' cried the priestess. 'Stand well apart. The whole grove must be free of your presence. You, Aeneas, must enter upon your journey. Draw your sword from the sheath. Now you need your courage. Now let your heart be strong.' With these words she moved in a trance into the open cave and step for step Aeneas strode fearlessly along behind her.

You gods who rule the world of the spirits, you silent shades, and Chaos, and Phlegethon, you dark and silent wastes, let it be right for me to tell what I have been told, let it be with your divine blessing that I reveal what is hidden deep in the mists beneath the earth.

They walked in the darkness of that lonely night with shadows all about them, through the empty halls of Dis and his desolate kingdom, as men walk in a wood by the sinister light of a fitful moon when Jupiter has buried the sky in shade and black night has robbed all things of their colour. Before the entrance hall of Orcus, in the very throat of hell, Grief and Revenge have made their beds and Old Age lives there in despair, with white faced Diseases and Fear and Hunger, corrupter of men, and squalid Poverty, things dreadful to look upon, and Death and Drudgery besides. Then there are Sleep, Death's sister, perverted Pleasures, murderous War astride the threshold, the iron chambers of the Furies and raving Discord with blood-soaked ribbons binding her viperous hair. In the middle a huge dark elm spreads out its ancient arms, the resting-place, so they say, of flocks of idle dreams, one clinging under every leaf. Here too are all manner of monstrous beasts, Centaurs stabling inside the gate, Scyllas – half dogs, half women – Briareus with his hundred heads, the Hydra of Lerna hissing fiercely, the Chimaera armed in fire, Gorgons and Harpies and the triple phantom of Geryon. Now Aeneas drew his sword in sudden alarm to meet them with naked steel as they came at him, and if his wise companion had not warned him that this was the fluttering of disembodied spirits, a mere semblance of living substance, he would have rushed upon them and parted empty shadows with steel.

Here begins the road that leads to the rolling waters of Acheron, the river of Tartarus. Here is a vast quagmire of boiling whirlpools which belches sand and slime into Cocytus, and these are the rivers and waters guarded by the terrible Charon in his filthy rags. On his chin there grows a thick grey beard, never trimmed. His glaring eyes are lit with fire and a foul cloak hangs from a knot at his shoulder. With his own hands he plies the pole and sees to the sails as he ferries the dead in a boat the colour of burnt iron. He is no longer young but, being a god, enjoys rude strength and a green old age. The whole throng of the dead was rushing to this part of the bank, mothers, men, great-hearted heroes whose lives were ended, boys, unmarried girls and young men laid on the pyre before the faces of their parents, as many as are the leaves that fall in the forest at the first chill of autumn, as many as the birds that flock to land from deep ocean when the cold season of the year drives them over the sea to lands bathed in sun. There they stood begging to be allowed to be the first to cross and stretching out their arms in longing for the further shore.

But the grim boatman takes some here and some there, and others he pushes away far back from the sandy shore.

Aeneas, amazed and distressed by all this tumult, cried out: 'Tell me, virgin priestess, what is the meaning of this crowding to the river? What do the spirits want? Why are some pushed away from the bank while others sweep the livid water with their oars?' The aged Sibyl made this brief reply: 'Son of Anchises, beyond all doubt the offspring of the gods, what you are seeing is the deep pools of the Cocytus and the swamp of the Styx, by whose divine power the gods are afraid to swear and lie. The throng you see on this side are the helpless souls of the unburied. The ferryman there is Charon. Those sailing the waters of the Styx have all been buried. No man may be ferried from fearful bank to fearful bank of this roaring current until his bones are laid to rest. Instead they wander for a hundred years, fluttering round these shores until they are at last allowed to return to the pools they have so longed for.' The son of Anchises checked his stride and stood stock still with many thoughts coursing through his mind as he pitied their cruel fate, when there among the sufferers, lacking all honour in death, he caught sight of Leucaspis, and Orontes, the captain of the Lycian fleet, men who had started with him from Troy, sailed the wind-torn seas and been overwhelmed by gales from the south that rolled them in the ocean, ships and crews.

Next he saw coming towards him his helmsman Palinurus who had fallen from the ship's stern and plunged into the sea while watching the stars on the recent crossing from Libya. Aeneas recognized this sorrowing figure with difficulty in the dark shadow and was the first to speak: 'What god was it, Palinurus, that took you from us and drowned you in mid-ocean? Come tell me, for this is the one response of Apollo that has misled me. I have never found him false before. He prophesied that you would be safe upon the sea and would reach the boundaries of Ausonia. Is this how he has kept his promise?' 'O great leader, son of Anchises,' replied Palinurus, 'the bowl on the tripod of Apollo has not deceived you and no god drowned me in the sea. While I was holding course and gripping the tiller which it was my charge to guard, it was broken off by some mighty force and I dragged it down with me as I fell. I swear by the wild sea that I felt no fear for myself to equal my fear that your ship might come to grief, stripped of its steering and with its pilot pitched into the sea and that great swell rising. Three long winter nights the wind blew hard from the south and carried me over seas I could not measure, till, when light came on the fourth day, and a wave lifted me to its crest, I could just make out the land of Italy. I swam slowly to shore and was on the point of reaching safety when a tribe of ruffians set upon me with their knives, weighed down as I was by my wet clothes and clinging by my finger tips to the jagged rocks at the foot of a cliff. Knowing nothing of me they made me their plunder, and now I am at the mercy of the winds, and the waves are turning my body over at the water's edge. But I beg of you, by the joyous light and winds of heaven, by your father, by your hopes of Iulus as he grows to manhood, you who have never known defeat, rescue me from this anguish. Either throw some earth on my body – you can do that. Just steer back to the harbours of Velia. Or else if there is a way and the goddess who gave you life shows it to you – for I do not believe you are preparing to sail these great rivers and the swamp of the Styx unless the blessing of the gods is with you – take pity on me, give me your right hand, take me aboard and carry me with you over the waves, so that in death at least I can be at peace in a place of quiet.' These were the words of Palinurus and this was the reply of the Sibyl: 'How did you conceive this monstrous desire, Palinurus? How can you, who are unburied, hope to set eyes on the river Styx and the pitiless waters of the Furies? How can you come near the bank unbidden? You must cease to hope that the Fates of the gods can be altered by prayers. But hear my words, remember them and find comfort for your sad case. The people who live far and wide in all their cities round the place where you died, will be driven by signs from heaven to consecrate your bones. They will raise a burial mound for you and to that mound will pay their annual tribute and the place will bear the name of Palinurus for all time to come.' At these words his sorrows were removed and the grief was driven from that sad heart for a short time. He rejoiced in the land that was to bear his name.

And so they carried on to the end of the road on which they had started, and at last came near the river. When the boatman, now in mid-stream, looked ashore from the waves of the Styx and saw them coming through the silent wood towards the bank, he called out to them and challenged them: 'You there, whoever you are, making for our river with a sword by your side, come tell us why you are here. Speak to us from where you stand. Take not another step. This place belongs to the shades, to Sleep and to Night, the bringer of Sleep. Living bodies may not be carried on the boat that plies the Styx. It gave me little enough pleasure to take even Hercules aboard when he came, or Theseus, or Pirithous, although they said they were born of gods and their strength was irresistible. It was Hercules whose hand put chains on the watchdog of Tartarus and dragged him shivering from the very throne of our king. The others had taken it upon themselves to steal the queen, my mistress, from the chamber of Dis.' The answer of the Amphrysian Sibyl was brief: 'Here there are no such designs. You have no need for alarm. These weapons of his bring no violence. The monstrous keeper of the gate can bark in his cave and frighten the bloodless shades till the end of time and Proserpina can stay chaste behind her uncle's doors. Trojan Aeneas, famous for his devotion and his feats of arms, is going down to his father in the darkest depths of Erebus. If the sight of such devotion does not move you, then look at this branch,' she said, showing the branch that had been hidden in her robes, 'and realize what it is.' At this the swelling anger subsided in his heart. No more words were needed. Seeing it again after a long age, and marvelling at the fateful branch, the holy offering, he turned his dark boat and steered towards the bank. He then drove off the souls who were on board with him sitting all along the cross benches, and cleared the gangways. In the same moment he took the huge Aeneas into the hull of his little boat. Being only sewn together, it groaned under his weight, shipping great volumes of stagnant water through the seams, but in the end it carried priestess and hero safely over and landed them on the foul slime among the grey-green reeds.

The kingdom on this side resounded with barking from the three throats of the huge monster Cerberus lying in a cave in front of them. When the priestess was close enough to see the snakes writhing on his neck, she threw him a honey cake steeped in soporific drugs. He opened his three jaws, each of them rabid with hunger, and snapped it up where it fell. The massive back relaxed and he sprawled full length on the ground, filling his cave. The sentry now sunk in sleep, Aeneas leapt to take command of the entrance and was soon free of the bank of that river which no man may recross.

In that instant they heard voices, a great weeping and wailing of the souls of infants who had lost their share of the sweetness of life on its very threshold, torn from the breast on some black day and drowned in the bitterness of death. Next to them were those who had been condemned to death on false charges, but they did not receive their places without the casting of lots and the appointment of juries. Minos, the president of the court, shakes the lots in the urn, summoning the silent dead to act as jurymen, and holds inquiry into the lives of the accused and the charges against them. Next to them were those unhappy people who had raised their innocent hands against themselves, who had so loathed the light that they had thrown away their own lives. But now how they would wish to be under high heaven, enduring poverty and drudgery, however hard! That cannot be, for they are bound in the coils of the hateful swamp of the waters of death, trapped in the ninefold windings of the river Styx. Not far from here could be seen what they call the Mourning Plains, stretching away in every direction. Here are the victims of unhappy love, consumed by that cruel wasting sickness, hidden in the lonely byways of an encircling wood of myrtle trees, and their suffering does not leave them even in death. Here Aeneas saw Phaedra, and Procris, and Eriphyle in tears as she displayed the wounds her cruel son had given her. Here he saw Evadne and Pasiphae with Laodamia walking by their side, and Caeneus, once a young man, but now a woman restored by destiny to her former shape.

Wandering among them in that great wood was Phoenician Dido with her wound still fresh. When the Trojan hero stopped beside her, recognizing her dim form in the darkness, like a man who sees or thinks he has seen the new moon rising through the clouds at the beginning of the month, in that instant he wept and spoke sweet words of love to her: 'So the news they brought me was true, unhappy Dido? They told me you were dead and had ended your life with the sword. Alas! Alas! Was I the cause of your dying? I swear by the stars, by the gods above, by whatever there is to swear by in the depths of the earth, it was against my will, O queen, that I left your shore. It was the stern authority of the commands of the gods that drove me on, as it drives me now through the shades of this dark night in this foul and mouldering place. I could not have believed that my leaving would cause you such sorrow. Do not move away. Do not leave my sight. Who are you running from? Fate has decreed that I shall not speak to you again.' With these words Aeneas, shedding tears, tried to comfort that burning spirit, but grim-faced she kept her eyes upon the ground and did not look at him. Her features moved no more when he began to speak than if she had been a block of flint or Parian marble quarried on Mount Marpessus. Then at last she rushed away, hating him, into the shadows of the wood where Sychaeus, who had been her husband, answered her grief with grief and her love with love. Aeneas was no less stricken by the injustice of her fate and long did he gaze after her, pitying her as she went.

From here they continued on their appointed road and they were soon on the most distant of these fields, the place set apart for brave warriors. Here Tydeus came to meet him, and Parthenopaeus, famous for his feats of arms, and the pale phantom of Adrastus. Here he saw and groaned to see standing in their long ranks all the sons of Dardanus who had fallen in battle and been bitterly lamented in the upper world, Glaucus, Medon and Thersilochus, the three sons of Antenor, and Polyboetes, the consecrated priest of Ceres, and Idaeus still keeping hold of Priam's chariot, still keeping hold of his armour. The shades crowded round him on the right and on the left and it was not enough just to see him, they wished to delay him, to walk with him, to learn the reasons for his coming. But when the Greek leaders and the soldiers of Agamemnon in their phalanxes saw the hero and his armour gleaming through the shadows, a wild panic seized them. Some turned and ran as they had run once before to get back to their ships, while others lifted up their voices and raised a tiny cry, which started as a shout from mouth wide open, but no shout came.

Here too he saw Deiphobus, son of Priam, his whole body mutilated and his face cruelly torn. The face and both hands were in shreds. The ears had been ripped from the head. He was noseless and hideous. Aeneas, barely recognizing him as he tried frantically to hide the fearsome punishment he had received, went up to him and spoke in the voice he knew so well: 'Deiphobus, mighty warrior, descended from the noble blood of Teucer, who could have wished to inflict such a

punishment upon you? And who was able to do this? I was
told that on that last night you wore yourself out killing the
enemy and fell on a huge pile of Greek and Trojan dead. At
that time I did all I could do, raising an empty tomb for you
on the shore of Cape Rhoeteum and lifting up my voice to call
three times upon your shade. Your name and your arms mark
the place but you I could not find, my friend, to bury your
body in our native land as I was leaving it.'

To this the son of Priam answered: 'You, my friend, have
left nothing undone. You have paid all that is owed to
Deiphobus and to his dead shade. It is my own destiny and
the crimes of the murderess from Sparta that have brought
me to this. These are reminders of Helen. You know how we
spent that last night in false joy. It is our lot to remember it
only too well. When the horse that was the instrument of Fate,
heavy with the brood of armed men in its belly, leapt over
the high walls of Pergamum, Helen was pretending to be
worshipping Bacchus, leading the women of Phrygia around
the city, dancing and shrieking their ritual cries. There she
was in the middle of them with a huge torch, signalling to the
Greeks from the top of the citadel, and all the time I was
sleeping soundly in our accursed bed, worn out by all I had
suffered and sunk in a sleep that was sweet and deep and like
the peace of death. Meanwhile this excellent wife of mine,
after moving all my armour out of the house and taking the
good sword from under my head, called in Menelaus and
threw open the doors, hoping no doubt that her loving husband would take this as a great favour to wipe out the memory
of her past sins. You can guess the rest. They burst into
the room, taking with them the man who had incited them to
their crimes, their comrade Ulixes – they say he is descended
from Aeolus. You gods, if the punishment I ask is just, grant
that a fate like mine should strike again and strike Greeks.
But come, it is now time for you to tell me what chance has
brought you here alive. Is it your sea wanderings that have

taken you here? Are you under the instructions of the gods? What fortune is dogging you, that you should come here to our sad and sunless homes in this troubled place?'

While they were speaking to one another, Dawn's rosy chariot had already run its heavenly course past the midpoint of the vault of the sky, and they might have spent all the allotted time in talking but for Aeneas' companion. The Sibyl gave her warning in few words: 'Night is running quickly by, Aeneas, and we waste the hours in weeping. This is where the way divides. On the right it leads up to the walls of great Dis. This is the road we take for Elysium. On the left is the road of punishment for evildoers, leading to Tartarus, the place of the damned.' 'There is no need for anger, great priestess,' replied Deiphobus. 'I shall go to take my place among the dead and return to darkness. Go, Aeneas, go, great glory of our Troy, and enjoy a better fate than mine.' These were his only words, and as he spoke he turned on his heel and strode away.

Aeneas looked back suddenly and saw under a cliff on his left a broad city encircled by a triple wall and washed all round by Phlegethon, one of the rivers of Tartarus, a torrent of fire and flame, rolling and grinding great boulders in its current. There before him stood a huge gate with columns of solid adamant so strong that neither the violence of men nor of the heavenly gods themselves could ever uproot them in war, and an iron tower rose into the air where Tisiphone sat with her blood-soaked dress girt up, guarding the entrance and never sleeping, night or day. They could hear the groans from the city, the cruel crack of the lash, the dragging and clanking of iron chains. Aeneas stood in terror, listening to the noise. 'What kinds of criminal are here? Tell me, virgin priestess, what punishments are inflicted on them? What is this wild lamentation in the air?' The Sibyl replied: 'Great leader of the Trojans, the chaste may not set foot upon the threshold of that evil place, but when Hecate put me in charge of the groves of Avernus, she herself explained the punishments the gods had imposed and showed me them all. Here Rhadamanthus, king of Cnossus, holds sway with his unbending laws, chastising men, hearing all the frauds they have practised and forcing them to confess the undiscovered crimes they have gloated over in the upper world – foolishly, for they have only delayed the day of atonement till after death. Immediately the avenging Tisiphone leaps upon the guilty and flogs them till they writhe, waving fearful serpents over them in her left hand and calling up the cohorts of her savage sisters, the Furies. Then at last the gates sacred to the gods below shriek in their sockets and open wide. You see what a watch she keeps, sitting in the entrance? What a sight she is guarding the threshold? Inside, more savage still, the huge, black-throated, fifty-headed Hydra has its lair. And then there is Tartarus itself, stretching sheer down into its dark chasm twice as far as we look up to the ethereal Olympus in the sky. Here, rolling in the bottom of the abyss, is the ancient brood of Earth, the army of Titans, hurled down by the thunderbolt. Here too I saw the huge bodies of the twin sons of Aloeus who laid violent hands on the immeasurable sky to wrench it from its place and tear down Jupiter from his heavenly kingdom. I saw too Salmoneus suffering cruel punishment, still miming the flames of Jupiter and the rumblings of Olympus. He it was who, riding his four-horse chariot and brandishing a torch, used to go in glory through the peoples of Greece and the city of Olympia in the heart of Elis, laying claim to divine honours for himself – fool that he was to copy the storm and the inimitable thunderbolt with the rattle of the horn of his horses' hooves on bronze. Through the thick clouds the All-powerful Father hurled his lightning – no smoky light from pitchy torches for him – and sent him spinning deep into the abyss. Tityos too I could see, the nurseling of Earth, mother of all, his body sprawling over nine whole acres while a huge vulture with hooked beak cropped his immortal liver and the flesh that was such a rich supplier of punishment. Deep in his breast it roosts and forages for its dinners, while the filaments of his liver know no rest but are restored as soon as they are consumed. I do not need to speak of the Lapiths, of Ixion or Pirithous; over whose heads the boulder of black flint is always slipping, always seeming to be falling. The gold gleams on the high supports of festal couches and a feast is laid in regal splendour before the eyes of the guilty, but the greatest of the Furies is reclining at table and allows no hand to touch the food, but leaps up brandishing a torch and shouting with a voice of thunder. Immured in this place and waiting for punishment are those who in life hated their brothers, beat their fathers, defrauded their dependants, found wealth and brooded over it alone without setting aside a share for their kinsmen – these are most numerous of all – men caught and killed in adultery, men who took up arms against their own people and did not shrink from abusing their masters' trust. Do not ask to know what their punishments are, what form of pain or what misfortune has engulfed them. Some are rolling huge rocks, or hang spreadeagled on the spokes of wheels. Theseus is sitting there dejected, and there he will sit until the end of time, while Phlegyas, most wretched of them all, shouts this lesson for all men at the top of his voice in the darkness: "Learn to be just and not to slight the gods. You have been warned." Here is the man who has sold his native land for gold, and set a tyrant over it, putting up tablets with new laws for a price and for a price removing them. Here is the man who forced his way into his daughter's bed and a forbidden union. They have all dared to attempt some monstrous crime against the gods and have succeeded in their attempt. If I had a hundred tongues, a hundred mouths and a voice of iron, I could not encompass all their different crimes or speak the names of all their different punishments.'

When the aged priestess of Apollo had finished her answer, she added these words: 'But come now, you must take the road and complete the task you have begun. Let us hasten. I can see the high walls forged in the furnaces of the Cyclopes and the gates there in front of us in the arch. This is where we have been told to lay the gift that is required of us.' After these words they walked the dark road together, soon covering the distance and coming close to the doors. There Aeneas leapt on the threshold, sprinkled his body with fresh water and fixed the bough full in the doorway.

When this rite was at last performed and his duty to the goddess was done, they entered the land of joy, the lovely glades of the fortunate woods and the home of the blest. Here a broader sky clothes the plains in glowing light, and the spirits have their own sun and their own stars. Some take exercise on grassy wrestling-grounds and hold athletic contests and wrestling bouts on the golden sand. Others pound the earth with dancing feet and sing their songs while Orpheus, the priest of Thrace, accompanies their measures on his seven-stringed lyre, plucking the notes sometimes with his fingers, sometimes with his ivory plectrum. Here was the ancient line of Teucer, the fairest of all families, great-hearted heroes born in a better time, Ilus, Assaracus and Dardanus, the founder of Troy. Aeneas admired from a distance their armour and empty chariots. Their swords were planted in the ground and their horses wandered free on the plain cropping the grass. Reposing there below the earth, they took the same joy in their chariots and their armour as when alive, and the same care to feed their sleek horses. Then suddenly he saw others on both sides of him feasting on the grass, singing in a joyful choir their paean to Apollo all through a grove of fragrant laurels where the mighty river Eridanus rolls through the forest to the upper world. Here were armies of men bearing wounds received while fighting for their native land, priests who had been chaste unto death and true prophets whose words were worthy of Apollo; then those who have raised human life to new heights by the skills they have

discovered and those whom men remember for what they
have done for men. All these with sacred ribbons of white
round their foreheads gathered round Aeneas and the Sibyl,
and she addressed these words to them, especially to
Musaeus, for the whole great throng looked up to him as he
stood there in the middle, head and shoulders above them all:
'Tell me, blessed spirits, and you, best of poets, which part of
this world holds Anchises? Where is he to be found? It is
because of Anchises that we have come here and crossed the
great rivers of Erebus.' The hero returned a short answer:
'None of us has a fixed home. We live in these densely wooded
groves and rest on the soft couches of the river bank and in
the fresh water-meadows. But if that is the desire of your
hearts, come climb this ridge and I shall soon set you on an
easy path.' So saying, he walked on in front of them to a place
from where they could see the plains below them bathed in
light, and from that point Aeneas and the Sibyl came down
from the mountain tops.

Father Anchises was deep in a green valley, walking among
the souls who were enclosed there and eagerly surveying
them as they waited to rise into the upper light. It so happened
that at that moment he was counting the number of his people,
reviewing his dear descendants, their fates and their fortunes,
their characters and their courage in war. When he saw Aeneas
coming towards him over the grass, he stretched out both
hands in eager welcome, with the tears streaming down his
cheeks, and these were the words that broke from his mouth:
'You have come at last,' he cried. 'I knew your devotion would
prevail over all the rigour of the journey and bring you to
your father. Am I to be allowed to look upon your face, my
son, to hear the voice I know so well and answer it with my
own? I never doubted it. I counted the hours, knowing you
would come, and my love has not deceived me. I understand
how many lands you have travelled and how many seas you
have sailed to come to me here. I know the dangers that have

beset you. I so feared the kingdom of Libya would do you harm.' 'It was my vision of you,' replied Aeneas, 'always before my eyes and always stricken with sorrow, that drove me to the threshold of this place. The fleet is moored in the Tyrrhenian sea on the shores of Italy. Give me your right hand, father. Give it me. Do not avoid my embrace.' As he spoke these words his cheeks were washed with tears and three times he tried to put his arms around his father's neck. Three times the phantom melted in his hands, as weightless as the wind, as light as the flight of sleep.

And now Aeneas saw in a side valley a secluded grove with copses of rustling trees where the river Lethe glided along past peaceful dwelling houses. Around it fluttered numberless races and tribes of men, like bees in a meadow on a clear summer day, settling on all the many-coloured flowers and crowding round the gleaming white lilies while the whole plain is loud with their buzzing. Not understanding what he saw, Aeneas shuddered at the sudden sight of them and asked why this was, what was that river in the distance and who were all those companies of men crowding its banks. 'These are the souls to whom Fate owes a second body,' replied Anchises. 'They come to the waves of the river Lethe and drink the waters of serenity and draughts of long oblivion. I have long been eager to tell you who they are, to show them to you face to face and count the generations of my people to you so that you could rejoice the more with me at the finding of Italy.' 'But are we to believe,' replied Aeneas to his dear father, 'that there are some souls who rise from here to go back under the sky and return to sluggish bodies? Why do the poor wretches have this terrible longing for the light?' 'I shall tell you, my son, and leave you no longer in doubt,' replied Anchises, and he began to explain all things in due order.

'In the beginning Spirit fed all things from within, the sky and the earth, the level waters, the shining globe of the moon and the Titan's star, the sun. It was Mind that set all this matter in motion. Infused through all the limbs, it mingled with that great body, and from the union there sprang the families of men and of animals, the living things of the air and the strange creatures born beneath the marble surface of the sea. The living force within them is of fire and its seeds have their source in heaven, but their guilt-ridden bodies make them slow and they are dulled by earthly limbs and dying flesh. It is this that gives them their fears and desires, their griefs and joys. Closed in the blind darkness of this prison they do not see out to the winds of air. Even when life leaves them on their last day of light, they are not wholly freed from all the many ills and miseries of the body which must harden in them over the long years and become ingrained in ways we cannot understand. And so they are put to punishment, to pay the penalty for all their ancient sins. Some are stretched and hung out empty to dry in the winds. Some have the stain of evil washed out of them under a vast tide of water or scorched out by fire. Each of us suffers his own fate in the after-life. From here we are sent over the broad plains of Elysium and some few of us possess these fields of joy until the circle of time is completed and the length of days has removed ingrained corruption and left us pure ethereal sense, the fire of elemental air. All these others whom you see, when they have rolled the wheel for a thousand years, are called out by God to come in great columns to the river of Lethe, so that they may duly go back and see the vault of heaven again remembering nothing, and begin to be willing to return to bodies.'

When he had finished speaking, Anchises led his son and the Sibyl with him into the middle of this noisy crowd of souls, and took up his stance on a mound from which he could pick them all out as they came towards him in a long line and recognize their faces as they came.

'Come now, and I shall tell you of the glory that lies in store for the sons of Dardanus, for the men of Italian stock who will be our descendants, bright spirits that will inherit our name, and I shall reveal to you your own destiny. That young warrior you see there leaning on the sword of valour, to him is allotted the place nearest to the light in this grove, and he will be the first of us to rise into the ethereal air with an admixture of Italic blood. He will be called Silvius, an Alban name, and he will be your son, born after your death. You will live long, but he will be born too late for you to know, and your wife Lavinia will rear him in the woods to be a king and father of kings and found our dynasty to rule in Alba Longa. Next to him is Procas, glory of the Trojan race, and Capys, and Numitor, and the king who will renew your name, Silvius Aeneas, your equal in piety and in arms if ever he succeeds to his rightful throne in Alba. What warriors they are! Look at the strength of them! Look at the oak wreaths, the Civic Crowns, that shade their foreheads! These are the men who will build Nomentum for you, and Gabii, and the city of Fidenae. They will set Collatia's citadel on the mountains, and Pometia too, and Castrum Inui, and Bola and Cora. These, my son, will be the names of places which are at this moment places without names. And Romulus, son of Mars, will march at his grand-father's side. He will be of the stock of Assaracus, and his mother, who will rear him, will be Ilia. Do you see how the double crest stands on his head and the Father of the Gods himself already honours him with his own emblem? Look at him, my son. Under his auspices will be founded Rome in all her glory, whose empire shall cover the earth and whose spirit shall rise to the heights of Olympus. Her single city will enclose seven citadels within its walls and she will be blest in the abundance of her sons, like Cybele, the Mother Goddess of Mount Berecyntus riding in her chariot turret-crowned through the cities of Phrygia, rejoicing in her divine offspring and embracing a hundred descendants, all of them gods, all dwellers in the heights of heaven.

'Now turn your two eyes in this direction and look at this family of yours, your own Romans. Here is Caesar, and all the sons of Iulus about to come under the great vault of the sky. Here is the man whose coming you so often hear prophesied, here he is, Augustus Caesar, son of a god, the man who will bring back the golden years to the fields of Latium once ruled over by Saturn, and extend Rome's empire beyond the Indians and the Garamantes to a land beyond the stars, beyond the yearly path of the sun, where Atlas holds on his shoulder the sky all studded with burning stars and turns it on its axis. The kingdoms round the Caspian sea and Lake Maeotis are even now quaking at the prophecies of his coming. The seven mouths of the Nile are in turmoil and alarm. Hercules himself did not make his way to so many lands though his arrow pierced the hind with hooves of bronze, though he gave peace to the woods of Erymanthus and made Lerna tremble at his bow. Nor did triumphing Bacchus ride so far when he drove his tiger-drawn chariot down from the high peak of Nysa, and the reins that guided the yoke were the tendrils of the vine. And do we still hesitate to extend our courage by our actions? Does any fear deter us from taking our stand on the shore of Ausonia?

'But who is this at a distance resplendent in his crown of olive and carrying holy emblems? I know that white hair and beard. This is the man who will first found our city on laws, the Roman king called from the little town of Cures in the poor land of the Sabines into a mighty empire. Hard on his heels will come Tullus to shatter the leisure of his native land and rouse to battle men that have settled into idleness and armies that have lost the habit of triumph. Next to him, and more boastful, comes Ancus, too fond even now of the breath of popular favour. Do you wish to see now the Tarquin kings, the proud spirit of avenging Brutus and the rods of office he will retrieve? He will be the first to be given authority as consul and the stern axes of that office. When his sons raise

again the standards of war, it is their own father that will call
them to account in the glorious name of liberty. He is not
favoured by fortune, however future ages may judge these
actions – love of his country will prevail with him and his
limitless desire for glory. Look too at the Decii and the Drusi
over there and cruel Torquatus with his axe and Camillus
carrying back the standards. Those two spirits you see gleaming there in their well-matched armour are in harmony now
while they are buried in night, but if once they reach the light
of life, what a terrible war they will stir up between them!
What battles! What carnage when the father-in-law swoops
from the ramparts of the Alps and his citadel of Monaco and
his son-in-law leads against him the embattled armies of the
East! O my sons, do not harden your hearts to such wars.
Do not turn your strong hands against the flesh of your
motherland. You who are sprung from Olympus, you must
be the first to show clemency. Throw down your weapons. O
blood of my blood! Here is the man who will triumph over
Corinth, slaughtering the men of Achaea, and will ride his
chariot in triumph to the hill of the Capitol. Here is the
man who will raze Argos and Agamemnon's Mycenae to the
ground, and will kill Perseus the Aeacid, descendant of the
mighty warrior Achilles, avenging his Trojan ancestors and
the violation of the shrine of Minerva. Who would leave you
unmentioned, great Cato? Or you, Cossus? Who would be
without the Gracchi? Or the two Scipios, both of them
thunderbolts of war, the bane of Libya? Or Fabricius, who
will find power in poverty? Or you, Serranus, sowing your
seed in the furrow? Where are you rushing that weary spirit
along to, you Fabii? You there are the great Fabius Maximus,
the one man who restores the state by delaying. Others, I do
not doubt it, will beat bronze into figures that breathe more
softly. Others will draw living likenesses out of marble. Others
will plead cases better or describe with their rod the courses
of the stars across the sky and predict their risings. Your task,

Roman, and do not forget it, will be to govern the peoples of the world in your empire. These will be your arts – and to impose a settled pattern upon peace, to pardon the defeated and war down the proud.'

Aeneas and the Sibyl wondered at what they heard, and Father Anchises continued: 'Look there at Marcellus marching in glory in spoils torn from the enemy commander he will fight and defeat. There he is, victorious and towering above all others. This is the man who will ride into battle and quell a great uprising, steadying the ranks of Rome and laying low the Carthaginian and the rebellious Gaul. He will be the third to dedicate the supreme spoils to Father Quirinus.'

At this Aeneas addressed his father, for he saw marching with Marcellus a young man, noble in appearance and in gleaming armour, but his brow was dark and his eyes downcast. 'Who is that, father, marching at the side of Marcellus? Is it one of his sons or one of the great line of his descendants? What a stir his escort makes! And himself, what a presence! But round his head there hovers a shadow dark as night.'

Then his father Anchises began to speak through his tears: 'O my son, do not ask. This is the greatest grief that you and yours will ever suffer. Fate will just show him to the earth – no more. The gods in heaven have judged that the Roman race would become too powerful if this gift were theirs to keep. What a noise of the mourning of men will come from the Field of Mars to Mars' great city. What a cortège will Tiber see as he glides past the new Mausoleum on his shore! No son of Troy will ever so raise the hopes of his Latin ancestors, nor will the land of Romulus so pride itself on any of its young. Alas for his goodness! Alas for his old-fashioned truthfulness and that right hand undefeated in war! No enemies could ever have come against him in war and lived, whether he was armed to fight on foot or spurring the flanks of his foaming war-horse. Oh the pity of it! If only you could break the harsh laws of Fate! You will be Marcellus. Give lilies from full hands. Leave me to scatter red roses. These at least I can heap up for the spirit of my descendant and perform the rite although it will achieve nothing.'

So did they wander all over the broad fields of air and saw all there was to see, and after Anchises had shown each and every sight to his son and kindled in his mind a love for the glory that was to come, he told them then of the wars he would in due course have to fight and of the Laurentine peoples, of the city of Latinus and how he could avoid or endure all the trials that lay before him.

There are two gates of sleep: one is called the Gate of Horn and it is an easy exit for true shades; the other is made all in gleaming white ivory, but through it the powers of the underworld send false dreams up towards the heavens. There on that night did Anchises walk with his son and with the Sibyl and spoke such words to them as he sent them on their journey through the Gate of Ivory.

Aeneas made his way back to his ships and his comrades, then steered a straight course to the harbour of Caieta. The anchors were thrown from the prows and the ships stood along the shore.

For lines 756–892, see Appendix One

❧ 7 ❧

WAR IN LATIUM

You too, Caieta, nurse of Aeneas, have given by your death eternal fame to our shores; the honour paid you there even now protects your resting-place, and your name marks the place where your bones lie in great Hesperia, if that glory is of any value.

Good Aeneas duly performed the funeral rites and heaped up a barrow for the tomb, and when there was calm on the high seas, he set sail and left the port behind him. A fair breeze kept blowing as night came on, the white moon lit their course and the sea shone in its shimmering rays. Keeping close inshore, they skirted the land where Circe, the daughter of the Sun, lives among her riches. There she sets the untrodden groves ringing with never-ending singing and burns the fragrant cedar wood in her proud palace to lighten the darkness of the night as her sounding shuttle runs across the delicate warp. From her palace could be heard growls of anger from lions fretting at their chains and roaring late into the night, the raging of bristling boars and penned bears and howling from huge creatures in the shape of wolves. These had all been men, but with her irresistible herbs the savage goddess had given them the faces and hides of wild beasts. To protect the devout Trojans from suffering these monstrous changes, Neptune kept them from sailing into the harbour or coming near that deadly shore. He filled their sails with favouring winds and took them past the boiling breakers to safety.

And now the waves were beginning to be tinged with red from the rays of the sun and Aurora on her rosy chariot glowed in gold from the heights of heaven, when of a sudden the wind fell, every breath was still and the oars toiled in a sluggish sea. Here it was that Aeneas, still well off shore, sighted a great forest and the river Tiber in all its beauty bursting through it into the sea with its racing waves and their burden of yellow sand. Around it and above it all manner of birds that haunted the banks and bed of the river were flying through the trees and sweetening the air with their singing. Aeneas gave the order to change course and turn the prows to the land, and he came into the dark river rejoicing.

Come now, Erato, and I shall tell of the kings of ancient Latium, of its history, of the state of this land when first the army of strangers beached their ships on the shores of Ausonia. I shall recall too, the cause of the first battle – come, goddess, come and instruct your prophet. I shall speak of fearsome fighting, I shall speak of wars and of kings driven into the ways of death by their pride of spirit, of a band of fighting men from Etruria and the whole land of Hesperia under arms. For me this is the birth of a higher order of things. This is a greater work I now set in motion.

King Latinus was by this time an old man and he had reigned over the countryside and the cities for many peaceful years. We are told that he was the son of Faunus and the Laurentine nymph Marica. The father of Faunus was Picus, and the father claimed by Picus was Saturn. Saturn then was the first founder of the line. By divine Fate Latinus had no male offspring. His son had been snatched from him as he was rising into the first bloom of his youth. An only daughter tended his home and preserved the succession for this great palace. She was now grown to womanhood and at the age for marriage and many were seeking her hand from great Latium and the whole of Ausonia, Turnus the handsomest of them all, his claim supported by the long line of his forbears. The queen Amata longed above all things to see him married to her daughter, but many frightening portents from the gods forbade it.

Deep in the innermost courtyard of the palace there stood a laurel tree. Its foliage was sacred and it had been preserved and held in awe for many years, ever since Father Latinus himself had found it, so the story went, when he was building his first citadel, and dedicated it to Phoebus Apollo, naming the settlers after it, the Laurentines. To this tree there came by some miracle a cloud of bees, buzzing loudly as they floated through the liquid air till suddenly they formed a swarm and settled on its very top, hanging there from a leafy branch with their feet intertwined. A prophet thus interpreted: 'What we see is a stranger arriving, and an army coming from the same direction, making for the same place and gaining mastery over the heights of the citadel.' Then again when Lavinia was standing by her father's side tending the altar with her chaste torches, another fearful sight was seen. Her long hair caught fire and all its adornment was crackling in the flames. The princess's hair was blazing, her crown with all its lovely jewels was blazing, and soon she was wrapped in smoke and a yellow glare, and scattering fire all over the palace. The horror and miracle of it were on everyone's lips, and it was prophesied that her own fate and fame would be bright, but that a great war would come upon the people.

Troubled by such portents, the king consulted the oracle of his prophetic father Faunus, visiting the grove under Mount Albunea, a huge forest sounding with the waters of its sacred fountain and breathing thick clouds of sulphurous vapour. Here the Italian tribes and the whole land of Oenotria came to consult the oracle in their times of doubt. Here the priest brought his offerings, and when he lay down to sleep in the silence of the night on a bed of the fleeces of slaughtered sheep, he would see many strange fleeting visions, hear all manner of voices, enjoy the converse of the gods and speak to Acheron in the depths of Avernus. Here too on that day Father Latinus himself came to consult the oracle, and after sacrificing a hundred unshorn yearling sheep as ritual prescribes, he was lying propped on a bed of their hides and fleeces, when suddenly a voice was heard from the depths of the forest: 'Do not seek to join your daughter in marriage to a Latin. O my son, do not place your trust in any union that lies to hand. Strangers will come to be your sons-in-law and by their blood to raise our name to the stars. The descendants of that stock will see the whole world turning under their feet and guided by their will, from where the rising Sun looks down on the streams of Ocean to where he sees them as he sets.' This was the reply of his father Faunus, the warning that came in the silence of the night. Latinus did not keep it locked in his heart, and Rumour as she flew had already spread it far and wide through the cities of Ausonia when the young warriors from Laomedon's Troy tied up their ships to the grassy ramparts of the river bank.

Aeneas, the leading captains of Troy and lovely Iulus had lain down on the grass under the branches of a tall tree and were starting to eat a meal, setting out their banquets on wheaten cakes – for Jupiter himself had so advised them – and heaping country fruits on these foundations, the gift of Ceres, the Goddess of Grain. When the fruit had all been eaten and the sparseness of the diet had driven them to sink their teeth into Ceres' bounty, scant as it was, to violate with bold hand and jaw the fateful circles of crust and show no mercy to the flat quarter-circles of bread, suddenly Iulus said, as a joke: 'Look! We are eating even our tables!' That was all. This was the first announcement they had received of the end of their sufferings. Astounded by the presence of the divine, Aeneas seized upon his son's first words while he was still speaking and made him be silent. In that instant he lifted up

his voice and cried out: 'Hail to the land owed to me by the
Fates, and hail to the household gods of Troy who have kept
faith with me! This is our home. This is our own land. For
now I remember it, my father Anchises left me this riddle of
the Fates. "When you sail to an unknown shore and your food
is so scanty that hunger forces you to eat your tables, that is
the time, weary as you are, to hope for a home. This is where
you must with your own hand lay down the foundations of
your first buildings and raise a rampart round them." This is
the hunger of which he spoke. This is the last hunger we had
to endure and it will put an end to our calamities. Come then,
with joy in your hearts, and at the first light of the sun let us
all go in different directions from the harbour to explore this
place and find out who are the men that live here and where
their cities are. And now pour libations from your goblets to
Jupiter, call upon my father Anchises with your prayers and
set the wine in due order on the tables.'

At these words he wound a branch of living green round
his forehead and offered up prayers to the Genius of the place
and to Earth the first of gods, to nymphs and rivers not yet
known, then to Night and the stars of Night then rising, to
Jupiter of Mount Ida and the Phrygian Mother in due order,
to his mother in the heavens and his father in Erebus. In reply
the All-powerful Father thundered clear three times from the
heights of the sky and with his own hand he displayed in
heaven a burning cloud, quivering with rays of golden light.
In that instant the word spread through the Trojan ranks that
the day had come for them to found their promised city.
Eagerly they renewed their feast, and delighting in this great
omen, they set up their mixing bowls and crowned the wine
with garlands.

When the next day first rose and began to traverse the earth
with its lamp, they set out in different directions to explore
the city and the boundaries and shores of this people. Here
were the pools where the river Numicus springs, here was

the river Tiber and here were the homes of the stalwart Latins. Then Aeneas, son of Anchises, ordered one hundred men chosen as spokesmen from every rank of his people to go to the sacred walls of king Latinus all bearing branches of Pallas Athene's olive wreathed in wool, carrying gifts and asking for peace for the Trojans. They made no delay, but hastened with all speed to do as they were bidden, while Aeneas himself was marking out the line of his walls with a shallow ditch and beginning to build on the site, surrounding this first settlement on the shore with a stockade and rampart as though it were a camp. The warriors, meanwhile, their long journey ended, were within sight of the towers and high roofs of the city of the Latins and came up to the wall. There in front of the city boys and young men in the first flower of their age were exercising with their horses, training chariot teams in clouds of dust, bending the springy bow, spinning the stiff-shafted javelin, racing and sparring, when a messenger riding ahead of the Trojans brought to the ear of the old king the news that huge men in strange costume had arrived. Latinus ordered them to be summoned into his palace while he took his seat in the middle on his ancestral throne.

A sacred building, massive and soaring to the sky with a hundred columns, stood on the highest point of the city. This was the palace of Laurentine Picus, a building held in great awe because of an ancestral sense of the presence of the divine in the grove that surrounded it. Here the omens declared that kings should receive their sceptres and take up the rods of office for the first time. This temple was their senate-house, this the hall in which they held their sacred banquets and here the elders would sacrifice a ram and sit down to feast at long tables. Here too, carved in old cedar wood, stood in order in the forecourt the statues of their ancestors from time long past: Italus and Father Sabinus planter of the vine, still holding in effigy his curved pruning knife, old Saturn, the image of Janus with his two faces, all the other kings since the foundation of the city and with them the men who had been wounded while fighting to defend their native land. Many too were the weapons hung on the posts of the temple doors, captured chariots, curved axes, crests of helmets, great bolts from the gates of cities, spears, shields and beaks broken off the prows of ships. Here too, with his short toga, and the augural staff of Quirinus in his left hand, sat the Horse-Tamer, Picus himself, whose wife Circe, possessed by lust, struck him with her rod of gold and changed him with her potions into a bird, sprinkling colours on his wings.

Such was the temple of the gods where Latinus sat in the seat of his fathers and called the Trojans to him in his palace. When they entered he was the first to speak, addressing them in these kindly words: 'Tell me, sons of Dardanus – you see we know your city and your family and had heard about you before you set your course here – what are you searching for? What has taken your ships over all the blue waters of ocean to the shore of Ausonia? What need has brought you here? Whether you have lost your way or been driven off course by the storms that sailors have to endure so often on the high seas, you have now sailed between the banks of our river and are sitting in harbour. Do not refuse the guest-friendship we offer you and do not forget that we Latins are Saturn's people, righteous not because of laws and restraints but holding of our own free will to the way of life of our ancient god. Besides, I myself remember that the Auruncan elders used to say – the story is dimmed by the mists of time – that Dardanus was born in these fields and went far away to the cities of Ida in Phrygia and the Thracian island of Samos now known as Samothrace. He set out from here, from his Tyrrhenian home in Corythus, and now sits on a throne in the palace of gold in the starry sky, and his altars add a name to the roll of the gods.'

He spoke these words, and these were the words in which Ilioneus made answer: 'Great king, son of Faunus, it is not

black storms and heavy seas that have driven us to this land
of yours, nor have we lost our way by mistaking a star or a
coastline. It is by design and with willing hearts that we all
sail to this city, driven from our own kingdom which was once
the greatest the journeying Sun could see from the highest part
of the heavens. Our race begins with Jupiter. The warriors of
Dardanus' Troy rejoice in Jupiter as their ancestor. Their king,
Aeneas himself, is descended from Jupiter's exalted stock,
and Trojan Aeneas has sent us to your door. The storm that
gathered in merciless Mycenae and swept across the plains
beneath Mount Ida, and the fate that drove the worlds of
Europe and of Asia to collide, these are known to all men,
those who live far to the north where the ends of the earth
beat back the stream of Oceanus, and those who are separated
from us by the zone of the cruel sun whose expanse covers
the middle zone of five. Since that cataclysm we have sailed
all those desolate seas, and now we ask for a little piece of
land for our fathers' gods, for harmless refuge on the beach,
for the air and sea which are there for all men. We shall not
bring discredit on your kingdom. Great fame will be yours,
and our gratitude for such a service will never fade. The men
of Ausonia will never regret taking Troy to their hearts. I
swear by the destiny of Aeneas and his right arm, strong in
the truth to all who have tested it, and strong in war and the
weapons of war, that many nations have asked to enter into
alliance with us. Do not despise us because we choose to
come to you with words of supplication and olive branches
wreathed in wool in our hands. Many races have wished to
be joined to ours, but the commands of divine destiny have
driven us to seek out your country. This was the first home of
Dardanus. This is the land to which Apollo calls us back, and
urges us with his mighty decrees towards the Tyrrhenian
Thybris and the sacred shallows of the fountain of Numicus.
These gifts, besides, Aeneas offers you, some small relics of
his former fortunes rescued from the flames of Troy. From

this gold cup his father Anchises used to pour libations at the altar. This was the sceptre Priam would hold in his hand as he gave solemn judgement before the concourse of the nations, and here are his sacred head-dress and the vestments woven for him by the women of Troy.'

When Ilioneus had finished speaking, Latinus kept his gaze fixed upon the ground and did not move. He never raised his burning eyes but they were never still. As a king he was moved to see the sceptre of Priam and his embroidered purple but much more was he moved by the thought of a marriage and a husband for his daughter, and long did he ponder in his heart the prophecy of old Faunus. So this was the fulfilment of the portents sent by the Fates! So this was the son-in-law who would come from a distant land and be called to share his kingdom with equal auspices. This was the man whose descendants would excel in valour and whose power would win the whole world. He spoke at last, and joyfully: 'May the gods give their blessing to what we begin today and to their own prophecies! You will receive what you ask, Trojan, and I do not refuse your gifts. While Latinus is king, you will have rich land to farm and you will never feel the lack of the wealth of Troy. Only Aeneas must come here himself if he is so eager and impatient to join us in friendship and be called our ally. He has no need to recoil from the face of his friends. It will be a condition of the peace I offer that I must clasp the hand of your king. But now I charge you to take back this answer to him. Tell him I have a daughter, and the oracles from my father's shrine agree with all the signs from heaven in forbidding me to join her in marriage to any man of our people. Strangers will come from a foreign land to be my sons-in-law – this is what is in store for Latium according to the prophecies – and by their blood they shall raise our name to the stars. This Aeneas is the man the Fates demand. This I believe, and this is my will, if my mind has any true insight into the future.' After these words, Father Latinus made a choice from his whole stable where three hundred well-groomed horses stood in their high-built stalls, ordering one to be brought out instantly for each of the Trojans in due order. Their hooves were swift as wings, their saddle-cloths were of embroidered purple. Gold medallions hung at their breasts, their caparisons were of gold and they champed bright golden bits between their teeth. For Aeneas in his absence, he chose a chariot and pair of heavenly descent breathing fire from their nostrils. They were sprung from a stock which cunning Circe had crossbred by stealing one of the stallions of her father the Sun to mate with a mare. With these gifts Aeneas' men returned riding high in the saddle and bringing messages of peace.

But at that very moment fierce Juno, wife of Jupiter, was coming back from Argos, city of Inachus, holding her course through the winds of the air, when from far away in the heavens, as far as Cape Pachynus in Sicily, she caught sight of the jubilant Aeneas and his Trojan fleet. When she saw that they were already at work on their buildings, having abandoned their ships and committed themselves to the land, she stopped in mid-flight, pierced by bitter resentment. Then, shaking her head, she poured out these words from the depths of her heart: 'A curse on that detested race of Phrygians and on their destiny, so opposed to our own! Could they not have died on the Sigean plains? They were defeated. Why could they not accept defeat? Troy was set alight. Could they not have burned with it? But no! They found a way through the press of the battle and the thick of the flames. They must think my divine powers are exhausted and discredited, or that I have glutted my appetite for hatred and am now at peace. After all, when they were cast out of their native land, I dared to hound them over the waves and wherever they ran across the face of the ocean I was there and set my face against them. I have used every resource of sea and sky against these Trojans, and what use have the Syrtes been to me? Or Scylla? Or the bottomless Charybdis? The Trojans are where they wanted to be in the valley of the Thybris, safe from the sea and safe from me. Mars had the strength to destroy the monstrous race of Lapiths. The Father of the Gods himself handed over the ancient kingdom of Calydon to the wrath of Diana, and what great crime had the Lapiths or Calydon committed? But here am I, great Juno, wife of Jupiter, thwarted, though I have tried everything that could be tried. Nothing has been too bold for me. And I am being defeated by Aeneas! But if my own resources as a goddess are not enough, I am not the one to hesitate. I shall appeal to whatever powers there are. If I cannot prevail upon the gods above, I shall move hell. I cannot keep him from his kingdom in Latium: so be it. The decree of the Fates will stand and he will have Lavinia to wife. But I shall be able to delay it all and drag it out, I shall be able to cut the subjects of both those kings to pieces. This will be the cost of the meeting between father-in-law and son-in-law, and their peoples will bear it. Your dowry, Lavinia, will be the blood of Rutulians and Trojans, and your matron-of-honour will be the Goddess of War herself, Bellona. Hecuba, daughter of Cisseus, was pregnant with a torch and gave birth to the marriage torches of Paris and Helen. But she is not alone. Venus, too, has a son, a second Paris, and torches will again be fatal, for this second Troy.'

With these words the fearsome goddess flew down to the earth and roused Allecto, bringer of grief, from the infernal darkness of her home among the Furies. Dear to her heart were the horrors of war, anger, treachery and vicious accusations. Her own father Pluto hated his monstrous daughter. Her own sisters in Tartarus loathed her. She had so many faces and such fearsome shapes, and her head crawled with so many black serpents. This was the creature Juno now roused to action with these words: 'Do this service for me, O virgin daughter of Night. It is a task after your own heart. See to it that my fame and the honour in which I am held are not impaired or slighted, and see to it that Aeneas and his men do not win Latinus over with their offers of marriage and are not allowed to settle on Italian soil. You can take brothers who love each other and set them at each other's throats. You can turn a house against itself in hatred and fill it with whips and funeral torches. You have a thousand names and a thousand ways of causing hurt. Your heart is teeming with them. Shake them all out. Shatter this peace they have agreed between them and sow the seeds of recrimination and war. Make their young men long for weapons, demand them, seize them!'

In that moment Allecto, gorged with the poisons of the Gorgons, went straight to Latium and the lofty palace of the king of the Laurentines and settled on the quiet threshold of the chamber of Amata. There the queen was seething with womanly anger and disappointment at the arrival of the Trojans and the loss of the wedding with Turnus. Taking one of the snakes from her dark hair the goddess Allecto threw it on Amata's breast to enter deep into her heart, a horror driving her to frenzy and bringing down her whole house in ruin. It glided between her dress and her smooth breasts and she felt no touch of its coils. Without her knowing it, it breathed its viper's breath into her and made her mad. The serpent became a great necklace of twisted gold round her neck. It became the trailing end of a long ribbon twined round her hair. It slithered all over her body. While the first infection of the liquid venom was still oozing through all her senses and winding the fire about her bones, before her mind in her breast had wholly consumed the fever of it, she spoke with some gentleness, as a mother might, and wept bitterly over the marriage of her daughter to a Phrygian: 'Is Lavinia being given in marriage to these Trojan exiles? You are her father. Have you no feelings for your daughter or her mother or yourself? When the first wind blows from the north, that lying brigand will take to the high seas and carry off my daughter, leaving me desolate. Is this not how the Phrygian shepherd wormed his way into Sparta and carried Leda's daughter Helen off to the cities of

Troy? Where is your sacred word of honour? Where is the care you used to have for your kinsmen? And what of all the pledges you have given Turnus, your own flesh and blood? But if you are searching for a son-in-law among strangers and that is decided, if the commands of your father Faunus weigh so heavily upon you, then I maintain that all peoples who are not subject to our sceptre are strangers. That is what the gods are saying. Besides, if you were to trace the house of Turnus back to its first, beginnings, his forefathers were Inachus and Acrisius of Argos and his home is in the heart of Mycenae.'

When with these words she had tried in vain to move Latinus and seen that he held, firm when the maddening poison of the serpent had soaked deep into her flesh and oozed all through her body, the unhappy Amata, driven out of her mind by her monstrous affliction, raged in a wild frenzy through the length and breadth of the city like a spinning top flying under the plaited whip when boys are engrossed in their play and make it go in great circles round an empty hall; the whip drives it on its curved course and the boys look down, puzzled and fascinated as they lash the spinning box-wood into life – as swift as any top Amata ran through the middle of the cities of the fierce Latian people. Not content with this, she flew into the forests, pretending that she was possessed by Bacchus, and rose to greater impieties and greater madness by hiding her daughter in the leafy woods, hoping to cheat the Trojans out of the marriage or delay the lighting of the torches. 'Euhoe, Bacchus!' she screamed. 'Only you are worthy of the virgin. For you she takes up the soft-leaved thyrsus. Round you she moves in ritual dance. She grows her hair to consecrate it to you.' Rumour flew fast. The same passion kindled in the hearts of all the mothers of Latium and drove them out to search for new homes. They left their houses, their throats bare and their hair streaming in the winds. Others, clad in animal skins and carrying vine shoots sharpened into spears, made the heavens ring with whimpering and wailing. Amata herself, in the fever of her madness, held high a burning torch in the midst of them and sang a wedding hymn for Turnus and her daughter, rolling her bloodshot eyes. Suddenly she gave a dreadful cry: 'Io, Io, all you mothers of Latins wherever you may be, if in your faithful hearts there remains any regard for unhappy Amata, if your minds are troubled by the thought of what is due to a mother, untie the ribbons of your hair and take to the secret rites with me.' This, then, was the queen whom Allecto drove with the lash of Bacchus through the forests and the desolate haunts of wild beasts.

After she saw that this first madness was well under way, and that she had subverted Latinus' plans and all his house, the deadly goddess rose on her dark wings and flew straight to the walls of the bold prince of the Rutulians. Danae is said to have been driven on to this coast by southern gales and to have founded this city for settlers who were subjects of her father Acrisius, king of Argos. Our ancestors long ago gave it the name of Ardea, and Ardea still keeps its great name though its fortune lies in the past. Here in his lofty palace in the darkness of midnight Turnus was lying deep in sleep. Allecto changed her appearance. No longer wild and raving, she took on the face of an old woman, with her brow furrowed by horrible wrinkles and her white hair tied in a sacred ribbon and bound in a chaplet of olive leaves. She became Calybe, the aged priestess of Juno and her temple, and appeared before the eyes of young Turnus saying: 'Are you going to stand by and see all your labours go for nothing, Turnus, and your crown made over to these incomers from Troy? The king is refusing to give you the marriage and the dowry you have earned in blood and is searching for a stranger to inherit his kingdom. So now, Turnus, go and expose yourself to danger! Your reward is to be laughed at. Go and cut down these Etruscans in their battle-lines! Go and cover the Latins with the shield of peace. These are the very words which the daughter of Saturn, All-powerful Juno, has commanded me to say and say clearly to you as you lie in the peace of night. So up with you, and with a light heart prepare to arm your young warriors and move them from inside the city gates and out to the fields to burn the Phrygian captains and their painted ships where they have made themselves at home on our lovely river. The mighty power of heaven demands it. If king Latinus does not agree to obey this command and allow you this marriage, he must learn, he must in the end face Turnus with his armour on.'

Turnus was laughing as he made his reply to the priestess: 'You are wrong. The report has not failed to reach my ears. I know a fleet has sailed into the waters of the Thybris. Do not invent these fears for me. Royal Juno has not entirely forgotten us. It is old age and decay that cause you all this futile agitation and distress and make you barren of truth, taking a prophetess among warring kings and making a fool of her with false fears. Your duty is to guard the statues of the gods and their temples. Leave peace and war to men. War is the business of men.'

When she heard the warrior's words Allecto burst into blazing anger, and while he was still replying, a sudden trembling came over his limbs and the eyes stared in his head as the Fury revealed herself in her full size and set all her hydras hissing. As he faltered and tried to go on speaking, she flung him back with her eyes flashing fire, two snakes stood up on her head and she cracked her whips as she spoke again from her now maddened lips: 'So I am old and decayed and barren of truth and old age is taking me among warring kings and making a fool of me with false fears! Have a look at these! I come here from the home of the dread Furies, my sisters, and in my hands I carry war and death.'

With these words she threw a burning torch at the warrior and it lodged deep in his heart, smoking with black light. A great terror burst in upon his sleep, and the sweat broke out all over his body and soaked him to the bone. In a frenzy of rage he roared for his armour. 'My armour!' he shouted, ransacking his bed and the whole palace for it. The lust for battle raged within him, the criminal madness of war and, above all, anger. It was as though a heap of brushwood were crackling and burning under the sides of a bronze vessel, making the water seethe and leap up, a great river of it raging in the pot, with boiling foam spilling over and dense steam flying into the air. The peace was violated. Turnus gave orders to the leaders of his army to march to king Latinus, to prepare for war, to defend Italy and thrust the enemy out of its borders. When he arrived, that would be enough for the Trojans, and enough for the Latins. These were his words and he called upon the gods to witness them. The eager Rutulians urged each other to arms, some of them inspired by the rare grace of his youthful beauty, some by the long line of kings that were his ancestors, some by his brilliant feats of arms.

While Turnus was filling the hearts of the Rutulians with boldness, Allecto flew off with all speed to the Trojans on her wings of Stygian black. Here, spying out the ground where lovely Iulus was hunting along the shore, trapping and coursing, she hatched a new plot. Into his hounds the virgin goddess of Cocytus put a sudden fit of madness by touching their nostrils with the familiar scent of a stag and sending them after it in full cry. This was the first cause of all the suffering. It was this that kindled the zeal for war in the hearts of the country people. It was a huge and beautiful stag with a fine head of antlers, which had been torn from the udders of its mother and fed by Tyrrhus and his young sons – Tyrrhus looked after the royal herds and was entrusted with the wardenship of the whole broad plain. Silvia, the boys' sister, had given this wild creature every care and trained it to obey her. She would weave soft garlands for its horns, combing and washing it in clear running water. It became tame to the hand and used to come to its master's table. It would wander through the woods and come back home of its own accord to the door it knew so well, no matter how late the night. This is the creature that was roaming far from home, floating down a river, cooling itself in the green shade of the bank when it was startled by the maddened dogs of the young huntsman Iulus. He himself, Ascanius, burning with a passionate love of glory, bent his bow and aimed the arrow. The god was with him and kept his hand from erring. The arrow flew with a great hiss and passed straight through the flank into the belly. Fleeing to the home it knew so well, the wounded stag came into its pen moaning, and stood there bleeding and filling the house with its cries of anguish, as though begging and pleading. Silvia was the first to call for help. She beat her own arms in grief and summoned the country people, who came long before she expected them, for savage Allecto was lurking in the silent woods. Some came armed with stakes burned to a point in the fire; some with clubs made from knotted tree trunks; each man searched for what he could find and anger taught him how to make a weapon of it. Tyrrhus was calling up the troops. He had been driving in wedges to split an oak into four and he snatched up his axe, breathing furiously.

The cruel goddess saw from her vantage point that this was a moment when harm might be done and, flying to the top of the farm roof, from the highest gable she sounded the herdsman's signal with a loud call on the curved horn, and its voice was the voice of Tartarus. The trees shivered at the noise and the whole forest rang to its very depths. Far away the lake of Trivia heard it. The white sulphur-laden streams of the river Nar heard it and its springs in Lake Velinus, and terrified mothers pressed their babies to their breasts. Swift to answer the call of that dread horn, the hardy countrymen snatched up their weapons and gathered from every side. The Trojans, for their part, opened the gates of their camp and streamed out to help Ascanius. They drew up in line of battle, and this was no longer a village brawl with knotted clubs and stakes sharpened in the fire. They fought with two-edged steel, and a dark crop of drawn swords sprouted all over the field while bronze gleamed in answer to the challenge of the sun and threw its light up to the clouds, like the sea whitening at the first breath of wind and slowly stirring itself, raising its waves higher and higher till it reaches from the depths of the sea-bed to the heights of heaven. Suddenly there was the hiss of an arrow and a young man standing out in front of the leading line of battle fell to the ground. It was Almo, the eldest son of Tyrrhus. The shaft had stuck deep in his throat, blocking the moist passage of the voice and closing off the narrow channel of his life in blood. The bodies of slain men soon lay around him, among them old Galaesus, who died when he stepped between the armies to make peace. He was the justest man in the broad fields of Ausonia in these far days, and the richest. Five flocks of sheep and five herds of cattle came back at evening to his stalls and he turned the soil with a hundred ploughs.

While the battle was evenly poised on the plain, the mighty goddess, having fulfilled her promise when the first blood was spilt in war and the first clash of arms had led to death, left Hesperia and returned through the breezes of the sky to address Juno in these words of proud triumph: 'You asked and I have given. Discord is made perfect in the horror of war. Now tell them to come together and form alliances when I have sprinkled the Trojans with Italian blood! And I shall do more than this, if such be still your will for me. I shall spread rumours to draw the neighbouring cities into the war. I shall set their hearts ablaze with a mad lust for battle and they will come from all sides to join in the fray. I shall sow a crop of weapons in all their fields.' Juno gave her answer: 'There is enough terror and lying. The causes of war are established. They are fighting at close quarters and fresh blood is staining whatever weapons chance first puts into their hands. Let this be the wedding they will celebrate, the noble son of Venus and great king Latinus. Let this be their wedding hymn. The Father of the Gods, the ruler of high Olympus, would not wish you to rove too freely over the breezes of heaven. You must withdraw. Should there be any need for further effort, I shall take the guidance into my own hands.' No sooner had the daughter of Saturn spoken these words than Allecto lifted up her wings, hissing with snakes, and flew down to her home on the banks of the Cocytus, leaving the steeps of the sky. At the foot of high mountains in the middle of Italy, there is a well-known place, whose fame has spread to many lands, the valley of Amsanctus. A dark forest presses in upon it from both sides with its dense foliage and in the middle a crashing torrent roars over the rocks, whipping up crests of foam. Here they point to a fearful cave which is a vent for the breath of Dis, the cruel god of the underworld. Into this cave bursts Acheron and here a vast whirlpool opens its pestilential jaws, and here the loathsome Fury disappeared, lightening heaven and earth by her absence.

But none the less the Queen of the Gods, the daughter of Saturn, was at that moment putting the finishing touches to the war. A whole crowd of herdsmen came rushing from the battlefield into the city, carrying the bodies of young Almo and Galaesus with his face mutilated. They were all imploring the help of the gods and appealing to Latinus. Turnus was there, and when the fire of their fury and the accusations of murder were at their height, he heaped fear upon fear by claiming that the Trojans were being invited to take a share in the kingdom; their own Latin blood would be adulterated by Phrygians while he was being turned from the door. At this there gathered from all sides, wearying Mars with their clamour for war, those whose mothers had been crazed by Bacchus and were now dancing in wild rout in the pathless forests – the name of Amata had great weight with them. In an instant they were all demanding this wicked war against all the omens, against divine destiny and contrary to the will of the gods. They rushed to besiege the palace of king Latinus, who stood unmoved like a rock in the ocean, like a solid rock in the ocean pounded by breakers, standing fast with the waves howling round it, while reefs and foam-soaked scars roar in helpless anger and the seaweed is forced against its side, then streams back with the undertow. But there was no resisting the counsels of blind folly. All things were taking their course according to the nod of savage Juno. Again and again the king, the father of his people, called upon the gods and the empty winds to witness: 'We are caught in the gale of Fate,' he cried. 'Our ship is breaking under us. You, my poor people, will pay for this sacrilege with your blood. You are the guilty one, Turnus, and a grim punishment lies in store for you. You will supplicate the gods but your prayers will be too late. I have already reached calm water and here at the harbour mouth I lose all the happiness I might have had in the hour of my death.' He said no more, but shut himself away in his palace and gave up the reins of power.

In Hesperia, in the lands of Latium, there was a custom, later inherited and revered in the cities of Alba, and now observed by Rome, the greatest of the great, when men first rouse Mars for battle, whether they are preparing to bring the sorrows of war to the Getae, the Hyrcani or the Arabs, or whether they are heading for India and the rising of the sun and reclaiming the standards from the Parthians. There are two gates known as the Gates of War, sanctified by religion and the fear of savage Mars. These gates are closed by a hundred bolts of bronze and the everlasting strength of iron, nor does their sentry Janus ever leave the threshold. When the Fathers are resolved on war, the consul himself, conspicuous in the short toga of Quirinus girt about him in the Gabine manner, unbars the doors. They grind in their sockets and he summons war. The whole army takes up the call and the bronze horns breathe their shrill assent. So too in those days Latinus was bidden to declare war upon the men of Aeneas by opening these grim gates. The old king, father of his people, would not lay his hand upon them, but recoiled from this wickedness and refused to perform the task, shutting himself up in the darkness away from the sight of men. At this, the Queen of the Gods came down from the sky and struck the stubborn doors, bursting the iron-bound Gates of War and turning them in their sockets. Till that moment Ausonia had been at peace and unalarmed, but now the foot-soldiers mustered on the plain and high in the saddle came the excited horsemen stirring up the dust. Every man was looking for weapons, polishing shields with rich fat till they were smooth, burnishing spears till they shone and grinding axes on the whetstone. What joy to raise the standards and hear the trumpets sound! Five great cities, no less, set up anvils to forge new weapons, mighty Atina, proud Tibur, Ardea, Crustumerium and Antemnae with its towers. They hollowed out helmets to protect the heads of warriors. They wove frames of willow shoots to form shields. They made bronze breastplates and smooth shields of ductile silver. This is what had become of all their regard for the sickle and the share. This is what had become of all their love for the plough – the swords of their fathers were now retempered in the furnace. Now the trumpets blew and out went the signal that called them to war. In high excitement they tore down their helmets from the roof, yoked their trembling horses to the chariot, buckled on their shields and their breastplates of triple-woven gold and girt their trusty swords about them.

Now goddesses, it is time to open up Mount Helicon, to set your songs in motion and tell what kings were roused to war, what armies followed each of them to fill the plains, the heroes that flowered and the weapons that blazed in those far-off days in the bountiful land of Italy. You are the divine Muses. You remember, goddesses, and can utter what you remember. Our ears can barely catch the faintest whisper of the story.

The first to enter upon the war and arm his columns was

cruel Mezentius from Etruria, scorner of the gods. At his side was his son Lausus, who for his beauty was second to none but the Laurentine Turnus. Lausus was a tamer of horses and a hunter of wild beasts, and he was at the head of a thousand men who had followed him and followed him in vain from the city of Agylla. He deserved a father whom it would have been more of a joy to obey, a father other than Mezentius.

Behind them, driving over the grassland and displaying his victorious horses and his chariot which proudly bore the palm of victory, came Aventinus, son of Hercules, fair son of a fair father, and on his shield he carried his father's blazon, the Hydra and its snakes, the hundred snakes encircling it. His mother, the priestess Rhea, had given birth to him in secret, bringing him into the land of light in the wood on the Aventine hill. She had lain with Hercules, a woman with a god, when he had come in triumph to the land of the Laurentines, the hero of Tiryns who had slain Geryon and washed the cattle of Spain in the river of the Etruscans. His men carried javelins and fearsome pikes into battle and used the Sabine throwing spear with its round tapering point. He himself was on foot, swinging a great lion skin about him as he walked. It was matted and bristling, and he had put it with its white teeth over his head and a fearsome sight he was as he came up to the palace with his father's garb tied round his shoulders.

Next came two bold Argive warriors, the twin brothers Catillus and fierce Coras, leaving the walls of Tibur, which took its name from their brother Tiburtus. They would charge out in front of the first line of battle through showers of missiles, like two cloud-borne Centaurs plunging down in wild career from the snow-clad tops of Mount Homole or Mount Othrys, crashing through the trees as the great forest opens to let them pass.

The founder of the city of Praeneste was also there, a king who ruled among the herds and flocks of the countryside.

Men have always believed that he was the son of Vulcan,
Caeculus, found as a baby on the burning hearth. His rustic
legion came from far and wide to follow him: from Praeneste
on its hill-top; from the fields round Juno's city of Gabii, from
the icy waters of the Anio and the streaming river rocks of the
Hernici; men nurtured by the rich city of Anagnia and by
your river, Father Amasenus. Not all of these came into battle
with shields and arms and chariots sounding: most of them
showered acorns of blue lead from slings; some carried a pair
of hunting spears in one hand and wore on their heads tawny
caps made from the hides of wolves, their left foot leaving a
naked print while a rawhide boot protected the right.

Now Messapus, breaker of horses, son of Neptune, whom
neither fire nor steel might lay low, suddenly took up his
sword again and called to arms tribes that had long lived at
ease and armies that had lost the habit of war. These were the
men who came from the ridges of Fescennium, from Aequum
Faliscum, from the citadel of Soracte and the Flavinian fields,
from the lake of Ciminius and its mountain and the groves
of Capena. They marched in regular formations singing the
praises of their king like white swans flying back from their
feeding grounds through wisps of cloud and pouring out the
measured music from their long necks while far and wide the
echo of their singing beats back from the river and the Asian
marsh. This great mingled swarm of men seemed not like a
bronze-clad army, but an aery cloud of clamorous birds on
the wing, straining in from the high seas to the shore.

There comes Clausus of the blood of the ancient Sabines,
leading a great army, and a great army in himself. From
Clausus are descended the tribe and family of the Claudii,
spread all over Latium ever since the Sabines were given
a share in Rome. With him came a large contingent from
Amiternum and the first Quirites, all the troops from Eretum
and from olive-bearing Mutusca, all who lived in the city of
Nomentum and the Rosean plains round Lake Velinus, on the

bristling rocks of Tetrica and its gloomy mountain, in Casperia and Foruli and on the banks of the Himella, men who drank the Tiber and the Fabaris, men sent by chilly Nursia, levies from Orta, tribes from old Latium and the peoples whose lands are cut by the Allia, that river of ill-omened name. They were as many as the waves that roll in from the Libyan ocean when fierce Orion is sinking into the winter sea, or as thick as the ears of corn scorched by the early sun on the plain of Hermus or the golden fields of Lycia. Their shields clanged and the earth quaked under the beat of their feet.

Halaesus next, one of Agamemnon's men and an enemy of all things Trojan, yoked his horses to his chariot and rushed a thousand fierce tribes to join Turnus: men whose mattocks turn the rich Massic soil for Bacchus: Auruncans sent by their fathers from their high hills; men sent from the nearby plains of Sidicinum; men who come from Cales and the banks of the Volturnus, river of many fords, and with them the tough Saticulan and bands of Oscans. Their weapon was the aclys, a light spear, and it was their practice to attach a supple thong to it. A leather shield protected their left side and for close fighting they used swords shaped like sickles.

Nor will you, Oebalus, go unmentioned in our song. Men say you were the son of Telon by the nymph of the river Sebethus, born when Telon was already an old man and ruling over Capreae, the island of the Teleboae. But the son no more than the father had been content with the lands he had inherited and by now he had long held sway over the tribes of the Sarrastes, the plains washed by the river Sarnus, men who lived in Rufrae, Batulum and the fields of Celemna and those on whom the walls of apple-bearing Abella look down. Their missile was the cateia, a weapon thrown like the Teuton boomerang. Their heads were protected by helmets of bark stripped from the cork oak. They carried gleaming half-moon shields of plated bronze and their swords too were of gleaming bronze.

You too, Ufens, famous for your feats of arms, were sent into battle from the mountains of Nersae. These Aequi live in a hard land and are the most rugged of races, schooled in hunting the forests. They work the soil with their armour on. Their delight is always to bring home new plunder and live off what they take.

Then came a priest from Marruvium, his helmet decorated by a sprig of fruitful olive, the bravest of men, Umbro by name, sent by king Archippus. By his spells and the touch of his hand he knew well how to sow the seed of sleep on nests of vipers and on water-snakes, for all their deadly breath. His arts could charm their anger and soothe their bites, but he had no antidote for the sting of a Trojan sword and not all his lullabies and herbs gathered in the Marsian hills could help him with his wounds. For you wept the grove of the goddess Angitia. For you wept the glassy waves and clear pools of Lake Fucinus.

There too, sent by his mother Aricia, glorious Virbius came to the war, the lovely son of Hippolytus. He had grown to manhood in the grove of Egeria around the dank lake-shores by the altar where rich sacrifices win the favour of Diana. For after Hippolytus had been brought to his death by the wiles of his stepmother Phaedra, torn to pieces by bolting horses and paying with his blood the penalty imposed by his father, men say he came back under the stars of the sky and the winds of heaven, restored by healing herbs and the love of Diana. Then the All-powerful Father was enraged that any mortal should rise from the shades below into the light of life and with his own hand he took the inventor of those healing arts, Asclepius, son of Apollo, and hurled him with his thunder-bolt down into the wave of the river Styx. But Diana Trivia, in her loving care, found a secret refuge for Hippolytus and consigned him to the nymph Egeria and her grove, where, alone and unknown, his name changed to Virbius, he might live out his days. Thus it is that horn-hooved horses are not admitted to the sacred grove of the temple of Trivia because in their terror at the monsters of the deep the horses of Hippolytus had overturned his chariot and thrown him on the shore. But none the less his son was driving fiery horses across the level plain as he rushed to the wars in a chariot.

There, looking around him and moving among the leaders, was Turnus himself, in full armour, the fairest of them all, and taller by a head than all the others. On the towering top of his triple-plumed helmet there stood a Chimaera breathing from its throat a fire like Etna's, and the fiercer and bloodier the battle, the more savagely she roared and belched the deadly flames. The blazon on his polished shield showed a mighty theme, a golden figure of Io, raising her horned head, with rough hair on her hide, already changed into a heifer. And there was Argus, guarding her, and her father Inachus pouring his river from an urn embossed on the shield. Behind Turnus came a cloud of foot-soldiers and the whole plain was crowded with columns of men bearing shields, the youth of Argos, bands of Auruncans, Rutulians, Sicani, that ancient race, Sacrani in battle order and Labici with their painted shields; men who ploughed the Tiber valley and the sacred banks of the Numicus; men whose ploughshare worked the Rutulian hills and the ridge of Circeii; men from the fields ruled by Jupiter of Anxur and the goddess Feronia delighting in her greenwood grove, and men from the black swamps of Satura where the icy river Ufens threads his way along his valley bottom to lose himself in ocean.

Last of all came Camilla, the warrior maiden of the Volsci, leading a cavalry squadron flowering in bronze. Not for her girlish hands the distaff and wool-basket of Minerva. She was a maid inured to battle, of a fleetness of foot to race the winds. She could have skimmed the tops of a standing crop without touching them and her passage would not have bruised the delicate ears of grain. She could have run over the ocean, hovered over the swell and never wet her foot in the waves.

Young men streamed from house and field and mothers came thronging to gaze at her as she went, lost in wonderment at the royal splendour of the purple veiling the smoothness of her shoulders, her hair weaving round its gold clasp, her Lycian quiver and the shepherd's staff of myrtle wood with the head of a lance.

ca 8 bo

AENEAS IN ROME

When Turnus raised the flag of war above the Laurentine citadel and the shrill horns blared, when he whipped up his eager horses and clashed his sword on his shield, there was instant confusion. In that moment the whole of Latium rose in a frenzy to take the oath and young warriors were baying for blood. Their great leaders Messapus and Ufens and the scorner of the gods Mezentius were levying men everywhere, stripping the fields of those who tilled them. They also sent Venulus to the city of great Diomede to ask for help and to let him know that Trojans were settling in Italy, that Aeneas had arrived with a fleet bringing the defeated household gods of Troy, claiming that he was being called by the Fates to be king; the tribes were flocking to join this Trojan, this descendant of Dardanus, and his name was on the lips of men all over Latium; what all this was leading up to, what Aeneas hoped to gain from the fighting if Fortune smiled upon him, Diomede himself would know better than king Turnus or than king Latinus.

This is what was happening in Latium. The Trojan hero, descendant of Laomedon, saw it all and great tides of grief flowed in his heart. His thoughts moved swiftly, now here, now there, darting in every possible direction and turning to every possible event, like light flickering from water in bronze vessels as it is reflected from the sun or its image the moon, now flying far and wide in all directions, now rising to strike the high coffers of a ceiling.

It was night, and over the whole earth the weary animals, all manner of birds and all manner of flocks, were already deep in sleep before Father Aeneas, on the bank of the river, under the cold vault of the sky, heart sick at the sadness of war, lay down at last and gave rest to his body. There on that lovely river he saw in his sleep the god of the place, old Tiber himself, rising among the leaves of the poplars. He was veiled in a blue-green cloak of fine-spun flax and dark reeds shaded his hair. He then spoke to Aeneas and lightened his sadness with these words: 'O you who are born of the race of the gods, who are bringing back to us the city of Troy saved from its enemies, who are preserving its citadel Pergamum for all time, long have we waited for you in the land of the Laurentines and the fields of Latium. This is the home that is decreed for you. This is the home decreed for the gods of your household. Do not give it up. Do not be intimidated by the threat of war. All the angry passions of the gods are now spent. But come now, so that you may not think what you are seeing is an empty dream, I tell you that you will find a great sow with a litter of thirty piglets lying beneath ilex trees on a shore. There she will lie all white on the ground and the young around her udders will be white. This will be a sign that after three times ten years revolve, Ascanius will found the city of Alba, white in name and bright in glory. What I prophesy will surely come to pass. Attend now and I shall teach you in few words how you may triumphantly resolve the difficulties that lie before you.

'The Arcadians are a race descended from Pallas. They came to these shores following the standards of their king Evander, chose a site here and established in these hills a city called Pallanteum after their founder Pallas. This people wages continual war with the Latin race. Welcome them into your camp as your allies. Make a treaty with them. I will take you to them straight up my river between these banks and you will be able to row upstream into the current. Up with you then, son of the goddess, for the first stars are beginning to set. Offer due prayers to Juno and overcome her angry threats with vows and supplications. To me you will give honour and make repayment when you are victorious. I am that full river whom you see scouring these banks and cutting through the rich farmland. I am the river Thybris, blue as the sky and favoured of heaven. Here is my great home. My head waters rise among lofty cities.'

So spoke the river-god and plunged to the bottom of a deep pool. The night was over and so was Aeneas' sleep. As he rose he looked up to the light of the sun rising in the sky, took up water from the river in cupped hands and poured out these words of prayer to the heavens: 'O you Laurentine nymphs, nymphs who are the mothers of rivers, and you, Father Thybris with your holy stream, receive Aeneas, and now after all his suffering keep him safe from peril. In whichever of your pools you may be, at whichever of your sources, you who pity our misfortunes, in whatever land you emerge in all your splendour, I will always pay you honour and always make offerings to you, O hornèd river, king of all the waters of Hesperia, only be with me and by your presence confirm your divine will.' So speaking he picked out two biremes from the fleet, manned them with rowers and at the same time put some of his comrades on board in full armour.

Now suddenly before his astonished eyes there appeared a portent. There through the trees he caught sight of a white sow with offspring of the same colour, lying on the green shore. This sow devout Aeneas offered to you as a sacrifice, even to you, O greatest Juno, leading her to your altar with all her young. And all that long night the Thybris calmed his flood, reversing his current, and was as still and silent as a peaceful lake or quiet marsh. There were no ripples on the surface of his waters, and no toiling for the oar. Thus they began their journey and made good speed, raising a cheerful noise as the caulked hulls glided over the water. The waves were amazed and the woods were full of wonder at the unaccustomed sight of far-glinting shields of warriors and painted prows floating on the river. So did they wear out the night and the day with rowing and mastered all the long windings of the river, moving under the shade of all manner of trees and cleaving green woods in smooth water. The fiery sun had climbed to the middle of the vault of heaven when they saw in the distance walls and a citadel and the roofs of scattered houses. What Roman power has now raised to the heights of the sky, in those days was a poor land ruled by Evander. Quickly they turned their prows to the bank and steered for the city.

It so happened that on that day the Arcadian king Evander was performing yearly rites in honour of the mighty Hercules, son of Amphitryon, and was sacrificing to the gods in a grove outside the city. His son Pallas was with him, and with him also were all the leading warriors and the senators, poor men as they were. They were offering incense and warm blood was smoking on the altars. When they saw the tall ships and saw them gliding through the dense grove with men bending to the oars in silence, they were seized with sudden fright and rose in a body, abandoning the sacred tables. Not so Pallas. Boldly he told them not to disturb their holy feast, and seizing a weapon he rushed off to face the strangers by himself. 'What is it, warriors, that has driven you to try these new paths?' he called out from the top of a mound while he was still at a distance. 'Where are you going? What race are you? Where is your home? Is it peace you are bringing us or war?' Then Father Aeneas replied from the high poop of his ship, holding out in his hand the olive branch of peace: 'We are of the Trojan race. These weapons you see are for use against our enemies the Latins. It is they who have driven us here, exiles as we are, with all the insolence of war. We are looking for Evander. Tell him of this. Say to him that the chosen leaders of the race of Dardanus have come to ask him to be their ally in battle.' At this great name Pallas was dumbfounded. 'Whoever you may be,' he cried, 'leave your ship and come and speak with my father face to face. Come as a guest into our house.' With these words he took Aeneas by the right hand in a long clasp, and they moved forward into the grove, leaving the river behind them.

Then Aeneas addressed the king with words of friendship: 'O noblest of the race of the Greeks, Fortune has willed that I should come to you as a suppliant with an olive branch draped with wool. I was not alarmed at the thought that you are a leader of Greeks, an Arcadian and joined by blood to the two sons of Atreus, for I am joined to you by my courage and by the holy oracles of the gods, by our fathers who were kinsmen and by your fame which is known throughout the world. All these have driven me here by the command of the Fates, and I have willingly obeyed. Dardanus, the first founder and father of the city of Troy, sailed to our Teucrian land. According to the Greeks he was the son of Electra, and that same Electra was the daughter of Atlas, the mighty Atlas who carries the circle of the heavens on his shoulder. On your side you are the son of Mercury and he was the son of Maia, conceived and born on the snow-clad top of Mount Cyllene. But the father of Maia, if we put any trust in what we hear, was Atlas, that same Atlas who supports the stars of the sky. And so we are of one blood, two branches of the same family. Trusting in this, I have not sent emissaries or made trial of you in advance by any form of subterfuge, but have come in person as a suppliant to your door, and laid my life before you. The same race harries us both in bitter war, the Rutulians of king Daunus, and they are persuaded that if they were to drive us away, nothing would prevent them from putting all the heartlands of Italy under their yoke and becoming masters of the Tyrrhenian sea to the south and the Adriatic to the north. Take the right hand of friendship I offer and give me yours. Our hearts are strong in war. Our spirits are high. Our fighting men are tried and proved.'

So spoke Aeneas. All the time he was speaking, Evander had been gazing at his face and his eyes and his whole body. He then replied in these few words: 'Bravest of the Trojans, I welcome you with great joy, and with great joy I recognize who you are. Oh how well do I recall the words of your father, the very voice and features of the great Anchises! For I remember that when Priam, son of Laomedon, was on a visit to his sister Hesione in the kingdom of Salamis, he came on to visit us in the cold lands of Arcadia. In those days the first bloom of youth was still covering my cheeks, and I was full of admiration for the leaders of Troy. Priam himself, too, I admired, but taller than them all walked Anchises. With all a young man's ardour, I longed to speak with him and put my right hand in his, so I approached him and led him with full heart to the walls of Pheneus. When he was leaving he gave me a wonderful quiver filled with Lycian arrows, a soldier's cloak interwoven with gold thread and a pair of golden bridles which now belong to my son Pallas. So then, the right hand of friendship for which you ask has already been given in solemn pledge, and as soon as tomorrow's sun returns to the earth, I shall send you on your way and you will not be disappointed with the reinforcements and supplies I shall give you. Meanwhile, since you are here as friends, come favour these annual rites of ours which it would be sinful to postpone, by celebrating them with us. It is time you began to feel at home at the tables of your allies.'

The food and drink had been cleared away, but as soon as he was finished speaking, he ordered them to be replaced, and the king himself showed the Trojans to seats on the grass, but took Aeneas apart to a couch of maple wood and seated him on a rough lion skin for a cushion. Then the priest of the altar and some chosen warriors served with great good will the roast flesh of bulls, loaded into baskets the grain which is the gift of Ceres worked by the hand of man, and poured out the juice of Bacchus. Aeneas and the warriors of Troy then feasted together on the whole chine and entrails of the sacrificial ox.

After their hunger was relieved and their appetite satisfied, king Evander spoke as follows: 'This annual rite, this set feast and this altar to a great divinity have not been imposed upon us by any vain superstition working in ignorance of our ancient gods. It is because we have been saved from desperate dangers, my Trojan friend, that we perform this worship and renew it yearly in honour of one who has well deserved it.

'First of all, look at this vaulted cavern among the rocks. You see how this great massive home inside the mountain has been torn apart and is now abandoned, with boulders lying everywhere in ruins. Here, deep in the vast recesses of the rock, was once a cave which the rays of the sun never reached. This was the home of a foul-featured, half-human monster by the name of Cacus. The floor of the cave was always warm with freshly shed blood, and the heads of men were nailed to his proud doors and hung there pale and rotting. The father of this monster was Vulcan, and it was his father's black fire he vomited from his mouth as he moved his massive bulk. Long did we pray and in the end we too were granted the help and the presence of a god. For the great avenger was at hand. Exulting in the slaughter of the triple-bodied Geryon and the spoils he had taken, the victorious Hercules was driving the huge bulls through our land and the herd was grazing the valley and drinking the water of the river. But Cacus was a robber, and thinking in the savagery of his heart not to leave any crime or treachery undared or unattempted, he stole from pasture four magnificent bulls and as many lovely heifers. So that there would be no hoof prints pointing forwards in the direction of the cave, he dragged them in by their tails to reverse the tracks, and was now keeping his plunder hidden deep in the darkness of the rock. There were no tracks leading to the cave for any searcher to see.

'Meanwhile, when his herd had grazed its fill, and the son of Amphitryon was moving them out of pasture and preparing to go on his way, the cows began to low plaintively at leaving the place, filling the whole grove with their complaints, and bellowing to the hills they were leaving behind them. Then, deep in the cave, a single cow lowed in reply. Cacus had guarded her well, but she thwarted his hopes. At this Hercules blazed up in anger. The black bile of his fury rose in him, and snatching up his arms and heavy knotted club, he made off at a run for the windswept heights of the mountain. Never before had our people seen Cacus afraid. Never before had there been terror in these eyes. He turned and fled, running to his cave with the speed of the wind, fear lending wings to his feet. There he shut himself up, dropping a huge rock behind him and breaking the iron chains on which it had been suspended by his father's art, so that its great mass was jammed against the doorposts and blocked the entrance. There was Hercules in a passion, trying every approach, turning his head this way and that and grinding his teeth. Three times he went round the whole of Mount Aventine in his anger. Three times he tried to force the great rock doorway without success. Three times he sat down exhausted in the valley.

'Above the ridge on top of the cave, there stood a sharp needle of flint with sheer rocks falling away on either side. It rose to a dizzy height and was a favourite nesting-place of carrion birds. Hercules put his weight on the right-hand side of it where it leaned over the ridge towards the river on its left. He rocked it, loosened it, wrenched it free from its deep base and then gave a sudden heave, a heave at which the great heavens thundered, the banks of the river leapt apart and the river flowed backwards in alarm. The cave and whole huge palace of Cacus were unroofed and exposed to view and his shadowy caverns were opened to all their depths. It was as though the very depths of the earth were to gape in some cataclysm and unbar the chambers of the underworld, the pale kingdom loathed by the gods, so that the vast abyss could be seen from above with the shades of the dead in panic as the light floods in.

'So Cacus was caught in the sudden rush of light and trapped in his cavern in the rock, howling as never before, while Hercules bombarded him from above with any missile that came to hand, belabouring him with branches of trees and rocks the size of millstones. There was no escape for him now, but he vomited thick smoke from his monstrous throat and rolled clouds of it all round his den to blot it from sight. Deep in his cave he churned out fumes as black as night and the darkness was shot through with fire. Hercules was past all patience. He threw himself straight down, leaping through the flames where the smoke spouted thickest and the black cloud boiled in the vast cavern. There, as Cacus vainly belched his fire in the darkness, Hercules caught him in a grip and held him, forcing his eyes out of their sockets and squeezing his throat till the blood was dry in it. Then, tearing out the doors and opening up the dark house of Cacus, he brought into the light of heaven the stolen cattle whose theft Cacus had denied, and dragged the foul corpse out by the feet. No one could have enough of gazing at his terrible eyes and face, at the coarse bristles on his beastly chest and the throat charred by fires now dead.

'Ever since that time we have honoured his name and succeeding generations have celebrated this day with rejoicing. This altar was set up in its grove by Potitius, the first founder of these rites of Hercules, and by the Pinarii, the guardians of the rites. We shall always call it The Greatest Altar, and the greatest altar it will always be. Come then warriors, put a crown of leaves around your hair in honour of this great exploit, and hold out your cups in your right hands. Call upon the god who is a god for all of us and offer him wine with willing hearts.' No sooner had he spoken than his head was shaded by a wreath and pendant of the green-silver leaves of Hercules' poplar woven into his hair, and the sacred goblet filled his hand. Soon they were all pouring their libations on the table and praying to the gods.

Meanwhile the Evening Star was drawing nearer as the day sank in the heavens and there came a procession of priests led by Potitius, wearing their ritual garb of animal skins and carrying torches. They were starting the feast again with a second course of goodly offerings, and they heaped the altar with loaded dishes. Then the Salii, the priests of Mars, their heads bound with poplar leaves, came to sing around the altar fires. On one side was a chorus of young warriors, on the other a chorus of old men, hymning the praise of Hercules and his great deeds: how he seized the two snakes, the first monsters sent against him by his stepmother, and throttled them, one in each hand; how also he tore stone from stone the cities of Troy and Oechalia, famous in war; how he endured a thousand labours under king Eurystheus to fulfil the fate laid upon him by the cruel will of Juno. 'O unconquered Hercules,' they sang, 'you are the slayer of the half-men born of the cloud, the Centaurs Hylaeus and Pholus; of the monstrous Cretan bull and the huge lion of Nemea in its rocky lair; the pools of the Styx trembled at your coming, and the watchdog of Orcus cringed where he lay in his cave weltering in blood on heaps of half-eaten bones. But nothing you have seen has ever made you afraid, not even Typhoeus himself, rising up to heaven with his weapons in his hands. Nor did reason fail you when the hundred heads of the Lernaean Hydra hissed around you. Hail, true son of Jupiter, the latest lustre added to the company of the gods, come to us now, to your own holy rite, and bless us with your favouring presence.' To end their hymn they sang of the cave of Cacus, and Cacus himself breathing fire, till the whole grove rang and all the hills re-echoed.

As soon as the sacred rites were completed, they all returned to the city. The king, weighed down with age, kept Aeneas and his son Pallas by his side as he walked, and made the way seem shorter by all the things he told them. Aeneas was lost in admiration and his eyes were never still as he looked about him enthralled by the places he saw, asking questions about them and joyfully listening to Evander's explanations of all the relics of the men of old. This is what was said that day by Evander, the founder of the citadel of Rome: 'These woods used to be the haunt of native fauns and nymphs and a race of men born from the hard wood of oak-tree trunks. They had no rules of conduct and no civilization. They did not know how to yoke oxen for ploughing, how to gather wealth or husband what they had, but they lived off the fruit of the tree and the harsh diet of huntsmen. In those early days, in flight from the weapons of Jupiter, came Saturn from heavenly Olympus, an exile who had lost his kingdom. He brought together this wild and scattered mountain people, gave them laws and resolved that the name of the land should be changed to Latium, since he had *lain* hidden within its borders. His reign was what men call the Golden Age, such was the peace and serenity of the people under his rule. But gradually a worse age of baser metal took its place and with it came the madness of war and the lust for possessions. Then bands of Ausonians arrived and Sicanian peoples, and the land of Saturn lost its name many times. Next there were kings, among them the cruel and monstrous Thybris, after whom we Italians have in later years called the river Thybris, and the old river Albula has lost its true name. I had been driven from my native land and was setting course for the most distant oceans when Fortune, that no man can resist, and Fate, that no man can escape, set me here in this place, driven by fearsome words of warning from my mother, the nymph Carmentis, and by the authority of the god Apollo.'

He had just finished saying this and moved on a little, when he pointed out the Altar of Carmentis and the Carmental Gate, as the Romans have called it from earliest times in honour of the nymph Carmentis. She had the gift of prophecy and was the first to foretell the future greatness of the sons of Aeneas and the future fame of Pallanteum. From here he pointed out the great grove which warlike Romulus set up as a sanctuary – he was to call it the Asylum – and also the Lupercal there under its cool rock, then called by Arcadian tradition they had brought from Parrhasia, the cave of Pan Lycaeus, the wolf god. He also pointed out the grove of the Argiletum, and, calling upon that consecrated spot to be his witness, he told the story of the killing of his guest Argus.

From here he led the way to the house of Tarpeia and the Capitol, now all gold, but in those distant days bristling with rough scrub. Even then a powerful sense of a divine presence in the place caused great fear among the country people, even then they went in awe of the wood and the rock. 'This grove,' said Evander, 'this leafy-topped hill, is the home of some god, we know not which. My Arcadians believe they have often seen Jupiter himself shaking the darkening aegis in his right hand to drive along the storm clouds. And then here are the ruined walls of these two towns. What you are looking at are relics of the men of old. These are their monuments. One of these citadels was founded by Father Janus; the other by Saturn. This one used to be called the Janiculum; the other, Saturnia.'

Talking in this way they were coming up to Evander's humble home, and there were cattle everywhere, lowing in the Roman Forum and the now luxurious district of the Carinae. When they arrived at his house, Evander said: 'The victorious Hercules of the line of Alceus stooped to enter this door. This was a palace large enough for him. You are my guest, and

you too must have the courage to despise wealth. You must
mould yourself to be worthy of the god. Come into my poor
home and do not judge it too harshly.' With these words he
led the mighty Aeneas under the roof-tree of his narrow house
and set him down on a bed of leaves covered with the hide of
a Libyan bear. Night fell and its dark wings enfolded the
earth.

But his mother Venus was terrified, and with good reason,
by the threats of the Laurentines and the savagery of the
fighting, so she spoke to her husband Vulcan. Coming to him
in his golden bedroom and breathing divine love into her
voice, she said: 'When the citadel of Troy was being ravaged
in war by the kings of Greece, it was owed to Fate and was
doomed to fall in the fires lit by its enemies, but I asked for
nothing for those who suffered. I did not call upon the help
of your art to make arms for them. Although I owed much to
the sons of Priam and had often wept at the sufferings endured
by Aeneas, I did not wish, O my dearest husband, that you
should exert yourself to no purpose. But now, in obedience to
the commands of Jupiter, Aeneas is standing on Rutulian soil
and so now I come to you as a suppliant. I approach that
godhead which I so revere, and as a mother, I ask you to make
arms for my son. You yielded to Thetis, the daughter of
Nereus, you yielded to the wife of Tithonus when they came
and wept to you. Look at all the nations gathering. Look at
the walled cities that have closed their gates and are sharpening their swords against me to destroy those I love.' She had
finished speaking and he was hesitating. The goddess took
him gently in her white arms and caressed him, and caressed
him again. Suddenly he caught fire as he always did. The old
heat he knew so well pierced to the marrow of his bones and
coursed through them till they melted, as in a thunderstorm,
when a fiery-flashing rift bursts the clouds and runs through
them in dazzling brightness. His wife knew and was pleased.
She was well aware of her beauty and she knew how to use

it. Father Vulcan, bound to her by eternal love, made this reply: 'You need not delve so deep for arguments. Where is that trust, O goddess, which you used to have in me? If your care for Aeneas was then as it is now, it would have been right for us even then to arm the Trojans. Neither the All-powerful Father nor the Fates were forbidding Troy to stand and Priam to go on living for ten more years. And now if you are preparing for war and this is what you wish, whatever care I can offer you in the exercise of my skill, whatever can be done by melting iron or electrum, anything that fire and bellows can achieve, you do not have to pray to me. You need not doubt your power.' At these words he gave his wife the embraces so much desired, and then, relaxed upon her breast, he sought and found peace and repose for all his limbs.

When the night had passed the middle of his course, when Vulcan's first sleep was over and there was no more rest, just when the ashes are first stirred to rouse the slumbering fire by a woman whose task it is to support life by the humble work of spinning thread on a distaff; taking time from the night for her labours, she sets her slave women going by lamplight upon their long day's work, so that she can keep her husband's bed chaste and bring her young sons to manhood – with no less zeal than such a woman and not a moment later did the God of Fire rise from his soft bed and go to work at his forge.

Between Lipari in the Aeolian Islands and the flank of Sicily, an island of smoking rocks rises sheer from the sea. Deep within it is a great vault, and in that vault caves have been scooped out like those under Etna to serve as forges for the Cyclopes. The noise within them is the noise of thunder. Mighty blows can be heard booming on the groaning anvils, the caves are filled with the sound of hissing as the Chalybes plunge bars of white-hot pig-iron into water and all the time the fires are breathing in the furnaces. This is the home of Vulcan, and Vulcania is the name of the island. Into these depths the God of Fire descended from the heights of heaven.

The Cyclopes were forging steel, working naked in that vast cavern, Brontes, Sterope and Pyracmon. In their hands was a thunderbolt which they had roughed out, one of those the Father of the Gods and Men hurls down upon the earth in such numbers from every part of the sky. Some of it was already burnished, some of it unfinished. They had attached three shafts of lashing rain to it, three shafts of heavy rain-clouds, three of glowing fire and three of the south wind in full flight. They were now adding to the work the terrifying lightning and the sound of thunder, then Fear and Anger with their pursuing flames. In another part of the cave they were working for Mars, busy with the wing-wheeled chariot in which he stirs up men and cities to war. Others were hard at work polishing the armour worn by Pallas Athene when roused, the fearsome aegis and its weaving snakes with their reptilian scales of gold, even the Gorgon rolling her eyes in the bodiless head on the breast of the goddess. 'Put all this away!' he cried. 'Whatever work you have started, you Cyclopes of Etna, lay it aside and give your attention here. Armour has to be made for a brave hero. You need strength and quick hands now. Now you need all your arts to guide you. Let nothing stand in your way.' He said no more, but instantly they all bent to the work, dividing it equally between them. The bronze was soon flowing in rivers. The gold ore and iron, the dealer of death, were molten in a great furnace. They were shaping one great shield to be a match for all the weapons of the Latins, fastening the seven thicknesses of it circle to circle. Bellows were taking in air and breathing it out again. Bronze was being plunged into troughs of water and hissing. The cave boomed with the anvils standing on its floor while the Cyclopes raised their arms with all their strength in time with one another and turned the ore in tongs that did not slip.

While Father Vulcan, the god of Lemnos, was pressing on

with this work in the Aeolian Islands, Evander was roused from sleep in his humble hut by the life-sustaining light of day and the dawn chorus of the birds under his eaves. The old man rose, put on his tunic and bound Etruscan sandals on the soles of his feet. He then girt on a Tegean sword with its baldric over the shoulder and threw on a panther skin to hang down on his left side. Nor did the sentinels from his high threshold fail to precede him – his two dogs went with their master – as the hero walked to the separate quarters of his guest Aeneas, remembering their talk and remembering the help he had promised to give. Aeneas was up and about just as early, walking with Achates. Evander had his son Pallas with him. They met, clasped right hands, and sitting there in the middle of Evander's house, they were at last able to discuss affairs of state.

The king spoke first: 'Great leader of the Trojans, while you are alive I shall never accept that Troy and its kingdom are defeated. Beside your mighty name, the power we have to help you in this war is as nothing. On one side we are hemmed in by the Tuscan river, on the other the Rutulians press us hard and we can hear the clang of their weapons round our walls. But I have a plan to join vast peoples and the armies of wealthy kingdoms to your cause. A chance that no man could have foreseen is showing us the path to safety. Fate was calling you when you came to this place.

'Not far from here is the site of Agylla, founded long ago on its ancient rock by the warlike Lydians who once settled there on the ridges of the Etruscan mountains. After this city had flourished for many years, Mezentius eventually took it under his despotic rule as king and held it by the ruthless use of armed force. I shall not speak of the foul murders and other barbaric crimes committed by this tyrant. May the gods heap equal suffering upon his own head and the heads of his descendants! He even devised a form of torture whereby living men were roped to dead bodies, tying them hand to hand and face to face to die a lingering death oozing with putrefying flesh in this cruel embrace. But at last his subjects reached the end of their endurance and took up arms against him. Roaring and raging he was besieged in his palace, his men were butchered and fire was thrown on his roof. In all this bloodshed he himself escaped and took refuge in the land of the Rutulians under the protection of the armies of his guest friend, Turnus. At this the whole of Etruria rose in righteous fury and has now come in arms to demand that Mezentius be given up for punishment. They have thousands of troops and I shall put you at their head. Their ships are massed all along the shore, clamouring for the signal for battle, but they are held in check by this warning from an aged prophet: "O you chosen warriors from Lydian Maeonia, flower of the chivalry of an ancient race, it is a just grievance that drives you to war, and Mezentius deserves the anger that blazes against him, but it is not the will of heaven that such a race as the Etruscans should ever obey an Italian. You must choose your leaders from across the seas."

'At this the Etruscan army has settled down again on the plain, held back by fear of these divine warnings. Tarchon himself has sent envoys to me with crown and sceptre, and offers me the royal insignia of Etruria if I agree to come to their camp and take over the kingdom. But my powers have passed with the passing of the generations. Age has taken the speed from my feet and the warmth from my blood. I am too old for command and no longer have the strength for battle. I would be urging my son to go, but he is of mixed stock through his Sabine mother and is therefore part Italian. It is you who are favoured of the Fates for your years and your descent. You are the man the gods are asking for. Go then, O bravest leader of all the men of Troy and Italy, and I shall send with you this my son Pallas, our hope and our comfort. Let him be hardened to the rigours of war under your leadership. Let him daily see your conduct and admire you from his earliest years. Two hundred horsemen I shall give him, the flower of our fighting men, and Pallas will give you two hundred more in his own name.'

He had scarcely finished speaking, and Aeneas, son of Anchises, and his faithful Achates were still looking sadly down at the ground, and long would they have pondered in the anguish of their hearts, had Venus not given a sign from the clear sky. There came from the heavens a sudden flash of lightning and a rumble of thunder and the whole sky seemed to be crashing down upon them with the blast of an Etruscan trumpet shrilling across the heavens. They looked up and again and again great peals broke over their heads and in bright sky in a break between the clouds they saw armour glowing red and heard it thunder as it clashed. The others were all astonished but the hero of Troy understood the sound and knew this was the fulfilment of the promise of his divine mother. At last he spoke: 'There is no need, my friend, no need to ask what these portents mean. This is heaven asking for me. The goddess who is my mother told me she would send this sign if war were threatening, and bring armour made by Vulcan down through the air to help me. Alas! What slaughter waits upon the unhappy Laurentines! What a punishment Turnus will endure at my hands! How many shields and helmets and bodies of brave men will Father Thybris roll down beneath his waves. Now let the Laurentines ask for war! Now let them break their treaties!'

When he had said this, he rose from his high throne. First of all he stirred the fires smouldering on the altar of Hercules and approached with joy the humble gods of home and hearth whom he had worshipped on the day before, and then Evander and the warriors of Troy made sacrifice together of duly chosen yearling sheep. When this was done Aeneas went back from Evander's house to his ships and his comrades, from whom he chose men of outstanding courage to follow him to war. The rest sailed downstream, floating effortlessly on the current, to bring Ascanius news of his father and tell him what had happened. The Trojans going to Etruria were given horses. The mount picked out for Aeneas was caparisoned in one great tawny lion skin with gleaming gold claws.

Swiftly round the little city flew the rumour that they were riding to the gates of the king of Etruria. Frightened mothers heaped prayer upon prayer, their fear increasing with the approach of danger, and the vision of Mars loomed ever larger before them. As they left, Evander took the right hand of his son Pallas and clung to it inconsolably: 'If only Jupiter would give me back the years that are past,' he cried, 'when I laid low the front rank of the enemy's battle line under the very walls of Praeneste, heaping up their shields and burning them to celebrate my victory, with this right hand sending down to Tartarus their king Erulus, whose mother Feronia had given him three lives at birth – I shudder to remember it – three sets of armour to carry into battle, and three times I had to lay him dead on the ground, but in those days this one right hand was able to take all his lives and strip him of all those sets of armour . . . no power on earth would be tearing me from your arms, O my beloved son, and Mezentius would never have been able to trample upon his neighbour, putting so many of my countrymen to the sword and emptying the city of so many of its people. But O you gods above, and you, Greatest Jupiter, ruler of the gods, I beseech you, take pity on an Arcadian king, and hear a father's prayers. If your divine powers and the Fates are keeping Pallas safe for me, if I am going to live to see him again and be with him again, then I pray for life and harden my heart to endure any suffering. But if Fortune has some horror in store, let me die now, let me break off this cruel life here and now, before I can put a name to my sorrow, before I know what the future will bring and while I still hold you in my arms, O my dear son, my only source of joy, given to me so late in life. I want no grim news to come and wound my ears.' These are the words that poured from the lips of Evander at his last parting with his son. When he had uttered them, he collapsed and was carried into his house by his attendants.

And now the gates had been opened and the horsemen had ridden out, Aeneas among the first of them and his faithful Achates with him, then the other Trojan commanders with Pallas conspicuous in the middle of the column in his Greek military cloak and brightly coloured armour. He was like the Morning Star, which Venus loves above all other starry fires, as he leaves his ocean bath and lifts up his holy face into the sky to scatter the darkness. Mothers stood on the city walls, full of dread and following with their eyes the cloud of dust and the glint of bronze from the squadrons. They were riding in their armour by the shortest route over rough scrub and their shouts rose to the sky as the four-hoofed beat of the galloping column drummed on the dusty plain. Near Caere's cold river there was a wide glade, revered for generations as a holy place by peoples near and far. It was enclosed on every side by a ring of hills clad in black firs. The story is told that the ancient Pelasgians, who in days long past were the first inhabitants of Latium, consecrated this grove and a holy day to be observed in it to Silvanus, the god of field and flock. Not far from here Tarcho and the Etruscans were occupying a strong position and their whole army could be seen from the heights of the hills, encamped on the broad fields. Aeneas and his chosen warriors had come down to the camp and, weary from the ride, were seeing to their horses and refreshing themselves.

But the goddess Venus, bringing her gifts, was at hand, shining among the clouds of heaven. When she saw her son at some distance from the others, alone in a secluded valley across the icy river, she spoke to him, coming unasked before his eyes: 'Here now are the gifts I promised you, perfected by my husband's skill. When the time comes you need not hesitate, my son, to face the proud Laurentines or challenge fierce Turnus to battle.' With these words the goddess of Cythera came to her son's embrace and laid the armour in all its shining splendour before him under an oak tree.

Aeneas rejoiced at these gifts from the goddess and at the honour she was paying him and could not have his fill of gazing at them. He turned them over in his hands, in his arms, admiring the terrible, crested, fire-spurting helmet, the death-dealing sword, the huge, unyielding breastplate of blood-red bronze like a dark cloud fired by the rays of the sun and glowing far across the sky, then the polished greaves of richly refined electrum and gold, the spear and the fabric of the shield beyond all words to describe. There the God of Fire, with his knowledge of the prophets and of time that was to be, had laid out the story of Italy and the triumphs of the Romans, and there in order were all the generations that would spring from Ascanius and all the wars they would fight.

He had made, too, a mother wolf stretched out in the green cave of Mars with twin boys playing round her udders, hanging there unafraid and sucking at her as she bent her supple neck back to lick each of them in turn and mould their bodies into shape with her tongue.

Near this he had put Rome and the violent rape of the Sabines at the great games in the bowl of the crowded Circus, and a new war suddenly breaking out between the people of Romulus and the stern Sabines from Cures led by their aged king Tatius. Then, after these same kings had put an end to their conflict, they stood in their armour before the altar of Jupiter with sacred vessels in their hands, sacrificing a sow to ratify the treaty.

Close by, four-horse chariots had been driven hard in opposite directions and had torn Mettus in two – the man of Alba should have stood by his promises – and Tullus was dragging the deceiver's body through a wood while a dew of blood dripped from the brambles.

There too was Porsenna ordering the Romans to take Tarquin back after they had expelled him, and mounting a great siege against the city while the descendants of Aeneas were running upon the drawn swords of the enemy in the name of liberty. There you could see him as though raging and blustering because Horatius Cocles was daring to tear the bridge down and Cloelia had broken her chains and was swimming the river.

At the top of the shield Manlius, the keeper of the citadel on the Tarpeian rock, stood in front of the temple and kept guard on the heights of the Capitol. The new thatch stood out rough on the roof of Romulus' palace, and here was a silver goose fluttering through the golden portico, honking to announce that the Gauls were at the gates. There were the Gauls close by, among the thorn bushes, climbing into the citadel under the cover of darkness on that pitch-black night. Their hair was gold, their clothing was gold, their striped cloaks gleamed and their milk-white necks were encircled by golden torques. In each right hand there glinted two heavy Alpine spears and long shields protected their bodies. Here too Vulcan had hammered out the leaping Salii, the priests of Mars, and the naked Luperci, the priests' conical hats tufted with wool, the figure-of-eight shields which had fallen from heaven and chaste matrons leading sacred processions through the city in cushioned carriages.

At some distance from these scenes he added the habitations of the dead in Tartarus, the tall gateway of Dis and the punishments of the damned, with Catiline hanging from his beetling crag and shivering at the faces of the Furies. There too were the righteous, in a place apart, and Cato administering justice.

Between all these there ran a representation of a broad

expanse of swelling sea, golden, but dark blue beneath the white foam on the crests of the waves, and all round it in a circle swam dolphins picked out in silver, cleaving the sea and feathering its surface with their tails.

In the middle were the bronze-armoured fleets at the battle of Actium. There before your eyes the battle was drawn up with the whole of the headland of Leucas seething and all the waves gleaming in gold. On one side was Augustus Caesar, leading the men of Italy into battle alongside the Senate and the People of Rome, its gods of home and its great gods. High he stood on the poop of his ship while from his radiant forehead there streamed a double flame and his father's star shone above his head. On the other wing, towering above the battle as he led his ships in line ahead, sailed Agrippa with favouring winds and favouring gods, and the beaks of captured vessels flashed from the proud honour on his forehead, the Naval Crown. On the other side, with the wealth of the barbarian world and warriors in all kinds of different armour, came Antony in triumph from the shores of the Red Sea and the peoples of the Dawn. With him sailed Egypt and the power of the East from as far as distant Bactria, and there bringing up the rear was the greatest outrage of all, his Egyptian wife! On they came at speed, all together, and the whole surface of the sea was churned to foam by the pull of their oars and the bow-waves from their triple beaks. They steered for the high sea and you would have thought that the Cycladic Islands had been torn loose again and were floating on the ocean, or that mountains were colliding with mountains, to see men in action on those ships with their massive, turreted sterns, showering blazing torches of tow and flying steel as the fresh blood began to redden the furrows of Neptune's fields. In the middle of all this the queen summoned her warships by rattling her Egyptian timbrels – she was not yet seeing the two snakes there at her back – while Anubis barked and all manner of monstrous gods levelled their weapons at Neptune and Venus and Minerva. There in the eye of battle raged Mars, engraved in iron, the grim Furies swooped from the sky and jubilant Discord strode along in her torn cloak with Bellona at her heels cracking her bloody whip. But high on the headland of Actium, Apollo saw it all and was drawing his bow. In terror at the sight the whole of Egypt and of India, all the Arabians and all the Shebans were turning tail and the queen herself could be seen calling for winds and setting her sails by them. She had untied the sail-ropes and was even now paying them out. There in all the slaughter the God of Fire had set her, pale with the pallor of approaching death, driven over the waves by the Iapygian winds blowing off Calabria. Opposite her he had fashioned the Nile with grief in every line of his great body, opening his robes and with every fold of drapery beckoning his defeated people into his blue-grey breast and the secret waters of his river.

But Caesar was riding into Rome in triple triumph, paying undying vows to the gods of Italy and consecrating three hundred great shrines throughout the city. The streets resounded with joy and festivities and applause. There was a chorus of matrons at every temple, at every temple there were altars and the ground before the altars was strewn with the bodies of slaughtered bullocks. He himself was seated at the white marble threshold of gleaming white Apollo, inspecting the gifts brought before him by the peoples of the earth and hanging them high on the posts of the doors of the temple, while the defeated nations walked in long procession in all their different costumes and in all their different armour, speaking all the tongues of the earth. Here Mulciber, the God of Fire, had moulded the Nomads and the Africans with their streaming robes; here, too, the Lelegeians and Carians of Asia and the Gelonians from Scythia with their arrows. The Euphrates was now moving with a chastened current, and here were the Gaulish Morini from the ends of the earth, the two-horned Rhine, the undefeated Dahae from beyond the Caspian and the river Araxes chafing at his bridge.

Such were the scenes spread over the shield that Vulcan made and Venus gave to her son. Marvelling at it, and rejoicing at the things pictured on it without knowing what they were, Aeneas lifted on to his shoulder the fame and the fate of his descendants.

For lines 626–728, see Appendix Two

ൽ 9 ൾ

NISUS AND EURYALUS

While this was happening far away in Etruria, Juno, daughter of Saturn, sent Iris down from the sky to bold Turnus, who chanced at that moment to be sitting in a grove sacred to his ancestor Pilumnus. These were the words that came to him from the rosy lips of Iris, daughter of Thaumas: 'There, Turnus, time in its ever-rolling course has brought you unasked what none of the gods would have dared to promise you if you had prayed for it – Aeneas has left his city, his allies and his fleet, and gone to visit the royal seat of Evander on the Palatine. And as though that were not enough, he has travelled as far as the remotest cities of Corythus and is arming a band of Lydians, some country people he has collected. What are you waiting for? This is the moment to call for your horses and chariots. Do not allow any delay. Make a surprise attack on their camp and seize it.' At these words she soared into the sky on poised wings, cutting in her flight a great rainbow under the clouds. The warrior knew her, and raising his hands palms upward to the stars, he called out to her as she flew: 'Iris, glory of the sky, who has sent you here to me, riding the clouds down to the earth? Why this sudden brightness in the air? I see the heights of heaven parting and stars wandering through the vault of the sky. I follow this great sign, whoever you are that call me to arms.' When he had spoken these words, he walked to the river's edge and scooped up in his hands the water from its surface as he offered up prayer upon prayer to the gods and burdened heaven with his vows.

The whole army was soon moving across the open plain, rich in its horses, rich in embroidered apparel, rich in gold. The vanguard was controlled by Messapus, the rear by the sons of Tyrrhus, while Turnus, the chief commander, was in the middle of the column. It was like the Ganges fed by the steady flow of its seven rivers and silently rising, or like the fertile waters of the Nile when it withdraws from the plains and settles back at last into its own channel. The Trojans saw this distant cloud of black dust suddenly gathering and the darkness rising on the plain. Caicus was on the rampart on that side and he was the first to raise the alarm: 'What is that ball of dark dust rolling along the plain? Fetch your weapons, fellow-citizens, and fetch them now! Give out missiles! Mount the walls! The enemy is upon us. To your posts!' With a great clamour the Trojans streamed in by all the gates to man the walls, for these were the orders they had received from Aeneas, the greatest of warriors, as he left them: if anything should happen in his absence, they were not to dare take up position for a pitched battle or trust themselves to the plain, but only to stay on the ramparts and defend the camp and the walls. So, though shame and anger urged them to join battle, they nevertheless obeyed orders and closed the gates against the enemy, waiting for them in full armour inside their towers.

By this time Turnus had taken wing and gone on ahead of the slow-moving column. With twenty picked horsemen he arrived at the city before he was expected, riding a piebald Thracian charger and wearing his gold helmet shaded by red plumes. 'Is there any man among you, my friends, will come with me and be first upon the enemy? There!' he cried, and sent his javelin spinning into the air as a signal for battle, then, rising in the saddle he charged across the plain. His comrades took up the cry and followed him with blood-curdling shouts.

They were amazed at the faint-heartedness of the Trojans. Why did they not commit themselves to a fair fight on the level plain? They were men. Why did they huddle in their camp and not meet arms with arms? Turnus in a fury prowled round the walls this way and that, searching for an approach where there was none, like a wolf in the dead of night, lying in wait in all the wind and rain by a pen full of sheep, and growling at the gaps in the fence, while the lambs keep up their bleating, safe beneath their mothers; beside himself with anger he storms and rages but cannot reach them; he is worn out by the ravening hunger he has been so long in gathering and many a day has passed since blood wet his throat – so did the Rutulian blaze with anger as he surveyed the walls of the Trojan camp and the pain burned him to the bone. How could he try to come at them? What device could shake out the Trojans shut up there behind their rampart and spill them on to the plain? Ah! The fleet! There it was moored in a sheltered position along the side of the camp, protected by the water of the river, and to the landward by ramparts. There he made his attack. Burning with fury himself he demanded fire from his exultant comrades and took up a great blazing pine torch in his hand. At this they all bent to the task, with Turnus there to urge them on. They plundered what fires they could find, and their reeking torches smouldered with a pitchy light as Vulcan whirled to the stars dense clouds of smoke shot through with sparks.

Tell me, Muses, what god turned these fierce flames away from the Trojans and drove such fire from their ships. The tale was told in times long past but the fame of it will live for ever. When Aeneas was first building his fleet on Mount Ida in Phrygia and preparing to take to the high seas, Berecyntian Cybele herself, the Mother of the Gods, is said to have addressed these words to great Jupiter: 'O my son, grant my prayer. Now that Olympus is subdued, grant what your dear mother asks of you. On top of my citadel I had a wood of pine trees which I had loved for many years, a dark grove of black pine and maple where men would bring their offerings. These trees I gladly gave to the Trojan warrior when he needed a fleet, but now my heart is seized by anxiety and dread. Put all my fears at rest and answer your mother's prayer. Grant that my ships should not be wrecked on any of their voyages or overwhelmed by any squall of wind. Let it stand to their favour that they were born on our mountains.' Her son, who turns the stars of heaven in their courses, made this reply to his mother: 'What is this you are calling on the Fates to do? What do these words of yours mean? Are ships made by mortal hands to have immortal rights? Is Aeneas to face all his doubts and dangers and never know uncertainty? Is there any god to whom such a privilege has been granted? No. But when the ships have done their duty, when in due course they reach the end of their voyaging and are safe in harbour in Ausonia, each one to survive the sea and reach the Laurentine fields with the Trojan leader will lose its mortal shape. I shall order all of them to become goddesses of the great ocean, like Galatea and Doto, daughters of Nereus, whose breasts cleave the foam of the waves of the sea.' Jupiter had spoken, ratifying his words by the waters of the Styx, his brother's river, by the banks and dark whirlpools of that pitch-black torrent, and at his nod the whole of Olympus shook.

And so the promised day had come and the Fates had completed the allotted time, when the violent attack of Turnus warned the Mother Goddess to defend her sacred ships from these burning brands. A strange light now shone before men's eyes and a great cloud seemed to cross the sky from the east, bearing with it votaries of the goddess from Mount Ida. A fearsome voice then fell from the air and filled the ears of Trojans and Rutulians in their armed ranks: 'Do not trouble, Trojans, to defend my ships. Do not take your weapons in your hands. Turnus will burn the sea dry before he can burn these sacred pine trees. Go then! You are freed. Go, you

goddesses of the sea! The Mother of the Gods commands.' In
an instant every ship burst the ropes that moored it to the
bank, and they plunged like dolphins, beak first to the bottom.
When they returned to the surface, they were miraculously
changed, each one a nymph swimming in the sea.

The Rutulians were astonished. Messapus himself was
afraid and his horses reared. Even Tiber checked his flow with
a harsh roaring of his waters as he called back his current
from the sea. But the boldness and confidence of Turnus never
wavered. Without hesitation he set about haranguing his men
and whipping up their spirits: 'These portents strike at the
Trojans: they mean that Jupiter has taken from them the help
they have become accustomed to. The ships did not wait to
taste Rutulian fire and sword! So now the seas are barred to
the Trojans and they have no hope of escape. By this they
have lost one half of the world, and the land is already in our
hands, so many thousands of men are marching under arms
from all the races of Italy. This Phrygian talk of destiny and
the oracles of the gods does not dismay me. Destiny and
Venus were satisfied the moment Trojans set foot on the fertile
fields of Italy. I too have a destiny, of a different sort – to cut
down with the sword this vicious people that has robbed me
of my bride. The sons of Atreus are not the only ones who
have suffered, and the people of Mycenae are not the only
men who can take up arms. Let them not imagine it is enough
to have been destroyed once! It should have been enough for
them to sin once. They had no need to show loathing and
contempt for every woman in the world. Look at them now,
all courage and confidence because of this rampart that keeps
us from them and these ditches they have dug to hold us back.
This is no sort of barrier to stand between them and death.
Did they not see the walls of Troy settling into the flames?
And those were fashioned by the hands of Neptune. You are
my chosen few. Which one of you is ready to cut through
their rampart with the sword and rush into that camp of

cowards? To fight Trojans I do not need the armour Vulcan made for Achilles. I do not need a thousand ships, not if every man in Etruria went and joined them as allies this instant. Nor do they need to be frightened of the dark. We shall not be creeping up on them like cowards to kill the guards all over their citadel and steal their Palladium. We shall not be hiding in the blind belly of a horse. Our plan is to come in daylight in full view and gird their walls with fire. I shall soon make sure they realize it is not Greeks they have to deal with or the army of Pelasgians Hector held off into a tenth year. But the best part of the day is already spent. For what remains of it you can now rest yourselves. You have done well. Be of good cheer, in high hopes that we can bring them to battle.'

Meanwhile Messapus was given the task of blockading the gates with a night guard and ringing the walls with watch-fires. Fourteen Rutulians were chosen to keep watch on the walls, each commanding a hundred men with purple crests on their helmets and gleaming with gold. They dispersed, some going to their various duties, others lying out on the grass, enjoying their wine and tipping up the bronze mixing bowls. The watch-fires burned and the guards kept awake by gaming the night away.

The Trojans looked out on all this from the top of their rampart and kept armed guards on all the high points while anxiously checking the gates, building bridges to their outlying fortlets, and bringing up missiles. Mnestheus and the zealous Serestus never relaxed their vigilance. They were the men Father Aeneas had appointed to take over the command of the troops and the government of the people should adversity require it. The whole legion was on the alert along the walls. Lots had been cast for posts of danger and each man was taking his turn to stand guard.

Nisus, son of Hyrtacus, was keeper of a gate. This formidable warrior, swift to throw the spear or send the arrow flying, had been sent by Ida, the hunters' mountain, to be the comrade of Aeneas, and with him came his own comrade, Euryalus, a boy with the first signs of manhood on cheeks as yet unshaven. There was no lovelier youth among the people of Aeneas, and no lovelier youth ever put on Trojan armour. They were one in love, and side by side they used to charge into battle. So now too, they were sharing guard duty on the gate, when Nisus said to Euryalus: 'Is it the gods who put this ardour into our minds, or does every man's irresistible desire become his god? My mind is not content to rest in peace and quiet but has long been driving me to rush into battle or into some great enterprise. You see the Rutulians there with just a few scattered lights piercing the darkness, how sure they are of everything, lying sunk in sleep and wine, and silence every-where. Just listen to what I am thinking and to the plan beginning to form in my mind. The people and the fathers, they are all clamouring for Aeneas to be summoned and messengers sent to tell him exactly what is happening. If they promise to give you what I ask – all I want is credit for the deed – I think I can find a way round the foot of that hill to the city of Pallanteum.' Euryalus was overcome, pierced to the heart with a great love of glory, and in an instant he replied in these words to his ardent friend: 'So you do not want me as your comrade on this great expedition, and I am to let you go alone into dangers like this? This is not how I was brought up by my father Opheltes during the Greek terror and our sufferings at Troy, and he knew all about war. Nor is this how I have conducted myself with you, in following to the end the Fates of great-hearted Aeneas. I have here a heart that despises the light, that would gladly spend life to buy the honour you are striving for.' To this Nisus replied: 'So may great Jupiter, or whatever god looks with favour on this undertaking, bring me back to you in triumph, I swear I never had any such fears about you. That would have been a sin. But if some chance or some god were to lead me into disaster – and you know how many things can happen in dangerous affairs like this – I would wish you to go on living. You are young and your claim on life is greater than mine. There would then be someone to consign my body to the earth if it is rescued from the battlefield or recovered by ransom, or if some fortune forbids that – and we know her ways – to make offerings for me here and honour me with an empty tomb. Besides, let me not be the cause of such heart-break to your mother, who of all the mothers of Troy is the only one who has dared to follow her son here with never a thought for the walls of great Acestes.' 'One feeble argument after another,' replied Euryalus, 'and all to no purpose. My mind is made up and you have done nothing to change it. Let us go, and quickly.' So saying, he woke sentries to take over and keep guard for Nisus and himself. They left their post and marched off side by side to look for prince Ascanius.

Over the whole world the creatures of the earth were relaxed in sleep, all resting from their cares, and their hearts had forgotten their labours; but the chosen warriors who were the great leaders of the Trojans were holding a council on matters of the highest importance to the kingdom. What were they to do now? Who would go as a messenger to Aeneas? As they stood there on the level ground in the middle of the camp, leaning on their long spears and carrying their shields, Nisus and Euryalus suddenly arrived in great haste and asked to be admitted, saying that their business was urgent and well worth listening to. Seeing their excitement, Iulus was the first to welcome them and invited Nisus to speak. These were the words of the son of Hyrtacus: 'Give us a fair hearing, sons of Aeneas. Do not judge what is said by the age of the speakers. The Rutulians have fallen quiet, deep in their drunken sleep, and we have seen a place for an ambush, some open ground where the two roads meet by the gate nearest the sea. There the ring of watch-fires is broken and the smoke is rising black to the stars. If you allow us to take this opportunity to go and look for Aeneas and the city of Pallanteum, you will soon see us coming back laden with booty and much slaughter done. We have no doubts about the way to go. We always hunt there and have seen the first houses of the city in the dark valleys. We have explored the whole river.'

It was Aletes, heavy with years and mature in judgement, who now replied: 'O gods of our fathers, in whose divine hands Troy still remains, in spite of all, it is not your will utterly to destroy the Trojans, if you have put such firmness of mind and heart into our young warriors,' and as he spoke he clasped the right hands of both of them and laid his hands on their shoulders while the tears ran down his cheeks and face: 'Can any recompense be found for you?' he cried. 'Can anything match the glorious deeds you propose? The first and richest reward will come from the gods and from your own virtue, but the others will soon follow from a grateful Aeneas, and young Ascanius for the rest of his life will never forget such a service.' 'More than that,' interposed Ascanius, 'my whole life hangs upon the return of my father and I call upon you both to witness, by the great Penates and Lar of Assaracus, and the shrine of white-haired Vesta, I now place all my fortunes and all my hopes for the future in your hands, Nisus. Call back my father. Bring him back to my sight. If he is restored there can be no cause for grief. I shall give you two solid silver embossed cups which he took at the fall of Arisba, and with them a pair of tripods, two great talents of gold and an ancient mixing bowl given him by Dido of Sidon. But if he succeeds in taking Italy and winning the crown, while he is presiding over the distribution of booty in his hour of victory – you have seen the horse that Turnus rides, you have seen him all golden in his armour – I shall exclude from the lot that horse, the shield and the scarlet plumes, and these will now be yours, Nisus, as your reward. In addition my father will give you twelve chosen matrons and twelve prisoners of war, each with his armour, and all the lands on the plain now held by king Latinus. But as for you, Euryalus, although you are a

boy and not so far ahead of myself in the race of life, I revere
you and take you wholly into my heart, embracing you as my
comrade, whatever may lie before us. Whatever I may do, I
shall look for no glory that is not shared with you. In war or
in peace, whatever I say or do, my whole trust will be placed
in you.'

To this Euryalus replied: 'The day shall never come when
I shall be found unequal to acts of courage like this, if only
the fall of fortune is in our favour tonight, and not against us.
But one thing I ask of you, more precious than any gifts: I
grieve for my mother of the ancient line of Priam. The land of
Troy could not hold her when she came away with me, nor
did the walls of king Acestes. As I now leave her, she knows
nothing of the danger I am entering upon, whether it be great
or small, and I have taken no farewell of her because – and
I swear it by the Night and your own right hand – I could
not bear to see my mother weep. But comfort her in her
helplessness, I beg you, and support her in her desolation. Let
me take with me the hope that you will do this and I shall go
all the more boldly into whatever dangers lie before me.' The
Trojans were overcome and wept, the fair Iulus most of all, as
this image of his love for his own father touched his heart,
and he replied: 'You can be certain that everything I do will
be worthy of your great enterprise. Your mother will be my
mother in everything but the name Creusa. The woman who
gave birth to such a son will receive no ordinary gratitude. I
have promised you rewards when you return in triumph.
Whatever the outcome of your bravery, I swear by this head
of mine, by which my father used to swear, that these same
promises will hold good for your mother and your kin.' So he
spoke, weeping, and in that moment he took from his shoulder
a gilded sword that Lycaon of Cnossus had fashioned with
consummate art and fitted in an ivory scabbard to hang per-
fectly at his side, while Mnestheus gave Nisus a rough hide
stripped from a lion, and trusty Aletes changed helmets with

him. As soon as they were armed they marched off, and all
the leading Trojans, young and old, escorted them to the gates
with their prayers. Foremost among them was the fair Iulus,
bearing beyond his years a man's load of cares and a man's
spirit. He gave them many commissions to bear to his father,
but they were all futile. The wind scattered them among the
clouds.

They moved off and crossed the ditch, making their way
under cover of night to the camp that would be their death,
but not before they had brought death to many others. They
could see men sprawling in drunken sleep all over the grass
and chariots standing along the river bank with their poles in
the air and a tangle of men's bodies and armour and wine
vessels among the reins and wheels. Nisus was the first to
speak: 'Now, Euryalus,' he said, 'my right hand must show
its mettle. The hour calls out for it. Our road goes this way.
You keep guard to the rear in case a party of men creeps up
on us from behind, and look well into the distance. I shall
make havoc here and clear a broad path for you.' So he spoke
and then had done with words. With sword drawn he made
for proud Rhamnes who happened to be propped up there
on a deep pile of rugs, his whole chest heaving as he slept. A
king he was, and a prophet cherished by a king, by Turnus.
But not all his prophesying could drive from him the plague
of death. Nisus then caught three of Rhamnes' attendants
lying in a heap among their weapons, then the armour-bearer
of Remus and his charioteer among the hooves of the horses.
Their heads were lolling. He cut them off. Next he removed
the head of their master Remus and left the blood gurgling
out of his trunk and warming the ground as the black gore
soaked through the bedding. Lamyrus also he slew, and
Lamus and young Serranus, a handsome youth who had
gambled late into the night. There he lay overcome by all the
wine of Bacchus he had drunk. He would have been happy if
he could have made his gambling last the night and kept it

up till daylight. Nisus was like a lion driven mad with hunger and ravening through pens full of sheep, dumb with fear, while he growls from jaws dripping with blood as he mauls and champs their soft flesh.

Meanwhile there was no less slaughter from the hand of Euryalus. He too was in a blazing frenzy as he crept up on a great crowd of nameless warriors lying unconscious in his path, Fadus and Herbesus, Rhoetus and Abaris. Rhoetus was awake and saw it all, so hid in panic behind a great mixing bowl. But when Euryalus came near him, he rose and Euryalus plunged his sword to the hilt in his chest. When he withdrew it, the whole life of Rhoetus flooded out after it. As he lay there dying, still vomiting his crimson life's breath and bringing up wine and gore together, Euryalus was already prowling on, hot for blood. He was soon making for Messapus and his comrades, where he saw the dying embers of the watch-fires and the horses tethered in good order cropping the grass, when Nisus had a few words to say to him – for he noticed that Euryalus was being carried away by bloodlust and greed: 'Let us make an end,' he said. 'Daylight is no friend of ours and it will soon be here. Our enemies have taken enough punishment and we have cut our path through the middle of them.' They left behind them many pieces of men's armour wrought in solid silver, and mixing bowls besides, and lovely rugs, but Euryalus took Rhamnes' medallions and his gold-studded belt. Long ago the wealthy Caedicus had sent them from his home as gifts to Remulus of Tibur to form a guest-friendship with him. When Remulus was dying, he gave them to his grandson, and after his death they passed to the Rutulians as spoils of war. Euryalus now snatched them up and put them round his brave shoulders, but little good were they to do him. He also put on the helmet of Messapus with its gorgeous plumes, and they left the camp and made for safety.

At this moment, while the rest of the Latin army was

waiting in battle order on the plain, a detachment of cavalry
had been sent out from their city and was now on its way
with dispatches to Turnus, three hundred of them, all carrying
shields, under the command of Volcens. They were approaching the camp and coming up to its ramparts when they saw
Nisus and Euryalus in the distance, veering off along the road
to the left. Euryalus had forgotten about the helmet, and its
glittering betrayed him, reflecting the rays of the moon in the
dim shadows of the night. The enemy saw and did not fail to
act. 'Halt there, you men!' shouted Volcens from the head of
his column. 'Why are you on the road? Who are you? Why
are you armed? Where are you going?' They offered no reply,
but ran off into the trees, putting their trust in the darkness of
the night. The horsemen spread out along each side of the
wood they knew so well, blocking the tracks that led in, and
putting guards on every approach. It was a rough wood full
of dense undergrowth and dark ilex trees, all of it choked
with thick brambles, and the path glimmered only here and
there among the faint tracks left by animals. Euryalus was
held back by the darkness under the trees and by the weight
of his booty, and in his fright he lost his way. But Nisus
escaped. Without knowing it he had come through the enemy
and the area later to be known as Alban, taking its name
from the city of Alba, but in those days king Latinus had
high-fenced enclosures there for his cattle. He now stopped
and looked back for his friend, but could not see him. 'Poor
Euryalus,' he cried. 'Where have I left you? Where can I look
for you?' and even as he spoke, he was beginning to go back
over his path through the wood with all its deceptive twists
and turns, retracing every remembered step as he wandered
through the silent undergrowth. He heard horses. He heard
the noise of the pursuers and their signals, and in no time
shouts reached his ears and he saw Euryalus. Lost in the
treacherous darkness of the wood and confused by the sudden
tumult, he had been caught by the whole enemy troop and

was now being carried off, still struggling desperately against all the odds. What was Nisus to do? How could he rescue his young friend? How should he attack? What weapons could he use? Should he throw himself into the thick of their swords and rush through wound upon wound to a glorious death? In that instant he drew back his arm, and brandishing his throwing spear, he looked up to the moon in heaven and prayed in these words: 'O goddess, daughter of Latona, O glory of the stars and guardian of the groves, be with me now and help me in my hour of trouble. If ever my father Hyrtacus has offered gifts for me at your altars, if ever I myself have enriched them with the spoils of my hunting, hanging my offerings in the dome of your temple or nailing them on your holy gables, guide my weapons through the air and grant that I may throw this troop of my enemies into confusion.' When he had spoken, he hurled his spear with the whole force of his body. Parting the shadows of the night it flew towards Sulmo, whose back was turned, and there it struck and broke, sending a splinter through his diaphragm. He rolled over, vomiting a stream of warm blood from his chest in the chill of death, and heaving his flanks in deep-drawn agonies. While the enemy were looking round in all directions, there was Nisus, emboldened by his success, with another shaft ready by his ear, poised to aim. They were still in tumult when the spear came whistling and caught Tagus in the middle of the forehead, went through the brain, and stuck there, growing warm. Volcens was wild with rage, but nowhere could he see the thrower and he could not decide where to direct the fury of his assault. 'Never mind!' he shouted. 'For the moment, you and your warm blood will pay me for both of them!' and he drew his sword and rushed at Euryalus. This was too much for Nisus. Out of his mind with terror and unable to endure his anguish, he broke cover, shouting at the top of his voice: 'Here I am! Here I am! I am the one who did it! Aim your weapons at me, you Rutulians! The whole scheme was mine.

He is innocent. He could not have done it. I swear by this sky above me and the stars who know the truth, his only offence is to have loved the wrong friend too much!' He was still speaking as the sword was driven through the ribs of Euryalus, full force, shattering his white breast. He rolled on the ground in death, the blood flowed over his beautiful body, his neck grew limp and the head drooped on his shoulders, like a scarlet flower languishing and dying when its stem has been cut by the plough, or like poppies bowing their heads when the rain burdens them and their necks grow weary. But Nisus rushed into the thick of the enemy, looking only for Volcens. Volcens was the only thought in his mind. The Rutulians gathered round their leader and in close fighting threw Nisus back again and again as he came at them from one side after another, but he bore on none the less, whirling a sword like lightning till he met the Rutulian face to face and buried it in his mouth as he opened it to shout. So, in the moment of his own dying, he cut off the breath of his enemy. Then, pierced through and through, he hurled himself on the dead body of his friend and rested there at last in the peace of death.

Fortune has favoured you both! If there is any power in my poetry, the day will never come when time will erase you from the memory of man, while the house of Aeneas remains by the immovable rock of the Capitol and the Father of the Romans still keeps his empire.

The victorious Rutulians had collected their booty and their spoils and carried the body of Volcens to their camp, weeping as they went. There was no less sorrow waiting for them there, when they found Rhamnes dead, and with him Serranus and Numa and all their other leaders who had been killed in that one night of slaughter. A great crowd gathered round the dead and dying heroes and the ground was running with rivers of newly shed blood, still warm and foaming. Between them they recognized the spoils, the shining helmet of Messapus, and the medallions which had cost so much sweat to recover.

By now Aurora was just leaving the saffron bed of Tithonus and sprinkling her new light upon the world. The sun was soon streaming over the earth and soon all things stood revealed in its light. Turnus, in full armour himself, was rousing his men to arm, and each of the leaders was taking his own troop into battle in ranks of bronze, whipping up their anger with different accounts of the night's work. They even stuck the heads of Euryalus and Nisus on spears – what a sight that was! – and paraded along behind them shouting. Aeneas' men, long-enduring, drew up in battle order to face them on the walls on their left flank – the right was guarded by the river – and they manned their great ditches and stood on their high towers stricken with grief and shocked by the sight of the heads of the comrades they knew so well, impaled on spears and dripping black gore.

Meanwhile Rumour flew with the news on her swift wings through the whole terrified city of the Trojans, and came gliding into the ears of the mother of Euryalus. In that instant the warmth left her very bones, the shuttle was dashed from her fingers and its thread unwound. Crazed with grief she rushed out, and wailing as women do and tearing her hair, she made for the front ranks of the army on the walls. With no thought for the presence of men, with no thought of the danger of flying weapons, she stood there on the ramparts and filled heaven with her cries of mourning: 'Is this you I am looking at, Euryalus? How could you leave me alone, so cruelly, you who were the last comfort of my old age? Could not your poor mother have been allowed a few last words with you, before you went on that dangerous expedition? So now you lie in a strange land, and your body is food for the dogs and the birds of Latium! I am your mother and did not walk before you at your funeral; nor close your eyes, nor wash your wounds, nor cover you with the robe I have been weaving for you day and night with what speed I could, finding in my loom some solace for the cares of age. Where am I to go to look for you, my son? What piece of earth holds your mutilated body and dismembered limbs? Is this head all you bring back to me? Is that what I have followed over land and sea? Strike me, you Rutulians, if you have any human feelings! Throw all your spears at me! Let me be the first to die. Or will you take pity on me, Great Father of the Gods, and blast my detested body into Tartarus with your lightning, since I can find no other way to end this bitter life?' Sorrow like this was too much for the Trojans to bear. The sound of mourning was heard all through the army. Their strength was broken. They were losing their appetite for battle and her presence was fanning the flames of their grief. At a word from Ilioneus and the bitterly weeping Iulus, Idaeus and Actor came and took her between them back into her house.

The ringing bronze of the trumpet gave out its shrill and terrible note from close at hand. The shouting rose and the heavens bellowed in reply. The Volsci all at once rushed the walls with their shields locked in tortoise formation and tried to fill in the ditches and tear down the rampart. Some were looking for a point of access and putting up scaling ladders where the line of defenders was strung out along the walls, and light could be seen in the breaks between them. From their side the Trojans showered down missiles of every kind, and pushed the ladders off with stout poles – in their long war they had learned how to defend walls – and they rolled great heavy rocks down on the enemy to try to break their armoured formations, but in their close-packed tortoise they cheerfully endured whatever fell on them. But they still did not succeed. For where a solid mass of Rutulians was threatening the walls, the Trojans rolled along a huge block of stone and sent it crashing down on them to loosen their interlocking shields and cut a great swathe through them. After this the bold Rutulians no longer cared to fight blind under cover of their shields but strove to clear the defenders off the ramparts with a barrage of missiles. At another section of the wall Mezentius was brandishing a torch of Etruscan pine and a fearful sight he was as he came at them with fire and smoke. Messapus, son of Neptune and tamer of horses, was cutting a way through the rampart and shouting for scaling ladders.

I pray to you, Calliope, and to your sister Muses, to breathe upon me as I sing of the death and destruction wrought by the sword of Turnus and to tell who sent down to Orcus each warrior that died. Unroll with me now the mighty scroll of war.

There was a tower, well placed and of commanding height, with high connecting bridges. The Latins were trying to take it by main force, striving with all their powers to bring it down, while the Trojans packed inside tried to defend it by throwing rocks and sending a hail of weapons through the loopholes. Turnus, who was leading the attack, hurled a blazing torch which set fire to the side of the tower. Fanned by the wind, the flames took hold of the planking and ate into the upright posts. Inside all was confusion, terror and desperate attempts to escape the heat. As everyone crowded together to take refuge on the side away from the flames, all at once the whole sky seemed to thunder and the tower toppled over with the weight, and men plunged to the ground in their death throes with the massive fabric following them down, impaling them on their own weapons and driving the broken timbers through their breasts. Only Helenor and Lycus were able to escape. Helenor was a young man, son of the king of Maeonia and the slave girl Licymnia, who had reared him in secret and sent him to Troy under arms although this had been forbidden. His equipment was light, a sword with no scabbard and an inglorious shield of plain white, and he found himself caught in the middle of the thousands of men who fought with Turnus, looking at the battle lines of the Latins drawn up on all sides of him, like a wild beast trapped in a dense ring of hunters; it rages against the steel, and with full understanding it hurls itself to its death by springing on to the hunting spears – just so did young Helenor leap into the middle of his enemies, rushing to his death where he saw the steel was thickest. But Lycus was far fleeter of foot. He ran the gauntlet of the enemy and their weapons as far as the wall. There as he was trying to take hold of the top of the outworks and reach the outstretched hands of his comrades, Turnus, who had been pursuing him with his javelin, came to gloat over him: 'You fool! Did you think you could escape my hands?' and even as he shouted, he seized hold of him where he hung and tore him down, taking a great section of the wall with him, like the eagle, the armour-bearer of Jupiter, seizing in his hooked talons a hare or the white body of a swan and soaring into the air with it; or like the wolf of Mars tearing a lamb out of the sheep pen, and loud and long will be the bleating of its mother, as she looks for it.

The shouting rose on every side. The attackers levelled the rampart, filled in the ditch and tossed blazing torches high on to the roofs. Lucetius, who was coming to set fire to a gate, was laid low by a rock thrown by Ilioneus, a huge block torn out of a mountain. Liger felled Emathion with a javelin; Asilas brought down Corynaeus with an arrow he never saw in all its long flight. Caeneus slew Ortygius; Turnus slew the victorious Caeneus; Turnus also slew Itys and Clonius, Dioxippus and Promolus, then Sagaris and Idas, who was standing out in front of the highest towers. Privernus was killed by Capys: Themillas had first grazed him with a light spear and the fool had thrown his shield away to put his hand to the wound. So the winged arrow flew and, plunging deep into his left side, it broke the passages of his life's breath with a mortal wound. The son of Arcens stood there in gorgeous armour, resplendent in his embroidered cloak and Spanish purple, a noble sight to see. He had been sent to war by his father, who had reared him in the grove of Mars on the banks of the river Symaethus where the people of Sicily made their offerings at the rich altar of the mild god Palicius. Mezentius laid down his spears. Then, whirling his sling three times round his head, he shot the hissing bolt and struck the son of Arcens full in the middle of the forehead. Melting in its flight, the lead bullet split his skull and stretched him full length on the sand.

It was then, men say, that Ascanius first shot in war the swift arrow which till this time had only driven wild animals to terror and flight, and his was the hand that laid the brave Numanus low. This was a warrior whose family name was Remulus, and not long before he had been joined in marriage to the younger sister of Turnus. His heart was swollen with pride at the royal rank he had newly acquired, and he stepped out in front of the battle line, swaggering and shouting abuse, some fit and some unfit to be repeated: 'You have been sacked twice already, you Phrygians! Are you not ashamed to be cooped up again in a siege behind ramparts with only a wall between yourselves and death! Are you the men who came here to fight us for our brides? Is it some god that has driven you to Italy? Or some madness? You will not find here the sons of Atreus or the fictions and fine words of Ulixes! We are men of a hardy stock. We take our babies down to the river the moment they are born and harden them in the icy water. Our boys stay awake all night and weary the woods with their hunting. For games they ride horses and stretch the bow to the arrow. Our men endure hard labour and live spare, subduing the land with the mattock and shaking the towns of their enemies with war. We are worn hard by iron all our lives and turn our spears to goad our oxen. There is no sluggish old age for us to impair the strength and vigour of our minds. We crush our grey hair into the helmet, and our delight is always to bring home new plunder and live off what we take. But you like your clothes dyed with yellow saffron and the bright juice of the purple fish. Your delight is in dancing and idleness. You have sleeves to your tunics and ribbons to keep your bonnets on. You are Phrygian women, not Phrygian men! Away with you over the heights of Mount Dindymus, where you can hear your favourite tunes on the double pipe. The tambourines are calling you and the boxwood fifes of the Berecyntian Mother of Mount Ida. Leave weapons to the men. Make way for the iron of our swords.'

So he hurled his abuse and threats till Ascanius could endure it no longer. Turning to face him, he drew his bow and stretched the horsegut string, and as he stood there with his arms straining wide apart, he prayed first to Jupiter with this vow: 'All-powerful Jupiter, bless now this my first trial of arms, and with my own hands I shall bring yearly offerings to your temple and set before your altar a milk-white bullock, with gilded horns, holding its head as high as its mother's, already butting with its horns and kicking up the sand with its hooves.' The Father heard and thundered on the left from a clear sky, and the sound of the death-dealing bow of Ascanius mingled with the sound of the thunder. The arrow had been drawn back, and it flew with a fearful hiss straight through the head of Remulus, its iron point piercing his hollow temples. 'Go, Remulus!' he cried, 'and mock brave men with proud words! This is the reply to the Rutulians from the twice-sacked Phrygians!' Ascanius said no more than this, but the Trojans followed it with a shout of joy, their spirits raised to the skies.

At that moment Apollo, the youthful god, whose hair is never cut, chanced to be seated on a cloud, looking down from the expanse of heaven on the armies and cities of Italy, and he addressed these words to the victorious Iulus: 'You have become a man, young Iulus, and we salute you! This is the way that leads to the stars. You are born of the gods and will live to be the father of gods. Justice demands that all the wars that Fate will bring will come to an end under the offspring of Assaracus. Troy is not large enough for you.' At these words he plunged down from the heights of heaven, parting the breathing winds, and made for Ascanius, taking on the features of old Butes. Butes had once been armour-bearer to the Dardan Anchises and the trusted guard of his door, and Aeneas had then appointed him as companion to his son Ascanius. This was the guise in which Apollo came, the old man Butes to the life – voice, colouring, white hair, weapons grimly clanking – and these were the words he spoke to Iulus in the flush of his victory: 'Let that be enough, son of Aeneas. Numanus has fallen to your arms and you are unhurt. Great Apollo has granted you this first taste of glory and does not grudge you arrows as sure as his own. You must ask for no more, my boy, in this war.' So began Apollo, but while speaking, he left the sight of men, fading from their eyes into the insubstantial air. The Trojan leaders recognized the god. They knew his divine arrows and the quiver that sounded as he flew. So, although Ascanius was thirsting for battle, they held him back, urging upon him the words of Phoebus Apollo and the will of the god. But they themselves went back into battle and put their lives into naked danger. The shouting rang round the ramparts all along the walls. They bent their deadly bows and twisted their spear thongs till the ground was strewn with missiles. Shield and round helmet rang with the blows as fiercer and fiercer raged the battle. It was like a great shower from the west drumming on the earth in the rainy season when the Kids are rising, or like hailstones dropping from the clouds into the sea when the south wind is blowing and Jupiter hurls down squalls of rain in his fury and bursts the hollow thunderclouds in the sky.

Pandarus and Bitias, sons of Alcanor of Mount Ida, had been brought up by the wood nymph Iaera in the grove of Jupiter and they were built like the pines and mountains of their fatherland. So sure were they of their weapons that they now flung open the gate that had been entrusted to them by their leader's commands, and took it upon themselves to invite the enemy to come within the walls. They themselves stood inside at the ready, like twin towers, one on the right and one on the left, armed in steel, with their crests flashing high on their heads. They were like a pair of tall oaks by a flowing river, on the banks of the Po or by the lovely Adige, holding their unshorn heads up to the sky with their high tops nodding in the breeze. As soon as they saw the gate open, the Rutulians came bursting in. Quercens and Aquiculus in splendid armour, impetuous Tmarus and Haemon, son of Mars, but instantly with all their men they either turned and ran or gave up their lives on the very threshold of the gate. The fury mounted in all their hearts as they fought. Trojans now came crowding to the spot and not only joined in the fray but also dared to sally out further and further in front of the gate.

Meanwhile Turnus, the Rutulian commander, was raging and storming and creating havoc in another part of the field, when a message arrived to say that the enemy were hot with the Rutulian blood they were now spilling and that open gates were on offer. Turnus instantly abandoned the work he had in hand and rushed to the Trojan gate in a savage rage to meet these arrogant brothers. The first man to fall to his javelin was Antiphates – for he was the first to confront him. Antiphates was the bastard son of great Sarpedon by a Theban mother. The spear of Italian cornel wood flew through the unresisting air, went in by his belly and twisted upwards deep into his chest. A wave of frothing blood welled out of the black hole of the wound, and the steel grew warm where it had lodged in the lung. Then Erymas and Meropes fell to his hand; then Aphidnus; then Bitias himself for all the fire that flashed from his eyes and the roaring fury of his heart. No javelin for him. He was not the man to yield his life to a javelin. It was an artillery spear with an iron head a cubit long and a ball of lead at its butt which came rifling through the air with a loud hiss and the force of a thunderbolt. The two bull-hides of his shield did not resist it, nor did his trusty breastplate with its overlapping scales of gold. His huge body collapsed and fell. The earth groaned and the mighty shield thundered as it came down on top of him. It was like the fall of a stone pile by the shore at Euboean Baiae; men first build it to its massive height and then they let it down into the sea, and it spreads ruin all along its length, grinding the sea-bed as it settles in the shallows; the water boils, the black sand rises, the high rock of Procida is shaken, and Inarime with it, the hard bed laid for Typhoeus at Jupiter's command.

Now Mars, mighty in war, put new spirit and strength into the Latins and twisted a sharp goad into their flesh, while sending Flight and black Fear upon the Trojans. Now that their chance had come to fight, the Latins gathered from all sides and the God of War stormed their hearts. When Pandarus saw his brother stretched out in death and knew how his fortunes stood and the turn events were taking, he put his broad shoulder to the gate with all his force and heaved it shut on its hinges, leaving many of his own people cut off outside the walls with a hard battle to fight, but taking in those who came running, and shutting them in with himself. Fool that he was! He did not see the Rutulian king bursting into the city in the middle of the press. By his own act he penned him in like a great tiger among helpless cattle. In that instant a new light shone from the eyes of Turnus. He clashed his armour with a fearsome noise, the blood-red crest trembled on his head, his shield flashed lightning. Suddenly Aeneas' men recognized him – the hated face, the huge body – and were thrown into confusion. But the giant Pandarus leapt forward to confront him, burning with anger at the death of his brother: 'This is not your bridal chamber in the palace of Amata!' he shouted. 'Turnus is not safe in the middle of Ardea behind his father's walls. This is the camp of your enemies and there is no way out.' Turnus replied, smiling calmly: 'If there is any courage in you, then come and fight.

You will soon be able to tell Priam that here too you found an Achilles!' At these words Pandarus took a spear of rough, knotted wood with its bark unplaned and hurled it with all his force. As it flew to wound Turnus, the winds caught it, Juno deflected it and it lodged in the gate. 'You will not escape this weapon of mine,' called out Turnus, 'which I brandish here in my right hand. This sword is wielded by a different arm, and gives a deeper wound.' With these words he lifted it above his head, rising with it, and struck Pandarus between the temples. The blade went straight through the middle of the forehead and parted the smooth, young cheeks. The wound was hideous. He fell with a crash and the ground shook with the weight of him. As he lay dying he strewed around his nerveless limbs and armour blooded with brains, and the two halves of his head hung on his two shoulders.

The Trojans turned and ran in terror. If at that moment the victor had thought of breaking the bolts and letting his comrades in through the gates, that would have been the end of the war and the end of the Trojan race, but instead his mad lust for blood drove him upon his enemies in an ecstasy of passion. First he caught Phaleris and Gyges, slitting his hamstrings. He then took their spears, and with Juno lending him strength and spirit, he hurled them into the backs of the retreating enemy. Next he sent Halys to keep them company and Phegeus, the spear passing through his shield; then Alcander, Halius, Noemon and Prytanis, who were on the walls in the thick of battle and did not know he was inside. Now Lynceus was coming at him and calling on his comrades for help. Turnus from the rampart on his right stopped him short with one flashing stroke of his sword, a blow from close range that severed the head and sent it flying far from the body, helmet and all. Next he brought down Amycus, that mighty hunter and slayer of wild beasts – no man better to charge the spear-point with poison or smear the tip of the arrow; then Clytius, son of Aeolus, and Cretheus, that dear companion of the Muses, Cretheus, a great lover of song and of the lyre, a great setter of poems to the strings, always singing of horses and armour and the battles of heroes.

At last the Trojan leaders, Mnestheus and the bold Serestus, hearing of the slaughter of their men, came on the scene to find their allies scattering and the enemy within the walls. 'Where are you running to now, citizens?' cried Mnestheus. 'Where is there to go? What other walls have you? What other defences when you leave these? Can one man, and one man hemmed in on every side by your ramparts, cause all this slaughter and send so many of your best fighting men to their deaths all over your city, and still live? Have you no spirit? Have you no shame? No thought for your fatherland in its anguish, for your ancient gods or for great Aeneas?' These words fired them. They rallied and held fast in close formation while Turnus gradually began to disengage, making for the river and the part of the camp in the bend of the river. Seeing this the Trojans laid on all the harder, shouting at the top of their voices and crowding him like a pack of huntsmen with levelled spears pressing hard on a savage lion; the lion is afraid and gives ground, but he is still dangerous, still glaring at his attackers; his anger and his courage forbid him to turn tail, and though he would dearly love to, he cannot charge through the wall of steel and the press of men – just so did Turnus give ground, uncertain but unhurried, and his mind was boiling with rage. Twice he even hurled himself into the middle of his enemies, breaking their ranks and sending them flying along the walls, but a whole army came together in a rush against him from the camp, and Juno, daughter of Saturn, did not dare to renew his strength to withstand them, for Jupiter sent Iris down from the sky bearing stern commands through the air for his sister Juno if Turnus did not withdraw from the high walls of the Trojans. So sword-arm and shield were of no avail. The warrior could no longer stand his ground in the hail of weapons that overwhelmed him from every side.

The helmet rang and rang again on his hollow temples and the solid bronze was cracked by rocks. The plumes were torn from his head and the boss of his shield gave way under the blows. The Trojans doubled their barrage and the spear of Mnestheus was like the lightning. Sweat poured off the whole body of Turnus like a river of pitch and he was given no breathing space. His lungs were heaving. He was shaking and sick with weariness. Then, and only then, he dived head first into the river in full armour. The Tiber took him when he came into his yellow tide, bore him up in his soft waves, washing away the blood of slaughter, and gave him back in high heart to his comrades.

PALLAS AND MEZENTIUS

Meanwhile the house of All-powerful Olympus was thrown open and the Father of Gods and King of Men summoned a council to his palace among the stars, from whose steep heights he looked down upon all the lands of the earth, upon the Trojan camp and the peoples of Latium. The gods sat in their chamber open east and west to the light, and Jupiter began to speak: 'O great dwellers in the sky, why have you gone back on your word? Why do you contend with such bitterness of heart? I had forbidden Italy to clash with the Trojans. Why is there discord against my express command? What has made them afraid and induced them to take up arms and make each other draw the sword? The time will come for war – there is no need to hasten it – when barbarous Carthage will let destruction loose upon the citadels of Rome, opening up the Alps and sending them against Italy. That will be the time for pillaging, and for hate to vie with hate. But now let it be. A treaty has been decided upon. Accept it, and be content.'

These were the few words spoken by Jupiter, but when golden Venus replied, her words were not few: 'O Father, imperishable power over men and over all the world – how could there be any other to whom we might address our prayers? – you see the Rutulians rampant and Turnus riding in glory in the midst of them, swollen with the success of his arms. A closed ring of fortifications no longer offers protection to the Trojans. They now have to fight hand to hand inside their gates, even on the ramparts of their walls, and their ditches are swimming with blood. Aeneas is far away and knows nothing of this. Will you never allow them to be free of besiegers? Even as Troy is being reborn, a new enemy is threatening its walls with a new army behind him, and from Arpi the Aetolian Diomede is once more rising against the Trojans. I suppose I shall soon be wounded again – after all, mortals are at war and your daughter stands in their way!

'If the Trojans have come to Italy without your approval, in defiance of your heavenly will, they must be punished for their sins and you must not raise a finger to help them. But if they have obeyed all the commands they have received from the gods above and the shades below, how can anyone over- turn what you have ordered or fashion a new destiny? You have seen their ships burned on the shores of my own son Eryx. You have seen the king of the storms and the raging winds roused out of their Aeolian island. You have seen Iris driven down from the clouds. And now she even turns to the one remaining part of the world and stirs up the powers below – Allecto has suddenly been let loose upon the earth and has run wild through all the cities in the middle of Italy! I no longer give a thought to empire. That was our hope, as you well know, while our fortunes remained. But those who must prevail are those you wish to prevail. If there is no region on earth that your cruel queen could concede to the Trojans, I beg of you, Father, by the smoking ruins of the sacred city of Troy, allow Ascanius to have a safe discharge from battle. Allow your own daughter's grandson to live. As for Aeneas, let him be tossed by storms in unknown waters and go the road that Fortune gives him, but grant me the power to protect Ascanius and take him out of this fearful battle. I have Amathus. I have lofty Paphos, and Cythera, and my palace at Idalium. Let him lay down his arms and live out his life in obscurity, while you give the order for Italy to be crushed beneath the mighty empire of Carthage. The cities of Tyre will have nothing to fear from Ascanius. What good has it done him to escape the plague of war and come safe through the middle of all the fires lit by the Greeks, to have drained the cup of danger on the sea and over all the earth while the Trojans have been searching for Latium and a new Pergamum? Would it not have been better for them to settle on the dead ashes of their native land, on the soil that was once Troy? Take pity on them, I beg you, and if the wretched Trojans must live again the fall of Troy, give them back their Xanthus and their Simois.'

At this Juno, Queen of Heaven, burst out, wild with rage: 'Why do you force me to break my deep silence? The scars have formed over my wounds. Why do you make me speak and reopen them? Neither man nor god compelled Aeneas to choose the ways of war and confront king Latinus as an enemy. We are told he has the authority of the Fates for coming to Italy. The Fates, indeed! He was goaded into it by the ravings of Cassandra! And did we urge him to abandon his camp or put his life at the mercy of the winds? Did we advise him to entrust his fortifications and the whole management of the war to a boy? To disturb the loyalty of the Etruscans and stir up a peaceful people? Was it a god that drove him to dishonesty? Was it some cruel power of mine? Where is Juno in all this? Where is Iris sent down from the clouds? It is wrong, we hear, for Italians to ring Troy with fire at the moment of its birth, and for Turnus to take his stand in the land of his fathers, Turnus, whose grandfather was Pilumnus and whose mother was the goddess Venilia. Why then is it right for Trojans to raise the black-smoking torches of war against Latins, to put other men's lands under their yoke, to carry off plunder, to pick and choose who are to be their fathers-in-law, to tear brides from their mothers' laps and to hold out the olive branch of peace with their weapons fixed on the high sterns of their ships? You can steal Aeneas away from the hands of the Greeks, and where there was a man you can spread a cloud with empty winds. You can change ships into sea nymphs. Is it an impiety if we in our turn have given some help to the Rutulians? Aeneas, you tell us, is far away and knows nothing of all this. Keep him in ignorance and let him stay away! You have Paphos and Idalium. You have the heights of Cythera. Why do you concern yourself with those rough-hearted Italians and their city teeming with war? You claim we are trying to overturn from the foundations the tottering fortunes of these Phrygians from Troy. No! Who was it who put your wretched Trojans at the mercy of the Greeks? What caused Europe and Asia to rise in arms and betray the sacred ties of friendship? Was I in the lead when the Trojan adulterer stormed the walls of Sparta? Did I hand him his weapons? Was it I who kindled the fires of war with lust? That was when you should have feared for your people. Now, when it is too late, you get to your feet with these complaints and lies, and hurl this empty abuse.'

As Juno was making her plea, all the gods began to murmur in support or in dissent. It was like the murmuring of a storm when the first breeze is caught in a wood and the rustling rolls through the trees unseen, warning sailors that winds are on the way. Then the All-powerful Father, the highest power in all the universe, began to speak, and at his voice the lofty palace of the gods fell silent, the earth trembled to its foundations and the heights of heaven were hushed. The winds in that moment were stilled and the sea kept its waves at peace. 'So be it,' he said. 'Hear my words and lay them to your hearts. Since you have not allowed the people of Ausonia to be joined in a treaty with the Trojans, and since there is no end to this discord of yours, this day let each man face his own fortune and set his course by his own hopes. Trojan and Rutulian I shall treat alike. Whether this camp is blockaded by the destiny of Italy or because of the folly and wickedness of the Trojans and false prophecies they have received, as each man has set up his loom, so will he endure the labour and the fortune of it – I do not exempt the Rutulians. Jupiter is the same king to all men. The Fates will find their way.' Then, swearing an oath by the waves of the Styx, his brother's river, by the banks and dark whirlpools of that pitch-black torrent, he nodded and his nod shook the whole of Olympus. There were no more words. He rose from his golden throne, and the heavenly gods thronged around him and escorted him to the threshold.

The Rutulians meanwhile were fighting hard round each of the gates to bring down their enemies in blood and ring their walls with fire, while Aeneas' legion was trapped inside its own ramparts with no hope of escape. Helpless and desperate, they stood on their high towers and manned the circle of their walls with a thin line of defenders. Asius, son of Imbrasus, Thymoetes, son of Hicetaon, the two Assaraci and old Thymbris alongside Castor were there in the forefront of the battle, and the two brothers of Sarpedon were with them, Clarus and Thaemon from the mountains of Lycia. Acmon of Lyrnesus, as great a warrior as his father Clytius or his brother Mnestheus, was putting out all his strength to carry a boulder, no small part of a mountain, while they strove to defend their camp by throwing rocks and javelins, or hurling fire and fitting arrows to the string. There in the middle of them, with his noble head bared, stood the boy Ascanius for whom the goddess Venus cares above all others, and rightly cares. He was like a gem sparkling in its gold setting, an adornment for a head or neck, or like glowing ivory skilfully inlaid in boxwood or Orician terebinth, and his long hair lay on his milk-white neck, held in place by a circlet of soft gold. There too was Ismarus. The warriors of those great-hearted peoples could see him tipping his arrows with poison and aiming them at the enemy. He was the offshoot of a noble house in Maeonia where men worked the rich lands and the river Pactolus watered them with gold. Mnestheus also was there, raised to the heights of glory for his recent repulse of Turnus out of the ring of the walls; Capys, too, who gives his name to the city of Capua in Campania.

These were the men who clashed that day in bitter fighting. In the middle of the night that followed, Aeneas was ploughing the waves of the ocean. After leaving king Evander, he had entered the Etruscan camp and gone to their king to tell him his name and nation, what he wanted, what he offered and what armed forces Mezentius was winning to his support. He told him too of the violent passions of Turnus and reminded him that in human affairs there is no room for certainty, and to all this he added his appeal for help. Tarchon instantly joined forces with him and made a treaty. Then these Etruscans, these men of Lydian stock, having paid their debts to destiny, put to sea and committed themselves to a foreign leader in accordance with the will of the gods. Aeneas' ship took the lead. Phrygian lions were yoked to it for a beak, and above them the figurehead was Mount Ida, a sight most dear to the Trojan exiles. Here sat great Aeneas, turning over in his mind the varied chances of war, and all the while young Pallas stayed close by his left side, asking him now about the stars and the course they were steering through the darkness of the night, now about all he had suffered by land and sea.

Now goddesses, it is time to open up Mount Helicon, to set your songs in motion and tell of the army which came that night with Aeneas from the shores of Etruria, to say who fitted out the ships and who sailed in them across the ocean.

Massicus was the first, cutting through the water on the bronze-plated *Tiger*. Under him sailed a band of a thousand warriors who had left behind them the walls of Clusium and the city of Cosae. Their weapons were arrows carried in light quivers on their shoulders, and death-dealing bows.

With them sailed grim Abas, whose whole troop shone in brilliant armour, and a gilded Apollo gleamed on the stern of his ship. Populonia, his motherland, had given him six hundred fighting men, skilful in the wars, while three hundred came from Ilua, the island of the Chalybes, teeming with its inexhaustible ores.

The third ship was sailed by Asilas, the great mediator between gods and men, master of the stars of the sky and the entrails of the beasts of the field, of bird cries and the prescient fires of lightning. He sped along leading a thousand men in close formation with their spears bristling. Pisa put them under his command, a city on Etruscan soil but founded by men from the Alpheus, the river of Olympia.

Next in line sailed fair Astyr, whose trust was in his horse and his iridescent armour. To him were joined three hundred men, and all were as one in their zeal to follow him, men whose home was Caere, men from the fields of Minio, from ancient Pyrgi and the unwholesome swamps of Graviscae.

Nor could I pass over Cunarus, so brave in war, the leader of the Ligurians, nor Cupavo with his small band of fighting men. High above his head tossed the swan feathers that were a token of his father's change of form – all the fault of the God of Love. They say that Cycnus sought comfort from the Muse for the sadness of his love, by singing of the loss of his dear Phaethon in the green shade of the poplars that had been Phaethon's sisters. There, when he grew old, he put on soft white plumage and rose from the earth, singing as he flew towards the stars. It was his son who now commanded the huge *Centaur*, driving it along under oar, and with him in his fleet he took a throng of his peers. The Centaur figurehead loomed over the water, threatening to hurl down a massive rock into the waves from its dizzy height, and the long keel ploughed its furrow deep in the sea.

There too was Ocnus, driving on an army from his fatherland. He was the son of Manto the prophetess and the Tuscan river Tiber. To you, Mantua, he gave your walls and the name of his mother – Mantua, rich in the roll of its forefathers, and not all of one race, but of three, and in each race four peoples.

Of all these peoples Mantua is the head, and its strength comes from its Etruscan blood. From here too, Mezentius had roused five hundred men to fight against him, and these the river Mincius, veiled in blue-green reeds, led down to the sea in their ships of war from his father, Lake Benacus. There sailed Aulestes, heavy in the water, but rising as his hundred oars thrashed the waves and churned the marble of the sea to foam. He sailed the monstrous *Triton*, which terrified the blue sea with its horn. As it swam along, its figurehead showed a shaggy front like a man as far as its flanks, but its belly ended in a monster of the deep, while under the breast of this creature, half-man half-beast, the waves foamed and murmured.

These were the chosen leaders who went to the help of Troy in their thirty ships, and ploughed the plains of salt with bronze.

By now the day had left the sky and Phoebe, the kindly Goddess of the Moon, was pounding the middle of Olympus with the hooves of her night-wandering horses. Duty allowed no rest to the limbs of Aeneas. As he sat controlling the tiller and seeing to the sails, a band of his old comrades came suddenly towards him in mid-voyage. They were nymphs, the nymphs into whom his ships had been changed at the bidding of the kindly Mother Goddess Cybele, and they now held divine power over the sea. There they were, swimming in line, as many of them now cleaving the waves as had then stood to the shore with bronze-plated prows. They recognized their king from a distance and danced around him in the water, and Cymodocea, the best speaker among them, came behind his ship and putting her right hand on its stern, raised her back out of the water, while her left hand was below the surface, oaring silently along. Aeneas was still bewildered when she began to speak to him: 'Are you awake, Aeneas,' she asked, 'son of the gods? Wake then and let out the sail-ropes. We are the pines from the sacred top of Mount Ida, now sea nymphs. We are your fleet. When the treacherous Rutulian was pressing us hard with fire and sword, against our wishes we had to break the moorings you gave us, and now we have been looking for you all over the ocean. Mother Cybele took pity on us and gave us this new form, allowing us to become goddesses and spend our lives beneath the waves. But your son Ascanius is trapped behind a wall and ditches, surrounded by missiles and by Latins bristling with war. The Arcadian cavalry from Pallanteum are in their places as ordered, along with the brave Etruscans, but Turnus has firmly resolved to prevent them joining forces with the Trojan camp by taking up position between them with his own troops. Up with you then, and at the coming of dawn, first order your allies to arms and then take up the invincible shield with its rim of gold given you by the God of Fire himself. Tomorrow's light, unless you think these are empty words of mine, will see the field of battle heaped high with Rutulian dead.' So she spoke, and as she left him she gave the high stern a push with her right hand – and well she knew the art of it. The ship flew through the waves faster than a javelin or wind-swift arrow, and the others sped along behind it. The leader of the Trojans, the son of Anchises, was struck dumb with bewilderment, but his heart lifted at the omen, and looking up to the vault of heaven, he uttered this short prayer: 'Kindly Mother of the Gods, dweller on Ida, who takes delight in Mount Dindymus, in cities crowned with towers and in the lion pair responsive to your chariot reins, be now my leader in this battle. Bring near to us the due fulfilment of your omen. Stand by the side of your Phrygians and give us your divine blessing.' These were his words, and even as he spoke them the revolving day was already rushing back in its full brightness and had put the darkness to flight. His first thought was to order his allies to follow the standards, to fit their minds for the use of their weapons and prepare themselves for battle.

And now, as soon as Aeneas, standing high on the stern of

his ship, could see the Trojans and his own camp, at that moment he lifted the shield on his left arm and made it flash. The Trojans on the wall raised a shout to heaven, fresh hope renewing their anger, and they hurled their spears, like cranes from the river Strymon in Thrace giving out their signals under the black clouds, trumpeting as they cross the sky and flying before the storm winds with exultant cries. The Rutulian king and the leaders of Italy were amazed until they turned round and saw a fleet making for the shore and a whole sea of ships coming in towards them. On the head of Aeneas there blazed a tongue of fire, baleful flames poured from the top of his crest and the golden boss of his shield belched streams of fire, like the gloomy, blood-red glow of a comet on a clear night, or the dismal blaze of Sirius the Dogstar shedding its sinister light across the sky and bringing disease and thirst to suffering mortals.

But the bold confidence of Turnus never wavered as he quickly took up position on the shore to repel the landing. 'This is the answer to your prayer,' he cried, 'now is the time to break them. Brave men have the God of War in their own right arms. Each of you must now think of his own wife and his own home and remember the great deeds which brought glory to our fathers. Let us go down to the sea to meet them while they are still in confusion and finding their feet after landing. Fortune favours the bold.' So he spoke and pondered in his mind who could be led against the fleet and who could be trusted to keep up the siege of the walls.

Meanwhile Aeneas was landing his allies by gang-planks from the high sterns. Many waited for the spent waves to be sucked back and then took a leap into the shallow water. Others were clambering down the oars. Tarchon, who had been looking out for a stretch of shore where there seemed to be no shoals and no grumbling of broken water, where the swelling tide could come in without obstruction, suddenly swung his ship round and appealed to his comrades: 'Now, my chosen band, now bend to your stout oars. Up with your ships out of the water. Take the weight of them. Split with your rams this land that we hate, and let each keel plough its own furrow. I do not care if my ship is wrecked by such a mooring, if only we take possession of this land.' When Tarchon had spoken, his comrades rose to their oars and drove their ships foaming at the prow, hard on to the soil at Latium, till their beaks struck home on dry land and their keels were safely settled. But not yours, Tarchon. You ran aground on a shoal and hung there see-sawing on a dangerous ridge of rock, till at last the waves were weary of you and your ship broke up, throwing your men into the sea to be tangled in smashed oars and floating thwarts, as the undertow of the waves kept taking the feet from them.

Turnus was no sluggard. Wasting no time he eagerly led his whole force to face the Trojans and drew them up at the ready on the shore. The trumpets sounded, and Aeneas was the first to move against the army of the country people of Latium and lay them low. This was an omen of the battle that was to come. Theron was the first to fall. He was the tallest of their warriors, and had taken it upon himself to attack Aeneas. Through the mesh of his chain mail of bronze, through his tunic stiffened with threads of gold, Aeneas tore a huge gash with his sword in the flesh of his side. He then struck Lichas. His mother was already dead when Lichas was cut from her womb and dedicated to Phoebus Apollo, the God of Healing. Little good did it do the baby to escape the hazard of steel at birth. Next Aeneas saw huge Gyas and tough Cisseus felling the embattled Trojans with their clubs, and sent them down to death. Nothing could help them now: not the weapons of Hercules, nor the strength of their hands, nor their father Melampus, who had stood by the side of Hercules as long as the earth supplied him with heavy labours to perform. There was Pharus, hurling his empty threats, till Aeneas spun the javelin and planted it in his throat even as he shouted. You too, Cydon, desperately following your latest beloved Clytius, with the first gold down on his cheeks, would have forgotten the young men you were always in love with. You would have fallen by the right hand of a Trojan and lain there for men to pity, had not Aeneas been confronted by seven brothers in serried ranks, the sons of Phorcus, hurling their seven spears. Some rebounded harmlessly from his helmet or his shield. Others his loving mother Venus deflected so that they only grazed his body, and Aeneas addressed his faithful Achates: 'Pile up some javelins for me. No weapon that has stood in the body of a Greek on the plains of Troy will spin in vain from my right hand against Rutulians!' He then caught up a great spear and hurled it. Flying through the air it beat through the bronze of Maeon's shield and shattered in one instant the breastplate and the breast. Alcanor came to help him as he fell, a brother's right hand to support a brother. Through Alcanor's arm went the spear of Aeneas and flew on its way dripping with his blood, while the dying arm hung by its tendons from the shoulder. Another brother, Numitor, snatched the weapon from Maeon's body and aimed at Aeneas in return, but was not allowed to strike him, only to graze the thigh of great Achates. Then came Clausus of Cures in all the pride of his youthful strength and with a long-range cast of his unbending spear he struck Dryops full force under the chin. It went straight through his throat and took from him in one moment, even as he spoke, his voice and his life's breath. His forehead struck the ground and his mouth vomited great gouts of blood. Then Aeneas laid three Thracians low, men from the exalted stock of Boreas, then three more sent by their father Idas from their fatherland Ismara, all by different forms of death. Halaesus came running to the spot with his Auruncans; Messapus too, son of Neptune, whose horses drew every eye. Trojans and Latins were battling on the very threshold of Italy, each striving to dislodge the other, like opposing winds fighting their wars in the great reaches of the sky, equal in spirit and equal in strength; they do not give way to one another, neither the winds themselves nor the clouds nor the sea, but long rages the fight, undecided, and they all stand locked in battle – just so clashed the armies of Troy and the armies of Latium, foot planted against foot, and man face to face with man.

In another part of the battle, where a torrent had rolled down boulders and trees uprooted from its banks and strewn them everywhere, Pallas saw his Arcadians, who had for once advanced on foot, now retreating with Latins in hot pursuit – the floods had so roughened the ground that they had decided to abandon their horses. One course alone remained – to fire the valour of his men by appeals and bitter reproaches: 'Where are you running to, comrades? I beg you by your pride in yourselves, by your bravery in time past, by the name of Evander your leader, by the wars you have won, by the hopes rising in me to gain glory like my father's, this is no time to trust to your feet! It is swords you need, to cut your way through the enemy. There, where the moil is thickest, where the attack is fiercest, that is where your proud fatherland requires you and your leader Pallas to go. These are not gods who are pressing you so hard; they are mortals pursuing mortals. Like us they have two hands, and like us they have one life to lose. Look about you! The great barrier of ocean closes us in. There is no more land to run to. Shall we take to the sea? Shall we set course for Troy?' With these words he threw himself into the thick of his enemies.

The first man to meet him, drawn there by an unkindly fate, was Lagus. While he was trying to tear loose a great heavy rock, Pallas hurled his spear and struck him in the middle of the back where the spine divides the ribs. Pallas was pulling out the weapon, which had wedged between the bones, when Hisbo swooped on him, hoping to take him by surprise, but Pallas caught him first in the fury of his charge, made reckless by the cruel death of his comrade. Hisbo's lungs were swollen. Pallas buried his sword in them. He then turned on Sthenius; then on Anchemolus of the ancient stock of Rhoetus, who had shamefully debauched his own step-mother. You too fell on the Rutulian fields, Larides and Thymber, sons of Daucus, identical twins, a source of confusion and delight to your parents. But Pallas made a grim difference between you: with the sword of his father Evander he removed the head of Thymber, and cut off the hand of Larides. As it lay there, it groped for its owner and the fingers twitched, still half alive, and kept clutching at the sword. The Arcadians were stung by Pallas' reproaches, and as they watched his glorious feats, remorse and shame armed them against their enemies.

Then Pallas put a spear through Rhoeteus as he fled past on his two-horse chariot, and gave that much respite and reprieve to Ilus. For it was against Ilus that Pallas had aimed a long throw with his mighty spear, but Rhoeteus had come between them and taken the blow while fleeing from great Teuthras and his brother Tyres. He rolled from his chariot, and died with his heels drumming on the Rutulian plough-land. Just as a shepherd fires a wood at different points when the summer winds get up at last, and suddenly all the flames merge in the middle to make one bristling battle-front of fire stretching over the broad plain, and there he sits in triumph looking down on the exulting blaze – just so, Pallas, did the valour of your men all come together in one, and put joy in your heart. But Halaesus was a fierce warrior, and he made straight for the enemies that stood in front of him, gathering all his strength behind his weapons. Ladon and Pheres and Demodocus he slew, and his flashing sword ripped off the right hand of Strymonius as it was poised to lunge at his throat. Thoas he struck with a rock in the face, shattering the bones and grinding them into the blood-soaked brains. Halaesus was next. His father, foreseeing the future, had hidden him in the woods, but when the father grew old and his whitening eyes dissolved in death, the Fates laid a hand on the son and consecrated him to Evander's spear. This was the prayer of Pallas before he attacked: 'Grant now, O Father Thybris, that the spear I am holding poised to throw may reach the mark and go through the stout breast of Halaesus, and I shall strip these arms of his from his body and hang them on your sacred oak as spoils.' The god heard his prayer. As the hapless Halaesus protected Imaon, he left his breast exposed to the Arcadian spear.

But Lausus, who was bearing the brunt of the battle, did not allow his men to be dismayed by all this slaughter done by Pallas. First of all he slew Abas as he stood before him, the very knot and stumbling block of war. The youth of Arcadia were laid low and the Etruscans fell beside them, and you too, Trojans, who had faced the Greeks unscathed. The armies clashed, equal in their leaders and in their strength, and the wings of the battle line were forced into the centre so that men could not raise a hand or a weapon in the crowd. On the one side Pallas thrust and pressed, on the other Lausus. They were almost of an age, and noble in appearance, but Fortune had denied each of them a homecoming. Yet the ruler of high Olympus did not yet allow their paths to cross, reserving for each his own death at the hand of a stronger enemy.

Meanwhile, after Juturna had advised her dear brother Turnus to take the place of Lausus, he cut through the middle of the ranks of warriors on his swift chariot, and as soon as he saw his allies he called out: 'Time now to stand down from the fighting. I am the only one who attacks Pallas. Pallas is mine, and mine alone. I wish his father were here to see it.' So he spoke and his allies left the ground clear as ordered. When the Rutulians withdrew, Pallas marvelled at these proud commands and stood amazed at the sight of Turnus, running his eyes all over that mighty body, his grim stare taking it in part by part from where he stood, and these were the words he hurled in reply to the words of the insolent prince: 'I shall win rich renown today, either for stripping the corpse of the leader of my country's enemies, or else for a glorious death. My father will bear the one fate as easily as the other. Do not waste your threats on me.' With these words he strode on to the level ground in the middle of the battlefield, and the blood of the Arcadians froze in their breasts. Turnus leapt down from his chariot and prepared to come to close quarters on foot, flying at him like a lion which has seen from some high vantage point a bull practising for combat far away on the plain – this is how Turnus appeared as he came on. Pallas made the first attack, judging that Turnus would be within range of a spearcast and hoping that Fortune would favour the weaker for his daring. Lifting up his voice to the wide expanse of heaven, he cried: 'I call upon you, Hercules of the stock of Alceus, by my father's table and by the friendship he offered you when you came as a stranger to his home, stand at my side now as I set my hand to this great task. May Turnus as he dies see me tear the blood-stained armour off his body, and may the last sight he endures be the face of the man who has defeated him!' Hearing the young warrior, Hercules checked the great groan rising from the depths of his heart and the helpless tears streamed from his eyes. Then Father Jupiter spoke these loving words to his son: 'Each man has his allotted day. All life is brief and time once past can never be restored. But the task of the brave man is to enlarge his fame by his actions. So many sons of gods fell under the high walls of Troy, and with them fell also my son Sarpedon. Turnus too is called by his own destiny and has reached the limits of the time he has been given.' So he spoke and instantly turned his eyes away from the Rutulian fields.

But Pallas hurled his spear with all his strength and tore his bright sword from its enclosing scabbard. The spear flew and fell where the armour stood highest on the shoulder of Turnus, forcing its way through the edge of the shield and grazing at last the skin of that huge body. Then Turnus took long aim at Pallas with his steel-pointed hardwood spear and threw it saying: 'Now see whether mine is any better at piercing!' With a shuddering blow it beat through the middle of the shield, through all the plates of iron and of bronze and all the ox-hides that covered it, and unchecked by the breastplate, it bored through that mighty breast. In desperation Pallas tore the warm blade out of the wound, and blood and life came out together after it, both by the same channel. He fell forward on the wound, his armour ringing on top of his body, and as he died his bleeding mouth bit the soil of his enemies. Turnus stood over him and said: 'Take this message of mine to Evander, you Arcadians, and do not forget it: I am giving him back the Pallas he deserves. Whatever honour there is in a tomb, and any comfort he finds in burying him, these I gladly give him. His hospitality to Aeneas will cost him dear!' With these words he planted his left foot on the dead body, and tore off the huge, heavy baldric. On this great belt an abominable crime was embossed, how in one dark night, the night of their marriage, a band of young men were foully slain, and their marriage chambers bathed in blood, all worked by Clonus, son of Eurytus, in a wealth of gold. This was the spoil in which Turnus now exulted and he gloried in the taking of it. The mind of man has no knowledge of what Fate holds in store, and observes no limit when Fortune raises him up. The time will come when Turnus would gladly pay, and pay richly, to see Pallas alive and unharmed. He will bitterly regret this spoil and the day he took it. A throng of Pallas' allies laid him on his shield and carried him back with tears of lamentation. O Pallas, a great grief and a great glory is coming home to your father! This one day gave you to war, and now takes you from it, and yet you leave behind you huge piles of Rutulian dead.

First a rumour of this calamity came flying to Aeneas and then a reliable messenger, to tell him his men were on the very edge of destruction; the Trojans were in retreat; now was the time to help them. Everything that stood before him he harvested with the sword, cutting a broad swathe through the enemy ranks, and burning with rage as he looked for this Turnus flushed with slaughter. Before his eyes he could see Pallas, Evander, everything, the table he had sat down to that day when he first came to their house, and the right hands of friendship they had given him. Four warrior sons of Sulmo he now captured alive and four reared by Ufens, to sacrifice them as offerings to the shade of Pallas and pour their captive blood on the flames of his pyre. Next he aimed his deadly spear from long range at Magus, who cleverly ran under it. The quivering spear flew over his head and he clasped the knees of Aeneas with this prayer: 'By the shade of your own father and the hopes you have of Iulus as he grows to manhood, I beg you to spare this life of mine for the sake of my son and my father. Our home is a high-built palace, and buried deep within it I have talents of engraved silver and great weights of gold, both worked and unworked. A Trojan victory does not depend on me. My one life will not make so great a difference.' This was Aeneas' reply: 'Keep for your children all those talents of silver and gold you talk about. Turnus put an end to such war-trading the moment he murdered Pallas. So judges the shade of my father Anchises. And so judges Iulus.' When he had spoken he took Magus' helmet in his left hand, and bending back his neck when he was still begging for mercy, he drove the sword home to the hilt. Not far away was Haemonides, priest of Phoebus Apollo and Diana Trivia, his temples bound by a headband of sacred wool, all shining white in his white robes and insignia. Aeneas closed with him, drove him across the plain, stood over him when he fell, darkening the whiteness with his great shadow, and took him as his victim. Serestus collected the spoils and carried them back on his shoulders as a trophy to Mars Gradivus.

Caeculus of the stock of Vulcan renewed the battle, and

Umbro from the Marsian mountains with him. Aeneas confronted them in all his fury. His sword had already struck off the left hand of Anxur – a stroke of the blade had sent the whole circle of his shield to the ground. He had uttered some great threat, imagining that the strength would be there to make it good. It seemed he was trying to raise his spirits to the skies, and had promised himself that he would live to enjoy grey hairs and a long life. Next Aeneas in his fury was faced by Tarquitus, glorying in his shining armour, the son of Faunus, God of the Woods, and the nymph Dryope. Drawing back his spear, Aeneas threw and pinned the great heavy shield to the breastplate. While he was still begging for mercy, and still had much to say, Aeneas smashed his head to the ground, and as he set the warm trunk rolling, these were the words he spoke with hatred in his heart: 'Lie there now, you fearsome warrior. Your good mother will not bury you in the earth or burden your body with the family tomb. You will be left for the wild birds, or thrown into the sea to be carried away by the waves, and the hungry fish will come and lick your wounds!' Next he pursued and caught Antaeus and Lucas, the front rank of Turnus, then brave Numa and yellow-haired Camers, son of great-hearted Volcens, who was richest in land of all the men of Italy and ruled over silent Amyclae. Aeneas was like Aegaeon, who they say had a hundred arms and a hundred hands, with fire flaming from fifty breasts and mouths, and fifty was the number of swords he drew against the lightning of Jupiter, fifty the number of identical shields he clashed – so seemed Aeneas, raging victorious all over the plain, when once his sword blade had warmed to the work. Imagine him next bearing down on the chariot of Niphaeus, with the four horses showing their chests as they stood to meet him, but when they saw Aeneas' great stride and heard his fearsome roar, they wheeled in panic and bolted, throwing their master out of the chariot and stampeding to the shore.

Meanwhile Lucagus was coming into the middle of battle

on a chariot drawn by two white horses. With him was his
brother Liger, handling the reins and controlling the horses
while Lucagus whirled his naked sword about him. Aeneas
could not endure to see such fury and such fervour, but rushed
forward and loomed huge before them with his levelled spear.
It was Liger who spoke: 'These are not the horses of Diomede
you are looking at, or the chariot of Achilles. These are not
the plains of Troy. Here in this land today there will be an
end to your wars and to your life.' Far flew these wild words
of Liger. The Trojan was preparing a reply to his enemy, but
it was not in words – it was his javelin he hurled. Lucagus
had been leaning forward over his horses to urge them on by
beating them with the flat of his spear. Now, when he had
planted his left foot to the front and was preparing for battle,
through the bottom rim of his shining shield came the spear
of Aeneas and pierced his left groin. He was pitched from his
chariot and as he lay dying on the ground, good Aeneas
addressed these bitter words to him: 'It is not the panic of
your horses, Lucagus, that has brought your chariot to grief.
They did not shy away from the shadow of their enemy. It is
your own doing, leaping off the car and abandoning your
team!' With these words Aeneas caught the horses' bridles.
The wretched brother of Lucagus fell from the chariot and
stretched out his helpless hands to Aeneas: 'Great Trojan, I
implore you by your own self and by the parents who brought
such a man as you into the world, spare this life of mine and
take pity on a suppliant.' Aeneas cut short his appeal. 'This is
not what I heard you say a moment ago. Die now. A brother's
place is with his brother.' And as he spoke the point of his
sword opened the breast of Liger, the hiding place of his soul.
So did the Trojan leader deal out death all over the plain like
a raging torrent of water or a storm of black wind, until at last
the young Ascanius and his warriors sallied forth and left the
camp. The siege was lifted.

In the meanwhile Jupiter came to Juno and said to her: 'O

my true sister and most pleasing of wives, you are right, it is Venus, as you thought, who is maintaining the strength of the Trojans, not the warlike vigour of their right arms nor their fierce and danger-hardened spirit.' Humbly Juno replied: 'O finest of husbands, why do you cause me anguish when I am in despair and in terror of your harsh commands? If your love for me had that power which once it had, and should have still, you who can do all things would not be refusing me this. I should be able to withdraw Turnus from the battle and keep him safe for his father Daunus. But as things are, let him die. Let him pay the penalty to the Trojans with his righteous blood. Nevertheless he is descended from our stock, Pilumnus was his ancestor in the fourth generation and his generous hand has often weighed down your threshold with abundant gifts.' The King of Heavenly Olympus made brief reply: 'If what you ask is a stay of the death that is upon him and respite for a young man who must die, and if you accept that this is what I ordain, then rescue Turnus. Let him flee. Snatch him from the Fates that tread upon his heels. There is room for me to grant you indulgence thus far. But if there is some deeper thought of mercy underlying these appeals of yours, and if you believe that the whole course of the war can be affected or its outcome changed, the hopes which you nourish are empty.' Juno replied, weeping as she spoke: 'What if your heart wished to give what your words refuse? What if you listened to me and let Turnus live? As it is, although he is innocent, a cruel death is waiting for him, unless I am wide of the mark and there is no truth in me. But oh how I wish my fears were false and I were deluded! How I wish you would recast your plans, for you can do so, and choose a better course!'

As soon as the goddess had finished speaking, she flew down from the heights of heaven swathed in cloud and driving a great storm before her towards the battle line of the Trojans and the Laurentine camp. Then she fashioned out of empty vapour an effigy in the form of Aeneas, a weird sight, a shade without strength or substance, armed with Trojan weapons. She copied his shield and the crest on his godlike head and gave the phantom power to speak its empty words. Sound without thought she gave it, and moulded its strides as it moved. It was like the flitting shapes which men say are the ghosts of the dead, or like the dreams which delude our sleeping senses. There in high glee in front of the first line of warriors pranced this apparition and goaded Turnus by brandishing weapons and shouting challenges. Turnus attacked, throwing his whirring spear from long range. The apparition turned tail and fled. At that moment Turnus believed that Aeneas had turned his back on him and was running away. Taking a wild draught from the empty cup of hope, he cried: 'Where are you running to, Aeneas? You must not leave. Your marriage is arranged. This is the land you crossed the seas to find and my right hand will give it to you!' Shouting such taunts, he went in pursuit with his sword drawn and flashing and did not see that all his exultation was scattering to the winds.

The ship which king Osinius had sailed from the land of Clusium happened to be moored to a high shelf of rock, with her ladders and gangway out. Here the panic-stricken phantom of Aeneas fled and hid itself, with Turnus hard behind it. Nothing could delay him. He leapt across the gangways, high above the water, and scarcely had he set foot on the prow when Saturnian Juno tore the ship from her moorings, breaking the ropes, and took her quickly out to sea on the ebbing tide. But by this time the phantom was no longer looking for a place to hide. It had flown high into the air and melted into a black cloud. Meanwhile, Aeneas was calling on Turnus to fight, and there was no Turnus, but every man who crossed his path he sent down to death, and all the time the wind was blowing Turnus round and round in mid-ocean. Looking back to the shore in bewilderment and thanking no one for his safety, he raised his arms in prayer and lifted up his voice to the stars of heaven: 'All-powerful Father, have you decided that I deserve this disgrace? Have you decreed that I must endure this punishment? Where am I being taken? What have I left behind me? How can I go back after running away? What sort of Turnus would that be? Shall I ever see my camp and the walls of the Laurentines again? And what about that band of great warriors who have followed me and followed my sword? The horror of it – I have left them all to die! I see them wandering about without a leader. I hear them groaning as they fall. What am I to do? If only the earth could open deep enough to swallow me! Or rather I pray to the winds, and pray to them from my heart, to take pity on me and drive my ship on to the rocks and cliffs, or run it aground on some shoal of deadly sand, where there will be no Rutulian and no word of my shame can follow me.' Even as he spoke, his mind was tossed this way and that, in despair at his disgrace. Should he fall on his sword and drive the raw steel through his ribs? Should he throw himself into the sea and try to swim from mid-ocean back into the curve of the bay to face the weapons of the Trojans once again? Three times he tried each way, and three times mighty Juno held him back, pitying the young man in her heart, and would not let him move. Cutting the deep water, he floated on a favouring tide and following waves, and came to land in the ancient city of his father Daunus.

But Mezentius meanwhile, by the promptings of Jupiter, took the place of Turnus in the battle and fell furiously on the triumphant Trojans. Instantly all the Etruscan troops converged on him alone, united in their hatred, and pressed him hard under a hail of weapons. He stood like a rock jutting out into the ocean wastes, exposed to the threats and fury of wind and wave and bearing all the violence of sea and sky, unmoved. He felled Hebrus, son of Dolichaon, and Latagus with him, and Palmus as he ran. Latagus he stopped by hitting him full in the face and mouth with a rock, a huge block broken off a mountain, but he cut the hamstrings of Palmus and left him rolling helpless on the ground. His armour he gave to Lausus to put on his shoulders, and his crest to fix on his helmet. Then it was the turn of Euanthes the Phrygian, and Mimas, the same age as Paris and his comrade in war. In one night Theano, wife of Amycus, brought him into the light of life, while Hecuba, daughter of Cisseus, pregnant with a torch, was giving birth to Paris. Paris fell in the city of his fathers, but Mimas lies a stranger on the Laurentine shore. Like the wild boar who has long kept his citadel among the pines of Mount Vesulus, and long have the Laurentine marshes fed him in the reed beds of the forest; when the great beast is driven down from the mountains with the dogs snapping at him, and is caught between the nets, he stands at bay snorting, and the bristles rise on his shoulders and no one has the courage to clash with him or go near him, but they attack from a safe distance with javelins and shouts, while he stands his ground unafraid and wondering in which direction to charge, grinding his teeth and shaking the spears out of his back – even so, none of those men who had just cause of anger against Mezentius was minded to draw the sword and run upon him, but instead they stood well back and bombarded him with missiles and deafening shouts.

Acron was a Greek who had come from the ancient land of Corythus, driven into exile while waiting to be married. Mezentius saw him from a distance causing havoc in the middle of the battle line in the purple feathers and purple cloak given him by his promised bride. Just as a ravening lion scouring the deep lairs of wild beasts, driven mad by the pangs of hunger, if he sights a frightened she-goat, or sees a stag's antlers rising, he opens his great jaws in delight, his mane bristles and he battens on the flesh with foul gore washing his pitiless mouth – just so did Mezentius charge hot-haste into the thick of the enemy and felled the unlucky

Acron, who breathed out his life drumming the black earth with his heels and blooding the weapons broken in his body. Orodes fled, but Mezentius did not deign to cut him down as he ran, or deal him a wound, unseen, from the back, but came to bar his way and meet him face to face, proving himself the better man by strength in arms and not by stealth. He then put his foot on his prostrate enemy and leaned on his spear, calling out: 'Here, comrades, lies no small part of their battle strength, Orodes, that stood so tall.' His men shouted their glad paean of victory after him, but with his dying breath Orodes replied: 'Whoever you are that have conquered me, I shall be revenged. You will not enjoy your victory for long. The same fate is looking out for you, and we shall soon be lying in the same fields.' Half smiling, half in anger, Mezentius replied: 'Die now. As for me, that will be a matter for the Father of the Gods and the King of Men,' and at these words he drew his spear out of the body of Orodes. A cruel rest then came to him, and an iron sleep bore down upon his eyes and closed them in everlasting night.

Caedicus cut down Alcathous, Sacrator Hydaspes; Rapo killed Parthenius and Orses, a strong and hardy warrior. Messapus put an end to Clonius and Erichaetes, son of Lycaon, Erichaetes being on foot, but Clonius lying on the ground, having lost his reins and fallen from his horse. On foot also was Agis the Lycian, who had come out in front of the battle line, but Valerus had some spark of his family's courage and overthrew him. Thronius was killed by Salius, and Salius by Nealces, shooting his arrows and javelins from ambush at long range.

Pitiless Mars was now dealing grief and death to both sides with impartial hand. Victors and vanquished killed and were killed and neither side thought of flight. In the halls of Jupiter the gods pitied the futile anger of the two armies and grieved that men had so much suffering, Venus looking on from one side and Saturnian Juno from the other, while in the thick of all the thousands raged the Fury Tisiphone, pale as death.

Then came Mezentius storming over the plain, brandishing a huge spear, and as tall as Orion who walks in mid-ocean cleaving his path through its deepest pools with his shoulders rising clear of the waves, or strides along carrying an ancient ash from the mountain tops with his feet on the ground and his head hidden in the clouds – so did Mezentius advance in his massive armour. Aeneas had picked him out in the long ranks of men in front of him and was going to meet him. Mezentius held his ground, unafraid, and the huge bulk of him stood fast waiting to receive his great-hearted enemy. Measuring a spear-cast with his eye, he cried: 'Let the right hand which is my god not fail me now, nor the spear which I brandish to throw. My vow is to strip the armour from that brigand's body and clothe you with it, Lausus. My trophy over Aeneas will be my own son!' With these words he threw his spear from long range. Hissing as it flew, it bounced off Aeneas' shield and struck the noble Antores as he stood some distance away, entering his body between flank and groin. Antores had been a comrade of Hercules. He had come from Argos but attached himself to Evander, settling with him in his city in Italy. And so, falling cruelly by a wound intended for another, he looked up at the sky and remembered his beloved Argos as he died.

Then the devout Aeneas hurled his spear. Through the circle of Mezentius' convex shield it flew, the triple bronze, the layers of linen, the three stitched bull hides, and it stuck low in Mezentius' groin, but it had lost its force. Exultant at the sight of the Etruscan's blood, Aeneas tore the sword from the scabbard at his thigh. Seeing Mezentius in distress and Aeneas bearing down on him in hot fury, Lausus moaned bitterly for the father whom he loved and the tears rolled down his face. Now Lausus, I shall tell of your cruel death and glorious deeds in the hope that the distance of time may lead men to believe your great exploit. Never will it be my wish to be silent about you, Lausus – you are a warrior who does not deserve to be forgotten. Mezentius was falling back, defenceless and encumbered, dragging his enemy's spear behind him, stuck in his shield, when young Lausus leapt forward and threw himself between them. Just as Aeneas was standing to his full height and raising his arm to strike, he came in beneath the sword blade, blocking Aeneas and checking his advance. Lausus' comrades raised a great shout and supported him by bombarding Aeneas and harassing him with their missiles from long range, till the father could withdraw protected by the shield of the son. Aeneas, enraged, kept under cover. Just as when the clouds descend in a sudden storm of hail, and all the ploughmen and all the workers in the fields scatter across the open ground and the traveller finds a sure fortress to hide in under a river bank or the arch of some high-vaulted rock till the rain stops falling on the earth, so that they can continue to do the work of the day when the sunshine is restored – just so Aeneas, overwhelmed by missiles from all sides, weathered the storm of war till the last roll of its thunder, and then it was Lausus he challenged, and Lausus he threatened: 'Why are you in such a haste to die? Why do you take on tasks beyond your strength? You are too rash. Your love for your father is deceiving you.' But Lausus was in full cry and his madness knew no check. At this the anger rose even higher in the heart of the leader of the Trojans and the Fates gathered up the last threads for Lausus. Aeneas drove his mighty sword through the middle of the young man's body, burying it to the hilt, the point going straight through his light shield, no proper armour to match the threats he had uttered. It pierced, too, the tunic his mother had woven for him with a soft thread of gold and filled the folds of it with blood. Then did his life leave his body and go in sorrow through the air to join the shades.

But when Aeneas, son of Anchises, saw the dying face and features, the face strangely white, he groaned from his heart in pity and held out his hand, as there came into his mind the thought of his own devoted love for his father, and he said: 'What will the devout Aeneas now give to match such merit? What gift can he give that will be worthy of a heart like yours? Take your armour, that gave you so much pleasure. Now I return you to the shades and the ashes of your ancestors, if that is any comfort for you. In your misfortune you will have one consolation for your cruel death, that you fell by the hand of the great Aeneas.' At this he turned on Lausus' comrades, railing at them as they hung back, while he lifted Lausus off the ground where he was soiling his carefully tended hair with blood.

Meanwhile by the bank of the river Tiber Lausus' father was staunching his wounds with water and leaning against the trunk of a tree to rest. Nearby, his bronze helmet hung from the branches and his weighty armour lay quiet on the grass. About him stood his chosen warriors as he bathed his neck, gasping with pain, and his great beard streamed down his chest. Again and again he asked about Lausus, and kept sending men to recall him and take him orders from his anxious father. But Lausus was dead and his weeping comrades were carrying him back on his shield, a mighty warrior laid low by a mighty wound. Mezentius had a presentiment of evil. He heard the wailing in the distance and knew the truth. Then, fouling his grey hair with dust, he raised both hands to heaven and flung himself on his son's body: 'Was I so besotted with the pleasure of living that I allowed my own son to take my place under my enemy's sword? Is the father to be saved by the wounds of the son? Have you died so that I might live? Now for the first time is death bitter to me! Now for the first time does a wound go deep. And I have even stained your name, my son, by my crimes. Men hated me and drove me from the throne and sceptre of my fathers. I owed a debt to my country and my people who detested me, and I would to heaven I had paid it with this guilty life of mine by every death a man can die! But I am still alive. I have still not left the world of men and the light of day. But leave it I shall!' Even as he was speaking, he was raising himself on his wounded thigh, and slow as he was with the violence of the pain deep in his wound, his spirit was unsubdued. He ordered his horse to be brought. This was his glory and his comfort, and on it he had ridden home victorious from all his wars. Seeing it pining, he spoke to it in these words: 'We have lived a long time, Rhaebus, if any mortal life is long. Either you will be victorious today and carry back the head of Aeneas with the blood-stained spoils stripped from his body, and you and I shall avenge the sufferings of Lausus; or else, if that road is barred and no force can open it, we shall fall together. I do not think, with courage like yours, that you will accept instructions from any other man or take kindly to Trojan masters.' With these words Mezentius mounted and Rhaebus took on his back the weight of the rider he knew so well. Both his hands were laden with sharp-pointed javelins and on his head he wore his helmet of gleaming bronze with its shaggy horsehair crest. So armed, he galloped into the thick of battle, fierce shame, frenzy and grief all seething together in his heart. Three times he shouted the name of Aeneas. Aeneas knew his voice and offered up this joyful prayer: 'Let this be the will of the Father of the Gods. Let this be the will of high Apollo. Stand and fight with me.' He said no more, but made for Mezentius with spear at the ready. Mezentius replied: 'Now that you have taken my son, you savage, you need not try to frighten me. That was the only way you could have found to destroy me. Death holds no terrors for us and we give not a thought for the gods. Enough words. I have come here to die. But first I have these gifts for you.' He spoke and hurled a spear at his enemy, then another and another, planting them in Aeneas' shield as he flew round him in a great circle, but the golden boss of the shield held fast. Aeneas stood there and Mezentius rode round him three times hurling his spears and keeping Aeneas on his left side. Three times the Trojan pivoted with him, turning his huge bronze shield, with its bristling forest of bronze spears. Then, weary of all the delay, weary of plucking javelins out of his shield and hard-pressed in this unequal battle, Aeneas, after turning many plans over in his mind, at last burst forward and threw his spear, catching Mezentius' warhorse in the hollow between its temples. Up it reared thrashing the air with its hooves and throwing its rider. Then as it came down with all its weight, dislocating its shoulder, it fell head first on top of Mezentius and pinned him to the ground. The sky blazed with the shouts of Trojans and Latins as Aeneas rushed up tearing his sword from the sheath and crying: 'Where is the bold Mezentius now? Where is that fierce spirit of his?' The Etruscan looked up, drinking in the bright air of heaven as he came back to his senses, and replied: 'You are my bitter enemy. Why jeer at me and threaten me with death? There is no sin in killing. I did not come into battle on those terms and my son Lausus struck no such bargain with you on my behalf. One thing I ask, if the defeated can ask favours from their enemies, to let my body be buried in the earth. I know the bitter hatred of my people is all about me. Protect me, I beg you, from their fury and let me lie in the grave with my son.' These were his last words. He then took the sword in the throat with full knowledge and poured out his life's breath in wave upon wave of blood all over his armour.

༼ 11 ༽

DRANCES AND CAMILLA

Meanwhile the Goddess of the Dawn had risen from Ocean, and anxious and eager as Aeneas was to give time to burying his comrades, distraught as he was in mind at their deaths, at first light the victor was paying his vows to the gods. Cutting all the branches off a huge oak, he set it up on a mound as a trophy to the great god mighty in war, and clothed it in the shining armour he had stripped from the body of the enemy leader Mezentius. There he set the hero's crest dripping its dew of blood, the broken spears and the breastplate struck and pierced through in twelve places. On the left he bound the bronze shield and from the neck he hung the ivoried sword. He then addressed his comrades (for all the Trojan leaders were pressing close around him), and these were the words he spoke to urge them on in their hour of triumph: 'The greatest part of our work is done, my friends. In what remains there is nothing to fear. These are spoils I have taken from a proud king, the first fruits of this war. This is Mezentius, and my hands have set him in this place. Our way now lies towards the king of the Latins and the walls of their city. Make ready your weapons. Fill your minds and your hopes with the thought of war, so that no man shall hesitate or not know what to do when the gods permit us to pull up our standards and lead the army out of camp. When that time comes, there must be no faintheartedness or sluggishness in our thoughts to slow us down. In the meanwhile, let us

consign the unburied bodies of our comrades to the earth, for
that is the only honour a man has in the underworld. Go,' he
said, 'and grace these noble spirits with their last rites, for
they have shed their blood to win this land for us. But first let
Pallas be sent back to the stricken city of Evander. This was a
warrior who did not fail in courage when his black day took
him from us and drowned him in the bitterness of death.'

So he spoke, weeping, and made his way back to his
own threshold where the body of Pallas lay guarded by old
Acoetes. Acoetes had once been the armour-bearer of
Arcadian Evander, but the auspices were no longer so favour-
able when he was appointed as companion to his dear ward,
Pallas. About them stood the whole throng of their attendants
and all the Trojans and the women of Troy with their hair
unbound in mourning after the manner of their people. But
when Aeneas entered his high doorway, they beat their
breasts and raised their wild lament to the sky till the palace
rang with the sound of their grief. When he himself saw the
head of Pallas cushioned there and his white face, and the
open wound torn in that smooth breast by the Italian spear,
the tears welled up and he spoke these words: 'Oh the pity of
it! Fortune came to me with smiles, but took you from me
while you were still a boy, and would not let you live to see
us in our kingdom, or to ride back in triumph to your father's
house. This is not what I promised Evander for his son, when
he took me in his arms as I left him, and sent me out to take
up this great command, warning me with fear in his heart
that these were fierce warriors, that this was a hardy race I
had to meet in battle. Even now, deluded by vain hopes, he
may be making vows and heaping altars with offerings, while
we bring him with tears and useless honours a young warrior
who owes no more debts to any heavenly power. With what
eyes will you look at the dead body of your son? Is this how
we return from war? Are these the triumphs expected of us?
Is this my great pledge? But you will not see a wound on him,

Evander, of which you need to be ashamed. You will not be a father who has the terrible wish that his son who is alive were dead. The land of Italy has lost a great bulwark, and great too is your loss, Iulus.'

After he had his fill of weeping, he ordered them to take up the pitiable corpse, and from the whole army he sent a thousand chosen men as escort to pay a last tribute and join their tears with those of Evander, a small comfort for a great sorrow, but a debt that was owed to the stricken father. Others were not slow to weave a soft wickerwork bier of arbutus and oak shoots to make a raised couch, shaded by a canopy of green, where they laid the young warrior high on his bed of country straw. There he lay like a flower cut by the thumbnail of a young girl, a soft violet or drooping lily, still with its sheen and its shape, though Mother Earth no longer feeds it and gives it strength. Then Aeneas brought out two robes stiffened with gold and purple threads which Sidonian Dido had long since made for him with her own hands, picking out the warp in fine gold, and the work had been a joy to her. With grief in his heart he put one of these on the young man's body as his last tribute and in a fold of it he veiled the hair that would soon be burned. Then he gathered a great heap of spoil from the battle on the Laurentine fields and ordered it to be brought to the pyre in a long procession, adding to it the horses and weapons he had taken from the enemy. Then came the captives, whose hands he had bound behind their backs to send them as offerings to the shades of the dead and sprinkle the funeral pyre with the blood of their sacrifice. He also commanded the leaders of the army to carry in their own arms tree trunks draped with weapons captured from the enemy and inscribed with their hated names. Acoetes, worn out with age, was led along in the procession, beating his breast with clenched fists and tearing his face with his nails, but he collapsed and lay all his length on the ground. Chariots were drawn along drenched with Rutulian blood, and then came Pallas' warhorse Aethon, stripped of all its trappings with the tears rolling down in great drops and soaking its face. There were men to carry his spear and his helmet. The victorious Turnus had the rest. A great phalanx of mourners followed, all the Trojans and the Etruscans and the Arcadians with their arms reversed. After this procession of all the comrades of Pallas had marched well clear of the camp, Aeneas halted, and with a deep groan he spoke these words: 'The same grim destiny of war calls us away from here to weep other tears. For ever hail, great Pallas, and farewell for ever.' He said no more but set off towards his high-built fortifications and marched back into camp.

And now envoys appeared from the city of the Latins bearing olive branches wreathed in wool and asking for a truce. The bodies of their dead were all over the plain where the steel had laid them, and they begged Aeneas to give them back and let them go to their graves in the earth, for he could have no quarrel with men who were defeated and had lost the light of life; he must show mercy to those who had once been called his hosts and the kinsmen of his bride. Good Aeneas could not refuse this petition. He honoured the envoys, granted what they asked and added these words: 'What cruel fortune is this, men of Latium, that has embroiled you in war and made you run away from us, who are your friends? You ask me for peace for the dead, whose destiny has been to die in battle: I for my part would have been willing to grant them peace when they were still alive. Nor would I ever have come to this land if the Fates had not offered me a place here to be my home. I do not wage war with your people. It was your king who abandoned our sworn friendship and preferred to put his trust in the weapons of Turnus. It is not these men who should have risked their lives but Turnus. If it is his plan to put an end to this war by the strength of his arm, and drive out the Trojans, he should have faced me and these weapons of mine in battle. One of us would have lived.

God or our own right hands would have seen to that. Go now and light fires beneath the bodies of your unfortunate citizens.' Aeneas had spoken. They were astonished and stood looking at each other in silence.

Then Drances, an older man who had always hated the young warrior Turnus, and spoken against him, began to make his reply: 'O Trojan great in fame, and greater still in arms, what words of mine could raise you to the skies? What shall I first praise? Your justice, or your labours in war? Gratefully shall we carry these words of yours back to our native city, and if Fortune shows us a way, we shall reconcile you to our king Latinus. Turnus can make his own treaties. We shall do more. We shall delight to raise the massive walls Fate has decreed for you and lift up the building stones of Troy on our shoulders!'

All to a man they murmured in agreement when he had finished speaking. Twelve days they decided on, and during that time, with peace as mediator between them, Trojans and Latins were together in the hills and wandered the woods, and no man harmed another. The iron axe rang upon tall ash trees and brought down skyward-thrusting pines. They never rested from their labours, splitting the oak and fragrant cedar with wedges and carrying down the ash trees on carts from the mountains.

But Rumour was already on the wing, overwhelming Evander and the house and city of Evander with the first warnings of anguish. The talk was no longer of Pallas, conqueror of Latium. The Arcadians rushed to the gates, snatching up funeral torches according to their ancient practice. The road was lit by a long line of flames which showed up the fields far on either side. Nearer and nearer came the throng of Trojans till it joined the columns of mourners. When the mothers of Pallanteum saw them entering the walls, the stricken city was ablaze with their cries. No power on earth could restrain Evander. Coming into the middle of the throng where the bier had been laid on the ground, he threw himself on the body of Pallas and clung to it weeping and moaning until at last grief freed a path for his voice: 'O Pallas, this is not what you promised your father! You said you would not be too rash in trusting yourself to the cruel God of War. I well knew the glory of one's first success in arms, the joy above all other joys of one's first battle. These are bitter first fruits for a young man. A hard schooling it has been in war, and you did not have far to go for it. None of the gods listened to my vows and prayers. O my dear wife, most blessed of women, you were fortunate in your death, in not living to see this day. But I have outstayed my time. A father should not survive his son. If only I had followed our Trojan allies into battle and the Rutulians had buried me under their spears! If only I had given up my own life and this procession was bringing home my body and not the body of Pallas. I would not wish to blame you, Trojans, nor our treaties, nor regret the joining of our right hands in friendship. The death of my son was a debt I was fated to pay in my old age. But if an early death was his destiny, I shall rejoice to think that first he killed thousands of Volscians and fell while leading the Trojans into Latium. Nor would I wish you any other funeral than this, Pallas, given you by good Aeneas and the great men from Phrygia, the leaders of the Etruscans and all the soldiers of Etruria, bearing the great trophies of the warriors your right hand has sent to their deaths. And you too, Turnus, would now be standing in the fields, a huge headless trophy, had Pallas been your equal in age, had the years given you both equal strength. But why does my grief keep the Trojans from their arms? Go now, take this charge to your king and do not forget it. If I drag out my hated life now that Pallas is killed, the reason, Aeneas, lies in your right arm. You know it owes the life of Turnus to the son and to the father. This is the one field where you must put your courage and your fortune to the test. I seek no joy in life – that is not what the gods have willed – only to take this satisfaction down to my son among the dead.'

Aurora meanwhile had lifted up her life-giving light for miserable mortals, bringing back their toil and sufferings. Both Tarchon and Father Aeneas soon built funeral pyres on the curving shore and carried there the bodies of their dead, each after the fashion of their fathers. They then set black-burning torches to the fires and the heights of heaven were plunged into pitchy darkness. Three times they ran round the blazing pyres in gleaming armour. Three times they rode in solemn procession round the fires of the dead with wails of lamentation. Tears fell upon their armour and fell upon the earth beneath. The clamour of men and the clangour of trumpets rose to heaven as some threw into the flames spoils torn from the corpses of the Latins, their splendid swords and helmets, the bridles of horses and scorching chariot wheels, while others burned the familiar possessions of their dead friends, the shields and spears which Fortune had not blessed. All around, oxen were being sacrificed and their bodies offered to the God of Death, while bristling swine and flocks carried off from the fields were slaughtered over the fires. All along the shore they watched the bodies of their comrades burn and tended the dying flames, nor would they be torn away till dank Night turned over the heavens and showed a sky studded with burning stars.

The mourning Latins too had built countless pyres some distance apart from the Trojans. Many bodies of men they buried in the earth; many they took up and carried back to the city or to their homes nearby in the countryside. The rest they burned uncounted and unhonoured, a huge pile of jumbled corpses, and all the wide land on every side was lit by fire upon fire, each brighter than the other. When the third day had risen and dispersed the chill darkness of the sky, the mourners levelled on the pyres the deep ash in which the bones of the dead were mingled, and weighed it down with mounds of warm earth. That day in their homes in the city of king Latinus, famous for his wealth, the noise of grief was at its loudest. That day their long mourning reached its height. Here were the mothers and heart-broken wives of the dead. Here were loving sisters beating their breasts, and children who had lost their fathers, all cursing this deadly war and Turnus' marriage; he was the man who should be deciding this matter with his own sword and shield since he was the man who was claiming the kingdom of Italy and the highest honours for himself. The bitter Drances heaped fuel on the fire and swore that Turnus was the only man whose name was being called; nobody else was being asked to fight. But at the same time many voices were raised for Turnus and much was said on his behalf. The great name of the queen cast its protecting shadow and also in his favour was all the fame and all the trophies he had won in his wars.

In the middle of this disturbance, while the dispute was still raging, to crown all, the envoys suddenly arrived back with a gloomy answer from the city of Diomede. They had achieved nothing for all the efforts they had expended; their gifts, their gold, their earnest prayers had failed; the Latins would have to look elsewhere for reinforcements or plead for peace with the Trojan king. At this bitter blow even king Latinus lost heart. Aeneas was chosen by Fate and brought there by the express will of heaven – this was what the anger of the gods was telling them; this was the message of these tombs newly raised before their eyes. With such thoughts in mind he summoned a great council, commanding the leaders of his people to come within his lofty doors. They duly gathered, filling the streets as they streamed to the royal palace. Greatest in age and first of those who carried the sceptre, Latinus sat in the middle with sadness on his brow and asked the envoys who had returned from the city of the Aetolians to tell what reply they brought, demanding to hear every

detail in due order. The assembly was called to silence. Venulus obeyed the command and began to speak: 'Fellow-
citizens, we have seen Diomede and the Argive camp. We
have paced out the road and lived through all the chances of
the journey. We have touched the hand that brought down
the land of Ilium. There in the fields near Mount Garganus,
in the Apulian kingdom of Iapyx, the victorious Diomede was
founding his city called Argyripa after the home of his fathers
at Argos. After we were admitted to his presence and given
leave to speak, we offered our gifts, telling him our names
and the land from which we came, who had brought war
among us and what had taken us to Arpi. He heard us out
and made this reply in words of peace:

' "The peoples of your land are blest by Fortune. Yours are
the kingdoms of Saturn, the ancient Ausonians, but what
Fortune is it that disturbs your peace and persuades you to
stir up wars you do not understand? Those of us whose
swords violated the fields of Ilium – let me not speak of all
we endured as we fought beneath her walls or of our men
drowned in her river Simois – we are scattered over the round
earth, paying unspeakable penalties and suffering all manner
of punishment for our crimes. We are a band of men that even
Priam might pity. The deadly star of Minerva knows us well.
So do the rocks of Euboea and Caphereus, the cape of vengeance. From that campaign we have been washed up on
many a different shore: Menelaus, son of Atreus, is in exile in
distant Egypt at the pillars of Proteus; Ulixes has seen the
Cyclopes on Etna; shall I speak of the kingdom of Neoptolemus in Epirus? Of the new home of Idomeneus in Calabria?
Of Locrians living on the shores of Libya? Even the leader of
the great Achivi from Mycenae was struck down by the hand
of his evil queen the moment he stepped over his own
threshold! The adulterous lover had been waiting for Asia to
fall. To think that the envious gods forbade me to return to
the altars of my fathers or to see the wife I longed for and my

beautiful homeland of Calydon. Even now I am pursued by the sight of hideous portents. My lost comrades have taken to the sky on wings. They have become birds and haunt the rivers – so cruelly have my people been punished – weeping till the rocks ring with the sound of their voices. From that moment of madness when I attacked the body of a goddess and my spear defiled the hand of Venus, I should have known that this was bound to come. Do not, I beg you, do not urge me to take part in any such battle. I have had no quarrel with the Trojans since the uprooting of their citadel of Pergamum, and I do not remember old wrongs or take any pleasure in them. As for the gifts you bring me from your country, give them rather to Aeneas. We have faced each other, spear against deadly spear, and closed in battle. Believe me, for I have known it, how huge he rises behind his shield, with what a whirr he spins his javelin. If the land of Ilium had borne two other such heroes, the Trojan would have come in war to the cities of the Greek, the Fates would have changed and Greece would now be in mourning. As for all the long delay before the stubborn walls of Troy, it was the hands of Hector and Aeneas – both men noble in their courage, noble in their skill in arms, but Aeneas the greater in piety – that held back the victory of the Greeks and did not let it come till the tenth year. Let your hands join in a treaty of peace while the chance is offered, but take care not to let your weapons clash on his!"

'You have heard, O best of kings, the answer of a king. You have heard his judgement on this great war.'

The envoys had scarcely finished before a confused roar was running through the troubled ranks of the Italians, as when rocks resist a river in spate and the trapped waters eddy and growl while the banks on either side roar with the din of the waves. As soon as calm returned to their minds and the words of fear were stilled on their lips, the king on his high throne addressed the gods and then began. 'For my part, O men of Latium, I would have wished, and it would have been better so, to have decided this great issue long since, and not be summoning a council at a time like this with the enemy sitting by our walls. We are fighting a misguided war, fellow-citizens, against unconquerable heroes and the sons of gods. Battle does not weary them, and even in defeat they cannot take their hands from the sword. If you had any hope of recruiting the Aetolians as your allies, lay it aside. To everyone his own hopes, but you can see how feeble this one is. All other resource is shattered and lies in ruins. You can see this with your own eyes. The whole truth is there at your finger tips. I accuse no one. Courage has done all that courage could do. The whole body of the kingdom has fought this fight. But now the time has come for me to express an opinion which has formed in my doubting mind. Give me your attention, and I shall tell it in a few words. Near the Tuscan river Tiber I have long owned some land which stretches away to the west beyond the land of the Sicani. Here Auruncans and Rutulians sow their seeds, wearying the stony hills with the plough and grazing the roughest of them. Let this whole area with the pine forests clothing its high mountains be given to the Trojans as a token of our friendship, and let us propose a treaty in just terms, inviting them to become partners in our kingdom. Let them settle here, if their hearts are so set on it, and build their walls. But if it is their wish to go elsewhere and seize the land of some other nation, and if it is within their power to leave this country of ours, let us weave the timbers of twenty ships in Italian oak, or more if they can man them. The wood is all lying on the shore. Let them say what ships they want and how many, and we can provide the bronze, the dockyards and the hands to do the work. I propose also that a hundred envoys, men of the highest rank in the Latin race, be sent to carry this message and conclude this treaty, holding out the branches of peace in their hands and bearing gifts, talents of gold and ivory, and the throne and robe which are the emblems of our royal power. Consider this together, and rescue our crippled fortunes.'

Then rose Drances, hostile as ever, who always looked askance at Turnus' great reputation and was goaded by bitter jealousy. He was generous with his wealth and readier still with his tongue, but his hand did not warm to battle. His voice had some weight in council and was always a force for discord. His mother's breeding gave him pride of rank; his father's origins were unknown. These were the words he spoke to add force and substance to their anger: 'What you propose, good king Latinus, is clear to all and needs no words of mine to support it. Everyone knows, and admits that he knows, what fortune has in store for the people, but they are all afraid to utter it. It is time for the man whose auspices the gods reject to blow a little less hard and give us freedom to speak. It is because of his fatal recklessness – I, for one, shall not be silent though he draw his sword and threaten me with death – we have seen so many of our leaders, who have been the lights of our people, extinguished, and the whole of our city now slumped in grief, while he storms the Trojan camp and frightens the sky with his weapons, knowing he can save his own life by taking to his heels. There is still one thing you must add, O best of kings, to all those many proposals and gifts you tell us to send to the sons of Dardanus, one thing only, and no man's violence should be able to overrule your right as a father to give your own daughter to a noble husband in a marriage that will be worthy of her, sealing this peace in a treaty for all time. But if our hearts and minds are so beset with fear of the man, let us beg and beseech him to give her up and restore to his king and to his fatherland the rights which are their due. Why do you keep throwing your unfortunate fellow-citizens into the jaws of danger, Turnus, you who are the single source and cause of all these sufferings of Latium? War will never save us. We are all asking you for peace, and the one inviolable pledge of that peace. I am the first to come to you as a suppliant – you imagine I am your enemy and that causes me no distress – look at me! I beg you to pity your people and lay down your pride. You are defeated. You must leave the field. We have been routed often enough and have seen enough funerals. We have stripped our wide fields bare. But if fame drives you on, if you have the strength in your heart, if you have such a yearning to receive a palace as a dowry, then be bold, have the confidence to go and stand face to face with your enemy. So that Turnus can get himself a royal bride, our lives are to be as chaff. We, the rank and file, are to litter the fields, unburied and unwept. But you too, if there is any strength in you, if you have any of the fighting spirit of your fathers, stand up to your challenger and look him in the face.'

At this, Turnus groaned, and blazed up into a violent rage. The words seemed to burst from the depths of his heart: 'You have always a good supply of words, Drances, when war calls for action. When the senate is summoned, you are the first to appear. But this is no time for filling the council chamber with talk, for pouring out high-flown speeches in comfort while our walls and ramparts are all that keep the enemy from us, and we are waiting for the ditches to fill with blood. By all means, Drances, you can thunder out your eloquence in your usual style and accuse me of cowardice, when your right hand has heaped up as many Trojan corpses as mine has and all the fields are studded with your trophies. But now is our chance to test our vigour and our valour. We do not have to look too far for enemies – they are standing all round the walls. Shall we advance to meet them? You hesitate? Where is your martial spirit? Will it always be in your long tongue and nimble feet? You say I have been defeated. You scum of the earth, who can say I am defeated when he sees the Thybris rising, swollen with Trojan blood, the house of Evander destroyed root and branch and the Arcadians stripped of their arms? This is not how Pandarus and Bitias found me, nor the thousand men I

sent down to Tartarus on my day of victory when I was
trapped inside the walls and rampart of the enemy. You say
that war will never save us. That prophecy is for the Trojan
and for yourself, you fool. But go on, stirring up panic everywhere and praising to the skies the strength of a race of men
who have been twice defeated. Go on insulting the armies of
Latinus. Now, it seems, the leaders of the Myrmidons are
afraid of Phrygian weapons! Now it seems that Diomede and
Achilles of Larisa are taking fright, and the river Aufidus is
flowing backwards in full retreat from the waves of the
Adriatic! Drances even pretends to be terrified when I speak
– a rogue's trick! The fear is a pretence to add sting to his
charges against me. But there is no need for you to be alarmed.
My hand will never take the breath of life from a man like
you. It is welcome to stay where it is in that breast of yours.

'But now, father, I come to you and to your great plan. If
you no longer hold out any hope for our arms, if we are left
to fight on utterly alone, if after one setback we are completely
destroyed, and Fortune has abandoned us never to return, let
us stretch out our defenceless arms and sue for peace. But if
only there were a spark of our old courage left in us! Any man
who has fallen and bitten the dust of death rather than live to
see such a thing, I count him fortunate in his life's labours,
the noblest spirit amongst us! Surely we still have untapped
resources and warriors who have not yet engaged and there
are still cities and peoples in Italy to help us? And surely the
Trojans have paid a heavy price in blood for the glory they
have won! They too have had their funerals. The same storm
has fallen on all of us. Why then do we disgrace ourselves by
stumbling on the threshold? Why do our knees start shaking
before we hear the trumpet? Many things change for the better
with the passing of the days and the ever-varying workings
of time. Fortune comes and goes. She has mocked many a man,
and then set his feet back on solid ground. So the Aetolian
Diomede and his city of Arpi will not help us. But Messapus

will, and Tolumnius, blessed by the gods, and all the leaders who have come to us from so many peoples, and great will be the glory for the chosen men of Latium and the Laurentine fields. We have Camilla too, from the noble Volscian race, leading her mounted column and her squadrons flowering with bronze. But if I am the only one the Trojans want to meet in battle, if that is your will and I am such a great obstacle to the good of all, then the Goddess of Victory has not entirely abandoned me, nor is she so ill-disposed to these hands of mine that I should refuse any undertaking for which I have such hopes. I shall go and face him with my spirits high were he mightier than Achilles and with armour the equal of his, made like his by the hands of Vulcan. To all of you, and to Latinus, father of my bride, I, Turnus, second in courage to none of those who have gone before me, have offered up my life. Is Aeneas challenging me, and me alone? Let him challenge. It is the answer to my prayer. If this is the anger of the gods I would not have Drances appease it; if it is a moment for courage and glory, I would not give it to Drances.'

So they disputed among themselves in deep uncertainty. Aeneas, meanwhile, had struck camp and was moving his army. Suddenly there came a messenger rushing wildly through the royal palace and causing panic all over the city: the Trojans, drawn up in line of battle, the Etruscan squadron with them, were coming down the valley of the Tiber and filling the whole plain. There was instant confusion and dismay among the people and hearts were roused by the sharp spur of anger. With wild gestures the young men asked for arms. 'Arms!' they shouted, while their fathers wept and murmured. On every side a great clamour of dissenting voices rose to the winds like the sound of flocks of birds settling in groves of tall trees, or swans whose harsh calls ring across the chattering pools of the river Padusa, so rich in fish. 'Do not disturb yourselves, citizens!' shouted Turnus, seizing the moment. 'Convene your council and sit there praising peace

while your enemies invade your kingdom with swords in
their hands.' These were his only words to them as he leapt
to his feet and rushed from the lofty palace shouting: 'You,
Volusus, tell the Volscian contingents to arm! And take the
Rutulians with you! Deploy the cavalry, Messapus, and you
too Coras with your brother, in battle array over the whole
plain! Some of you reinforce the approaches to the city
and man the towers. The rest of you come and advance with
me where I order.'

In an instant they poured on to the walls from all over the
city. Father Latinus himself left the council and abandoned
his high designs till a later time, in deep distress at the troubles
of the hour. Again and again he blamed himself for not eagerly
welcoming Trojan Aeneas and taking him into the city as his
son-in-law. Meanwhile men were digging pits in front of the
gates and bringing up rocks and stakes. The shrill trumpet
blew the signal for bloody battle and mothers and sons went
to make a motley ring all round the city walls. Their last
struggle called them and they came. The queen too, with a
great retinue of the mothers of the city, rode in her carriage to
bring offerings to the temple of Pallas on the heights of the
citadel. With her went the maiden Lavinia, the cause of all
this suffering, her lovely eyes downcast. The mothers followed them and filled the temple with the smoke of incense,
pouring out their sad prayers from its high threshold: 'Mighty
in arms, ruler of the battle, Tritonian maiden, break with your
hand the spear of the Phrygian pirate and throw him to the
ground. Spread out his body beneath your high gates.' Turnus
in a fury was eagerly arming himself for battle, and soon had
on his breastplate glowing red with bristling scales of bronze,
and his golden greaves. His head was still bare, but the sword
was girt to his side as he ran down from the heights of the
citadel in a blaze of gold, ardent and exulting and already
grappling with the enemy in hope and expectation. He was
like a stallion that has broken his tether and burst from his

stall; free at last he gains the open plain and runs to the fields where the herds of mares are pastured or gallops off to bathe in the river which he used to know so well, tossing high his head and whinnying with delight while the mane streams over his neck and flanks.

The princess Camilla came to meet him with her Volscians in battle order. Under the very gates of the city she leapt down from her horse, and all her squadron followed her example, dismounting in one flowing movement. These were her words: 'Turnus, if the brave are right to have faith in themselves, I dare to meet the Trojan cavalry – this is my undertaking – and go alone against the horsemen of Etruria. Give me leave to try the first hazard of war, while you stay on foot by the walls and guard the city.'

At these words Turnus fixed his eyes on this formidable warrior maiden and replied: 'O Camilla, glory of Italy, I cannot hope to express my gratitude in words or deeds. But now, since that spirit of yours knows no limits, come share with me the heat of battle. According to a firm report my scouts have brought me, that scoundrel Aeneas has sent his light-armed cavalry ahead to scour the plains, while he himself is coming to the city along a ridge in deserted mountain country. I am planning an ambush where there is a sunken path through a wood, and shall post armed men where the road enters and where it leaves the gorge. You go to meet the Etruscan cavalry and engage them. Bold Messapus will be with you with the horsemen of Latium and the squadron of Tiburtus, and you will have the task of leading them.' So he spoke and with like words urged Messapus and the leaders of his allies into battle, while he went to meet his enemy.

There is a winding valley well suited to stealth and stratagem in war. Hemmed in on both sides, it is darkened by the dense foliage of trees, and a narrow path leads into it making a treacherous approach through a ravine. Above this valley, among the viewpoints on the hilltop, there lies a little-known

plateau which gives safe cover whether you wish to engage
the enemy on your right flank or on your left or stand on the
ridges rolling down great boulders. Marching by paths he
knew, Turnus took up position here and settled into ambush
in this dangerous forest.

Meanwhile in the palace of the heavens Diana, daughter of
Latona, spoke to swift Opis, one of the sacred company of
girls who were her companions, and these were her sad
words: 'Camilla is going to a cruel war. Dear as she is to me
above all others, she has put on our armour, and it will avail
her nothing. This is no new love, believe me, that has come
to move the heart of Diana with sudden sweetness. When
Metabus, hated by his people for his arrogant use of power,
was driven from his throne, he left the ancient city of Priver-
num and took his infant daughter with him through all his
wars and battles, to be his companion in exile. He called her
Camilla, changing part of her mother's name, Casmilla.
Carrying her in his arms, he made for the long ridges and the
lonely woods, cruel spears pressing him hard on every side
and Volscian soldiers on the move all about him. Suddenly
he found his way blocked by the river Amasenus in full spate,
foaming to the top of its banks – such a deluge of rain had
burst from the clouds. He was about to leap into the water to
swim across, but checked himself out of love for his child and
fear for the burden he so loved. As he pondered all the
dangers, a painful resolve soon formed in his mind. He took
the warrior's spear he chanced to have in his hand, a mighty
weapon of solid, knotted, well-seasoned wood, and wrap-
ping the baby in cork-tree pith and bark, he lashed her tightly
to the middle of the spear. Then brandishing it in his mighty
hand, he cried out to heaven: "To you, kindly maiden, lover
of woods and daughter of Latona, I dedicate my daughter as
your handmaiden. She is your suppliant, and as she flies
through the air to escape her enemies, the first weapon she
holds in her hands is yours. O goddess, I solemnly pray,

receive her as your own as I now commit her to the hazard of the winds." At these words he drew back his arm and sent the weapon spinning. The waters rang with the sound as helpless Camilla flew over the wild river on the whistling javelin. But by now a great throng of his enemies was pressing Metabus even closer, and he threw himself into the water. Then, in triumph on the other side, he wrenched from the turf spear and maiden together, his dedication to Diana.

'No cities took him under their roofs or within their walls – he himself was too savage to have submitted to them – but he spent his whole life on the lonely mountains among the herdsmen. There in the scrub among the rough dens of beasts he fed his daughter with milk from the udders of wild broodmares, putting the teats to her soft lips, and as soon as she had taken the first steps on her infant feet, he put a keen-edged javelin in her hand and slung a bow and arrows from her little shoulder. Instead of gold in her hair and a long cloak to cover her, a tiger skin hung from her head all down her back. While her hand was still soft, she was spinning her baby javelins and whirling the sling round her head on its tapering thong to shoot the white swan or crane from the river Strymon. Many a mother in the towns of Etruria longed in vain to see her married to her son, but all she cared for was Diana. Undefiled, she preserved a constant love for her weapons and her chastity. If only she had never been caught up in such a war as this, daring to challenge the Trojans! I would have loved her and she would now have been one of my companions. But come now, since a bitter fate is closing in on her, glide down from the sky, Opis my nymph, and visit the land of Latium, where a dreadful battle is being fought and all the omens are adverse. Take these weapons, and draw an avenging arrow from my quiver. Then, with that same shaft, whoever violates that sacred body with a wound, be he Trojan or Italian, must pay to me an equal penalty in blood. Then I shall put a cloud round her poor body and her armour and

take them undespoiled to lie in a tomb in her own country.'
The goddess spoke, and Opis, veiled in a dark storm, glided
lightly down through the breezes of the sky, whirring as she
flew.

But all this time nearer and nearer to the walls came the
Trojan column, the Etruscan leaders and the whole cavalry
army drawn up in regular squadrons. Horses were prancing
and snorting all over the plain, fretting at the reins that held
them in and plunging to one side after another. Far and wide
the field bristled with the steel of the spears, and all the land
was a blaze of light from uplifted weapons. There too, coming
to oppose them, appeared Messapus and the swift Latins,
Coras with his brother, and the squadron of Camilla. Their
right arms were drawn back, their lances thrust forward with
tips quivering. Men were arriving. Horses were neighing. The
whole plain was ablaze. They had now come within
a spear-cast of each other and stopped. Then, with a sudden
shout, they galloped forward, urging their horses to frenzy,
and showering weapons thick as snow till the sky was cur-
tained with shadow. Tyrrhenus and bold Aconteus were first
to charge each other, riding full force with levelled spears,
and great was the din and fearful the fall as they crashed
their warhorses against each other, smashing breast on breast.
Aconteus was thrown forward a great distance and fell like a
thunderbolt, or a rock hurled from a catapult, scattering his
life's breath into the breezes.

In that instant the battle lines were thrown into disorder.
Putting their shields on to their backs, the Latins turned and
rode back towards the city walls driven by the Trojan squadrons under Asilas. But when they were almost at the gates,
they raised another shout and pulled round the supple necks
of their horses, while the Trojans fled in their turn, galloping
with slack reins in a long retreat. As the sea advances wave
by wave, now rushing to the land, throwing foam over the
rocks and soaking the edge of the sand in the bay; now turning

and hurrying back, sucking down the stones and rolling them along in its undertow while the shallows retreat and the shore is left dry – just so the Etruscans twice turned and drove the Rutulians to the city walls, and twice they were repulsed and had to cover their backs with their shields and look over their shoulders at their enemies. But when they clashed in battle for the third time, and all the ranks were embroiled together, each man singled out his own enemy, and then the groans of the dying could be heard, weapons and bodies lay deep in blood, half-dead horses rolled about entangled with the corpses of men, and ever fiercer and fiercer grew the battle. Orsilochus did not dare go near Remulus, but hurled his spear at his horse and its steel point stuck under its ear. Maddened by the blow, it reared, heaving its chest high and lashing its hooves, unable to endure the pain of the wound. Remulus was thrown and sent rolling on the ground, Catillus felled Iollas and then Herminius, great in stature, in spirit, and in arms. His head of golden hair was bare, his shoulder bare, and he had no fear of wounds, so vast he stood and open to the weapons of his enemies. Catillus' spear drove right through him and stood out between his broad shoulders quivering, and Herminius doubled up in agony. Black blood was flowing everywhere as they dealt out slaughter with the steel, searching for death and glory among the wounds.

There in the middle of all this bloodshed, exulting in it, was the Amazon Camilla with the quiver on her shoulder, and one side bared for battle. Sometimes the pliant spears came thick from her hand; sometimes, unwearied, she caught up her mighty double axe, and the golden bow and arrows of Diana rang on her shoulder. Whenever she was forced to retreat, she turned her bow and aimed her arrows while still in flight. The girls she had chosen as her companions were all about her, Larina, Tulla, and Tarpeia brandishing her bronze axe, all of them daughters of Italy, chosen by the servant of the gods Camilla to do her honour by their beauty and to be her own trusted attendants in peace and war. They were like the Amazons of Thrace whose horses' hooves drum on the frozen waters of the river Thermodon when they fight round Hippolyte in their brightly coloured armour, or when Penthesilea, daughter of Mars, rides home in her chariot and her army of women with their crescent shields exult in a great howling tumult.

Whom first did your spear bring down from his horse? Whom last, fierce warrior maiden? How many bodies of dying men did you strew on the ground? Eunaeus, son of Clytius, was the first. When he stood face to face with Camilla and she drove the long pine shaft of her spear through his unprotected chest, he vomited rivers of blood and champed the gory earth with his teeth, twisting himself round his wound as he died. Then she brought down Liris and Pagasus on top of him: Liris when he was trying to collect the reins after his wounded horse had reared and thrown him, Pagasus when he came and stretched out an undefended right hand to support Liris as he fell; but they both went flying head over heels. Then she sent Amastrus, the son of Hippotas, to join them, and raced after Tereus and Harpalycus, Demophoon and Chromis, pressing them hard even at long range with her spear, and for every dart that flew from her hand, a Trojan hero fell. The huntsman Ornytus was rushing past in strange armour, mounted on his horse Iapyx. This was a warrior who wore on his broad shoulders the hide of a bullock, while his head was encased in the huge gaping jaws of a wolf, complete with cheekbones and white teeth. A country spear shaped like a sickle armed his hand as he moved in the middle of the press, taller by a head than them all. She caught him – it was not difficult, for the whole column had turned and run – and when she had pierced him through, she spoke these bitter taunts over him: 'So you thought you were driving game in the woods, my Etruscan friend? The day has come when you have been proved wrong by a woman's weapons! But it is no mean name you will be taking to your fathers when you tell them you fell by the spear of Camilla.'

Instantly then she struck Orsilochus and Butes, the two tallest of the Trojans. Butes was turned away from her and the tip of her spear went in between helmet and breastplate where his neck shone white as he sat in the saddle with the shield hanging loose on his left arm. She fled from Orsilochus, but after he had driven her in a great circle, she cut inside the arc and began to pursue her pursuer. Then, rising above him, she struck again and again with her mighty axe, hacking through his armour and his bones as he begged and pleaded with her and the axe-blows spilt the hot brains down his face. The warrior son of Aunus of the Apennines then came upon her and stood stock still in sudden terror at the sight. He was not the least of the Ligurians while the Fates gave him leave to tell his lies. So, when he saw that it was too late to save himself by running away, and that the princess was upon him and would not be deflected, he began to play his tricks, using all his cunning and calculation. 'What is so wonderful,' he said, 'if a woman depends on the courage of a horse? Give up your chance of running away, and risk your life in close combat with me on level ground. Gird yourself to fight on foot and you will soon discover that the winds are blowing you only the illusion of glory.' These words stung Camilla to a burning fury of resentment. Handing her horse to a companion, she stood there to face him without a trace of fear, armed like her enemy with a naked sword and a plain light shield. The moment he thought his ruse had succeeded, the warrior took to his heels himself. Jerking the reins around, he made off, driving his horse to the gallop with steel spurs. 'You Ligurian fool!' she cried. 'You are the one who has been carried away by the empty winds of pride! You have taken to the slippery arts of your ancestors, but little good will they do you. Trickery will not bring you safe back home to your treacherous father Aunus.' These were her words, and on nimble feet she ran as swift as fire in front of the horse and stood full in its path. Then, seizing the reins, she exacted punishment from her enemy in blood, as easily as the sacred falcon flies from his crag to pursue a dove high in the clouds, catches it, holds it and rips out its entrails with hooked claws while blood and torn feathers float down from the sky.

But the Father of Gods and Men was not blind to this as he sat high above on the top of Olympus, and he roused Tarchon the Etruscan to bitter battle, laying on him the sharp goad of anger. So Tarchon rode among the slaughter in the ranks of his retreating squadrons, whipping them up with all manner of cries, calling on each man by name and rallying the routed to do battle: 'What are you afraid of, you Etruscans? Will you never know shame? Will you always be so spiritless? This is rank cowardice! One woman has turned this whole army and is scattering you to all points of the compass! What are weapons for? Why do we carry swords in our hands and not use them? You are not so sluggish when it comes to lovemaking and night campaigns, or when the curved pipe calls you up to the dancing chorus of Bacchus! Wait, then, for feasts and goblets from groaning tables. That is what you love. That is what you care about. Do nothing till the sooth-sayer gives his blessing and announces the festival and the fat victim calls you into the deep groves.' When this harangue was over, he spurred his horse into the thick of the enemy – he too was willing to die – and made a wild charge at Venulus. Tearing him off his horse and clasping him in his right arm, he rode off at full gallop with his enemy held in front of him. A shout rose to the sky and all the Latins turned to look as Tarchon flew like fire across the plain carrying man and armour with him. Then he broke off the steel head of Venulus' spear and with it probed for exposed flesh where he could give the fatal wound. Venulus fought back to keep Tarchon's hand from his throat, pitting strength against violence, just as when a tawny eagle has seized a snake and flown up into the sky, winding its talons round it and digging in its claws; meanwhile the wounded serpent writhes in sinuous coils, its scales stiff and rough, and hisses as it reaches up with its head; but for all its struggles, the eagle never stops tearing at it with its great hook of a beak, beating the air all the time with its wings – just like such an eagle did the victorious Tarchon carry off his prey from the Tiburtine ranks. Following their leader's example, and seeking like success, the Etruscans, the men from Maeonia, rushed into battle. Then Arruns, whose life was owed to the Fates, circled round Camilla to find where Fortune would offer the easiest approach. She was swift of foot, but he was more than her equal with the javelin and far superior in cunning. Wherever she went on her wild forays through the thick of battle, Arruns was behind her, quietly following in her tracks. Wherever she went as she returned in triumph and withdrew from her enemies, Arruns pulled on his swift reins and kept out of sight. Round a whole circle he went, trying now one approach, now another, brandishing the fatal spear that never missed its mark.

It then so chanced that Chloreus appeared, a man who had been consecrated to Cybele on her mountain, and in days long past had been a priest. She saw him a long way off, resplendent in his Phrygian armour and spurring his foaming warhorse. The horse-cloth was of hide with gold stitching and over-lapping brass scales in the shape of feathers. He himself shone with exotic indigo and purple. The arrows he shot from his Lycian bow were from Gortyn in Crete and the bow hanging from his shoulder was of gold. Gold too was the helm on the head of the priest, and on that day he had gathered the rustling linen folds of his saffron-yellow cloak into a knot with a golden brooch. He wore an embroidered tunic and barbaric embroidered trousers covered his legs. Whether her intention was to nail his Trojan armour to the temple doors or to sport captive gold on her hunting expeditions, she picked him out in the press of battle, and blind to all else and unthinking, she tracked him through the whole army, burning with all a woman's passion for spoil and plunder. At last the lurking Arruns saw his moment and hurled his spear, offering up this prayer to heaven: 'O highest of the gods, guardian of the holy mountain of Soracte, Apollo, we are the first to worship you. We heap up the wood of the pine to feed your flames, and in your holy rites, sure in our faith, we walk on fire, sinking our feet deep in the hot ash. Grant now, All-powerful Father, that our arms be wiped clean of this disgrace. My mind is not set on spoils won from a girl or a trophy set up for routing her or for any form of booty. My fame will come from my other feats of arms. But let this deadly scourge be defeated and fall to my spear, and I shall go back to the cities of my fathers and claim no credit.'

Phoebus Apollo heard, and part of his prayer he decided to answer, part he scattered to the swift breezes of air. He granted his prayer to surprise Camilla and lay her low in death, but did not allow the mountains of his native land to see him ever again. A sudden squall took these words and blew them far away to the winds of the south. So, when the spear that left his hand went whirring through the air and the Volscians, all of them, turned their minds and eyes intently to their queen, she was not thinking of whirring or of air or of weapons coming out of the sky, and the shaft struck home beneath her naked breast and lodged there drinking deep of her virgin blood. Her companions rushed in panic to support their falling queen, and Arruns fled, more terrified than any one, joy mixed with his fear. He had lost his faith in his spear and was afraid to face the weapons of the warrior maiden. As when a wolf has killed a shepherd or a great ox, and goes at once to hide high in the trackless hills before the avenging spears can come to look for him; he knows what he has done, and takes fright, comforting his quivering tail by tucking it under his belly as he makes for the woods – just so did Arruns disappear from sight in wild confusion, happy to escape and mingle in the press of battle. Camilla was dying. She tried to pull out the spear, but its steel point stood deep in the wound between the bones of her ribs. She was swooning from loss of blood, her eyes dimming in the chill of death, and the flush had faded from her cheeks. With her dying breath she spoke to Acca, alone of all her young friends. She was her most faithful companion and to her alone she used to open her heart. 'I can do no more, Acca my sister. This cruel wound is taking all my strength, and everything is going dark around me. Run from this place and take my last commands to Turnus. He must come into battle and keep the Trojans away from the city. And now, farewell.' Even as she was speaking she was losing her hold on her reins and in spite of all her efforts she slid to the ground. Then, growing cold, she little by little freed herself from her body. Her neck drooped and she laid down her head, yielding to death and letting go her weapons, as her life left her with a groan and fled in anger down to the shades. At this a measureless clamour rose and struck the golden stars. Now that Camilla had fallen, the battle raged as never before. Charging in one solid mass came the whole army of the Trojans, the Etruscan nobles and the Arcadian squadrons of Evander.

Opis, Diana's sentinel, had long been at her post high in the mountains, watching the fighting and knowing no fear. But when, far beneath her in the press of warriors shouting in the frenzy of battle, she saw Camilla receive the bitter stroke of death, she groaned and spoke these words from the depths of her heart: 'Alas, Camilla! You have paid too cruel a price for daring to challenge the Trojans in war, nor has it profited you that alone in the wild woods you have worshipped Diana and worn our quiver on your shoulder. But your queen has not left you unhonoured now at your last hour. This death of yours will not be forgotten among the peoples of this earth, and no one shall say that you have died unavenged. Whoever has desecrated your body with a wound will pay just penalty with his life.'

At the foot of a high mountain there was a huge mound of earth shaded by dense ilex trees. It was the tomb of Dercennus, an ancient king of the Laurentines. Here the lovely goddess first alighted on her swift flight, keeping watch for Arruns from the high mound. When she saw him gleaming in his armour and swollen with empty pride, she called out: 'Why are you leaving? Turn round and come in this direction. Come here and die! You must receive your reward for Camilla. Come, even a man can die by the weapons of Diana!' When she had spoken, the Thracian nymph took a winged arrow from her gilded quiver and drew her deadly bow. Far back she stretched the string until the curved horns of the bow were close together, her hands level, the left on the steel point of the arrow, the right holding the string against her breast. Arruns heard the hiss of the arrow and the whirr in the air, and in that same moment the steel was planted in his flesh. His comrades paid no heed. They left him breathing his last and groaning in some place unknown in the dust of the plain, while Opis soared on her wings to heavenly Olympus.

The light-armed squadron of Camilla were the first to flee when they lost their queen; then the Rutulians in a rout; then bold Asilas and all the scattered leaders and leaderless columns made for safety, wheeling their horses and galloping for the walls. No weapon could check the deadly onset of the Trojans and no one could stand against them. Back rode the Latins with slack bowstrings on slumped shoulders, and the four-hooved beat of their galloping horses drummed on the crumbling plain. As the black cloud of swirling dust rolled up to the walls, the mothers stood on the watch-towers beating their breasts and the wailing of women rose to the stars in the sky. The first Latins to burst into the open gates were pressed hard by a pursuing column of enemies mingled with friends and did not escape a pitiable death. There, on the very threshold, within the walls of their native city and in the safe refuge of their own homes, their bodies were pierced and they breathed out their life's breath. Some shut the gates and dared not open them to take their own people within the walls for all their pleading, and there was piteous slaughter of the armed men guarding the approaches and of men rushing to death on their weapons. Of those who were shut out before the weeping eyes of their own parents, some rolled headlong down into the ditches with the weight of the rout behind them, while others came on blindly at full gallop and crashed into the massive gates with their firm-set posts. Even the mothers strove their utmost – the true love of their native land showed them the way and Camilla was their example. Wildly they hurled missiles from the walls and rushed to do the work of steel with stumps and stakes of oak wood hardened in the fire, longing to be the first to die in defence of the walls of their city.

Meanwhile the warrior Turnus was still in the wood when the bitter news came and filled his heart to overflowing. The words of Acca brought him great turmoil of spirit: the battle forces of the Volscians were destroyed; Camilla had fallen; the enemy were attacking fiercely and had carried everything irresistibly before them; panic was already reaching the city walls. In a frenzy – and this is what the implacable will of Jupiter decreed – he came down from the hills where he had kept his ambush and left the wild woods behind him. Scarcely was he out of sight and moving on to the plains when Father Aeneas entered the open pass, came over the ridge and then emerged from the woods. So then they were both making for the walls at speed, with their whole armies marching not many paces from each other. Aeneas saw the Laurentine columns and the long line of dust smoking on the plains at one and the same moment as Turnus recognized Aeneas advancing relentlessly under arms and heard the drumming of approaching hooves and the breathing of horses. They would have joined battle instantly and tried the fortunes of war if the rose-red sun had not been dipping its weary horses in the Iberian sea, drawing down the light of day and bringing on the night. They both encamped before the city and built stockades on their ramparts.

☙ 12 ❧

TRUCE AND DUEL

When Turnus saw the line of the Latins broken, the battle going against them and their spirits flagging, when he realized that the time had come to honour his promises and that all eyes were upon him, no more was needed. He burned with implacable rage and his courage rose within him. Just as a lion in the fields round Carthage, who does not move into battle till he has received a great wound in his chest from the hunters, and then revels in it, shaking out the thick mane on his neck; fearlessly he snaps off the shaft left in his body by the ruffian that threw it, and opens his gory jaws to roar – just so did the violent passion rise in Turnus. At last he spoke these wild words to the king: 'Turnus keeps no man waiting. There is no excuse for Aeneas and his cowards to go back on their word or fail to keep their agreement. I am coming to meet them. Bring out the sacraments, father, and draw up the terms of the treaty. Either this right hand of mine will send this Trojan who has deserted Asia down into Tartarus – the Latins can sit and watch – and one man's sword shall refute a charge brought against a whole people, or else he can rule over those he has defeated and have Lavinia as his wife.'

Latinus answered him, and his voice was calm: 'You are a great-hearted young warrior. The more you excel in fierce courage, the more urgent is my duty to take thought, to weigh all possible chances and to be afraid. You have the kingdom of your father Daunus. You have all the cities your right hand has taken. I too, Latinus, have some wealth and some generosity of spirit. In Latium and the Laurentine fields there are other women for you to marry, and of the noblest families. This is not easy to say. Allow me to speak openly and honestly, and as you listen, lay these words to your heart. For me it would have been wrong to unite my daughter with any of those who came to ask for her in the past. It was forbidden by all the prophecies of gods and men. But I gave way to my love for you. I gave way to the kinship of blood and to the grief and tears of my wife. Breaking all the ties that bound me, I seized Lavinia from the man to whom she had been promised and took up arms in an unjust cause. From that moment you see the calamities of war that fall upon me, and the suffering that you bear more than any other. Twice we have been crushed in great battles, and we can scarcely protect within our city the future hopes of Italy. The current of the Thybris is even now warm with our blood and the broad plains white with our bones. Why do I always give way? Why do I change my resolve? What folly this is! I am ready to accept them as allies if Turnus is killed; why not put an end to the war while he is still alive? What will your kinsmen the Rutulians, what will the whole of the rest of Italy say if I betray you and send you to your death – which Fortune forbid – when you are asking to marry my daughter? Remember the many accidents of war and take pity on your old father waiting with heavy heart far away in your native Ardea.' These words had no effect on Turnus. The violence of his fury mounted. The healing only heightened the fever. As soon as he could bring himself to speak, out came his reply: 'This concern you are so kind as to show for my sake, I beg of you for my sake, forget it, and allow me to barter my life for glory. We too have weapons, father. We too have some strength in our right arm to throw the steel around, and when we strike a man, the blood flows from the wound. His mother the goddess will not be at hand with her woman's tricks, lurking in the treacherous shadows and trying to hide him in a cloud when he turns tail!'

Terrified by this new turn in the fortunes of battle, queen Amata began to weep. Seeing her own death before her, she tried to check the frenzy of Turnus, the man she had chosen to be the husband of her daughter: 'By these tears, Turnus, by any respect for me that touches your heart, Amata begs of you this one thing. You are the one hope and the one relief of my old age. In your hands rest the honour and the power of Latinus. Our whole house is falling and you are its one support. Do not persist in meeting the Trojans in battle. Whatever fate awaits you in that encounter, waits also for me. If you die, I too will leave the light I loathe. I shall never live to be a captive and see Aeneas married to Lavinia.' When Lavinia heard these words of her mother, her burning cheeks were bathed in tears and the deep flush glowed and spread over her face. As when Indian ivory has been stained with blood-red dye, or when white lilies are crowded by roses and take on their red, such were the colours on the maiden's face. Turnus was distraught with love and fixed his eyes on Lavinia. Burning all the more for war, he then spoke these few words to Amata: 'Do not, I beg of you, mother, send me to the harsh encounters of war with tears and with such an evil omen. Turnus is not free to hold back the day of his death. Go as my messenger, Idmon, and take these words of mine to the leader of the Phrygians, and little pleasure will they give him: when tomorrow's dawn reddens in the sky, borne on the crimson wheels of Aurora's chariot, let him not lead Trojans against Rutulians. Let the Trojan and Rutulian armies be at peace. His blood, or mine, shall decide this war. This is the field where the hand of Lavinia shall be won.'

When he had finished speaking and rushed back into the palace, he called for his horses and it gladdened his heart to see them standing there before him neighing. Orithyia, wife of Boreas, had given them to Turnus' grandfather Pilumnus to honour him, and they were whiter than the snow and swifter than the winds. The impatient charioteers stood round them, drumming on the horses' chests with cupped hands and combing their streaming manes. Then Turnus himself drew over his shoulders the breastplate with scales of gold and pale copper and fitted on his sword and shield and his helmet with its red crests in horned sockets. The God of Fire himself had made the sword for Turnus' father Daunus, dipping it white-hot in the waters of the Styx. Then instantly he snatched up his mighty spear which was leaning there against a great column in the middle of the palace, spoil taken from Actor the Auruncan, and brandished it till it quivered, shouting: 'You, my spear, have never failed me when I have called upon you. Now the time is here. Mighty Actor once wielded you. Now it is the right of Turnus. Grant me the power to bring down that effeminate Phrygian, to tear the breastplate off his body and rend it with my bare hands, to foul in the dust the hair he has curled with hot steel and steeped in myrrh!' Such was the blazing fury that drove him on. Sparks flew from his whole face and his piercing eyes flashed fire. He was like a bull coming into his first battle, bellowing fearfully and gathering his anger into his horns by goring a tree-trunk and slashing the air, pawing the sand and making it fly as he rehearses for battle.

Aeneas meanwhile, arrayed in the arms his mother had given him, was no less ferocious. He too was sharpening his spirit and rousing himself to anger, rejoicing that the war was being settled by the treaty he had proposed. He then reassured his allies and comforted the fears and anxieties of Iulus, telling of the future that had been decreed, ordering envoys to return a firm answer to Latinus and lay down the conditions for peace.

The next day had scarcely risen, sprinkling the mountain tops with brightness. When the horses of the Sun first reared up from the deep sea and raised their nostrils to breathe out the light, the Rutulians and Trojans were measuring a field for the duel under the walls of the great city, setting out braziers between the two armies and building altars of turf to the gods they shared. Others, wearing sacrificial aprons, their foreheads bound with holy leaves, brought fire and spring water. The Ausonian legion advanced, armed with javelins, filling the gateways as they streamed out of their city in serried ranks. On the other side the whole Trojan and Etruscan army came at the run in all their varied armour, drawn up with weapons at the ready as though it were the bitter business of battle that was calling them out. There too, in the middle of all these thousands, the leaders hovered in the pride of purple and gold, Mnestheus of the line of Assaracus, brave Asilas and Messapus, tamer of horses, son of Neptune. The signal was given. They all withdrew to their places, planting their spears in the ground and propping their shields against them. Then in a sudden rush the mothers, those who could not bear arms and the weak old men took up their seats on the towers and roofs of the city or stood high on the gates.

But Juno looked out from the top of what is now the Alban Mount – in those days it had neither name nor honour nor glory – and saw the plain, the two armies of Laurentines and Trojans, and the city of Latinus. Immediately the goddess Juno addressed the goddess who was the sister of Turnus, the ruler of lakes and roaring rivers, an honour granted by Jupiter the High King of Heaven as the price of her ravished virginity: 'Nymph, pride of all rivers, dearest to our heart, you know how I have favoured you above all the other women of Italy who have mounted the ungrateful bed of magnanimous Jupiter, and have gladly set you in your place in the skies, learn now the grief which is yours, Juturna, and do not lay the blame on me. As long as Fortune seemed to permit it, as long as the Fates allowed all to go well with Latium, I have protected the warrior Turnus and your walls. But now I see he is confronting a destiny to which he is not equal. The day of the Fates and the violence of his enemy are upon him. My eyes cannot look at this battle or at this treaty. If you dare to stand closer and help your brother, go. It is right and proper. You suffer now. Perhaps a better time will come.' She had scarcely spoken when the tears flooded from Juturna's eyes, and three times and more she beat her lovely breasts. 'This is no time for tears,' said Juno, daughter of Saturn. 'Go quickly and if you can find a way, snatch your brother from death or else stir up war and dash from their hands this treaty they have drawn up. You dare. I sanction.' With these words she urged her on, then left her in doubt and confusion and wounded to the heart.

Meanwhile the kings arrived, Latinus mighty in his four-horse chariot, with twelve gold rays encircling his shining temples, proof of his descent from his grandfather the God of the Sun. Turnus was in his chariot drawn by two white horses, gripping two broad-bladed spears in his hand. From the other side, advancing from the camp, came Father Aeneas, the founder of the Roman race, with his divine armour blazing and his shield like a star. Beside him were Ascanius, the second hope for the future greatness of Rome, and a priest arrayed in pure white vestments, driving to the burning altars a yearling ewe as yet unshorn and the young of a breeding sow. Turning their eyes towards the rising sun, the leaders stretched out their hands with offerings of salted meal, marked the peak of their victims' foreheads with their blades and poured libations on the altars from their goblets.

Then devout Aeneas drew his sword and prayed: 'I now call the Sun to witness, and this land for which I have been able to endure such toil; I call upon the All-powerful Father of the Gods, and you his wife, Saturnian Juno – and I pray you, goddess, from this moment look more kindly on us – and you, glorious Mars, under whose sway all wars are disposed; I call upon springs and rivers; I call upon all the divinities of high heaven and all the gods of the blue sea: if

victory should chance to fall to Ausonian Turnus, it is agreed
that the defeated withdraw to the city of Evander. Iulus will
leave these lands, and after this the people of Aeneas will not
rise again in war, or bring their armies here, or disturb this
kingdom with the sword. But if Victory grants the day to us
and to our arms – as I believe she will, and may the gods so
rule – I shall not order Italians to obey Trojans, nor do I seek
royal power for myself. Both nations shall move forward into
an everlasting treaty, undefeated, and equal before the law. I
shall give the sacraments and the gods. Latinus, the father of
my bride, will have the armies and solemn authority in the
state. For me the Trojans will build the walls of a city and
Lavinia will give it her name.'

So prayed Aeneas, and Latinus followed him, looking up
and stretching his right hand towards the sky: 'I too swear,
Aeneas, by the same: by earth and sea and stars; by the two
children of Latona and by two-browed Janus; by the divine
powers beneath the earth and the holy house of unyielding
Dis; and let the Father himself, who sanctions treaties by the
flash of his lightning, hear these my words. I touch his altar. I
call to witness the gods and the fires that stand between us.
The day shall not come when men of Italy shall violate this
treaty or break this peace, whatever chance will bring. This is
my will and no power will set it aside, not if it dissolve the
earth in flood and pour it into the sea, not if it melt the sky
into Tartarus, just as this sceptre' – at that moment he was
holding his sceptre in his hand – 'will never sprout green or
cast a shadow from delicate leaves, now that it has been cut
from the base of its trunk in the forest, leaving its mother tree
and losing its limbs and leafy tresses to the steel. What was
once a tree, skilled hands have now clad in the beauty of
bronze and given to the fathers of Latium to bear.' With such
words they sealed the treaty between them in full view of the
leaders of the peoples. Then, taking the duly consecrated
victims, they cut their throats on to the altar fires, and, tearing

the entrails from them while they still lived, they heaped the altars from laden platters.

But it had long seemed to the Rutulians that this was not an even contest and their hearts were still more confused and dismayed when the two men appeared before their eyes and they saw at close range the difference in their strength. Their fears were increased by the sight of Turnus stepping forward quietly with downcast eyes to worship at the altar like a suppliant. His cheeks were like a boy's and there was a pallor over all his youthful body. As soon as his sister Juturna saw that such talk was spreading and that men's minds were weakening and wavering, she came into the battle lines in the guise of Camers, whose family had been great from his earliest ancestors, whose father had won fame for his courage, and who himself was the boldest of the bold in the use of arms. Into the middle of the battle lines she advanced, well knowing what she had to do, and there with these words she sowed the seeds of many different rumours: 'Is it not a disgrace, Rutulians, to sacrifice the life of one man for all of us? Are we not their equals in numbers and in strength? Look, these few here are all they have, the Trojans, Arcadians and the army sent by Fate – the Etruscans who hate Turnus! We are short of enemies, even if only half our number were to engage them in battle. As things are, the fame of Turnus will rise to the gods on whose altars he now dedicates himself, and he will live on the lips of men, but if we lose our native land, we shall be forced to obey proud masters, who now sit here idling in our fields!'

By such words she more and more inflamed the minds of the warriors, and murmurs crept through their ranks. Even the Laurentines had a change of heart, even the Latins, and men who a moment ago were longing for a rest from fighting and safety for their people, now wanted their weapons and prayed that the treaty would come to nothing, pitying Turnus and the injustice of his fate. At this moment Juturna did even more and showed a sign high in the sky, the most powerful portent that ever confused and misled men of Italy. The tawny eagle of Jupiter was flying in the red sky of morning, putting to clamorous flight the winged armies of birds along the shore, when he suddenly swooped down to the waves and seized a noble swan in his pitiless talons. The men of Italy thrilled at the sight, the birds all shrieked and – a wonder to behold – they wheeled in their flight, darkening the heavens with their wings, and formed a cloud to mob their enemy high in the air until, exhausted by their attacks and the weight of his prey, he gave way, dropping it out of his talons into the river below and taking flight far away into the clouds.

The Rutulians greeted the portent with a shout and their hands were quick to their swords. Tolumnius, the augur, was the first to speak: 'At last!' he cried. 'At last! This is what I have so often prayed to see. I accept the omen and acknowledge the gods. It is I who will lead you. Now take up your arms, O my poor countrymen, into whose hearts the pitiless stranger strikes the terror of war. You are like the feeble birds and he is attacking and plundering your shores. He will take to flight and sail far away over the sea, but you must all be of one mind, mass your forces into one flock and fight to defend your king whom he has seized.' When he had spoken he ran forward and hurled his cornel-wood spear at the enemy standing opposite. It whirred through the air and flew unerringly. In that moment a great shout arose. In that moment all the ranks drawn up in wedge formation were thrown into disorder, and in the confusion men's hearts blazed with sudden passion. The spear flew on. By chance nine splendid brothers had taken their stand opposite Tolumnius, all of them sons borne by the faithful Tyrrhena to her Arcadian husband Gylippus. It struck one of these in the waist where the sewn belt chafed the belly and the buckle bit the side-straps. He was noble in his looks and in the brilliance of his armour, and the spear drove through his ribs and stretched him on the yellow sand. Burning with grief, his brothers, a whole phalanx of spirited warriors, drew their swords or snatched up their throwing spears and rushed blindly forward. The ranks of the Laurentines ran to meet them while from the other side the massed Trojans came flooding up with Etruscans from Agylla and Arcadians in their brightly coloured armour. One single passion drove them on – to settle the matter by the sword. They tore down the altars and a wild storm of missiles filled the whole sky and fell in a rain of steel. The mixing bowls and braziers were removed, and now that the treaty had come to nothing even Latinus took to flight with his rejected gods. Some bridled the teams of their chariots; some leapt on their horses and stood at the ready with drawn swords.

Messapus, eager to wreck the treaty, rode straight at the Etruscan Aulestes, a king wearing the insignia of a king, and the charging horse drove him back in terror. He fell as he retreated, and crashed violently head and shoulders into the altar behind him. Riding furiously, Messapus flew to him and, towering over him with a lance as long as a housebeam, he struck him his death blow even as he poured out prayers for mercy. 'So much for Aulestes!' cried Messapus. 'This is a better victim to offer to the great gods!' and the men of Italy ran to strip the body while it was still warm. Corynaeus came to meet them, snatching a half-burnt torch from an altar. Ebysus made for him, but before he could strike a blow, Corynaeus filled his face with fire. His great beard flared up and gave off a stench as it burned. Corynaeus pressed his attack and, clutching the hair of his helpless enemy in his left hand, he forced him to the ground, kneeling on him with all his weight, and sunk the hard steel in his flank. Meanwhile Podalirius had been following the shepherd Alsus as he rushed through the hail of missiles in the front line of battle and was now poised over him with the naked sword. But, drawing back his axe, Alsus struck him full in the middle of the forehead and split it to the chin, bathing all his armour in a shower of blood. It was a cruel rest then for Podalirius. An iron sleep bore down upon him and closed his eyes in everlasting night.

But true to his vow Aeneas, unhelmeted, stretched out his weaponless right hand and called to his allies: 'Where are you rushing? What is this sudden discord rising among you? Control your anger! The treaty is already struck and its terms agreed. I alone have the right of conflict. Leave me to fight and forget your fears. We have a treaty, and my right hand will make it good. The rituals we have performed have made Turnus mine.' While he was still speaking, while words like these were still passing his lips, an arrow came whirring in its flight and struck him, unknown the hand that shot it and the force that spun it to its target, unknown what chance or what god brought such honour to the Rutulians. The shining glory of the deed is lost in darkness, and no man boasted that he had wounded Aeneas.

When Turnus saw him leaving the field and the leaders of the allies in dismay, a sudden fire of hope kindled in his heart. Horses and arms he demanded both at once, and in a flash he leapt on his chariot with spirits soaring and gathered up the reins. Then many a brave hero he sent down to death as he flew along, and many half-dead bodies he sent rolling on the ground, crushing whole columns of men under his chariot wheels as he caught up their spears and showered them on those who had taken to flight. Just as Mars, spattered with blood, charges along the banks of the icy river Hebrus, clashing sword on shield and giving full rein to his furious horses as he stirs up war; they fly across the open plain before the winds of the south and the west, till Thrace roars to its furthest reaches with the drumming of their hooves as his escort gallops all round him, Rage, Treachery and the dark faces of Fear – just so did bold Turnus lash his horses through the thick of battle till they smoked with sweat, and as he trampled the pitiable bodies of his dead enemies, the flying hooves scattered a dew of blood and churned the gore into the sand. Sthenelus he sent to his death with a throw from long range; then Thamyrus and Pholus, both in close combat. From long range, too, he struck down the Imbrasidae, Glaucus and Lades, whom their father Imbrasus himself had brought up in Lycia, and gave them armour that equipped them either to do battle or to outstrip the winds on horseback.

In another part of the field, Eumedes was charging into the fray. He was a famous warrior, son of old Dolon, bearing his grandfather's name, but his spirit and his hand for war were his father's. It was Dolon who dared to ask for the chariot of Achilles as a reward for going to spy on the camp of the Greeks. But Diomede provided a different reward for his daring, and he soon ceased to aspire to the horses of Achilles. When Turnus caught sight of Eumedes far off on the open plain, he struck him first with a light javelin thrown over the vast space that lay between. Then, halting the two horses that drew his chariot, he leapt down and stood over his dying enemy with his foot on his neck. He wrenched the sword out of Eumedes' hand, and it flashed as he dipped it deep in his throat, saying: 'There they are, Trojan. These are the fields of Hesperia you tried to take by war. Lie there and measure them! This is my reward for those who test me by the sword. This is how they build their cities.' Next, with a throw of his javelin, he sent Asbytes to join him, then Chloreus, Sybaris, Dares, Thersilochus and Thymoetes, whose horse had fallen and thrown him over its head. Just as when the breath of Thracian Boreas sounds upon the deep Aegean as he pursues the waves to the shore, and wherever the winds put out their strength the clouds take to flight across the sky, just so, wherever Turnus cut his path, the enemy gave way before him, their ranks breaking and running, and his own impetus carried him forward with the plumes on his helmet tossing as he drove his chariot into the wind. Phegeus could not endure this onslaught of Turnus and his wild shouting, but leapt in front of the chariot and pulled round the horses' heads as they galloped at him, foaming at their bits. Then, as he was dragged along hanging from the yoke, the broad blade of Turnus' lance struck his unprotected side, piercing and breaking the double mesh of his breastplate and grazing the skin of his body. He put up his shield and was twisting round to face his enemy when he fell and was caught by the flying wheel and axle and stretched out on the ground. Turnus, following up, struck him between the bottom of the helmet and the top edge of the breastplate, cutting off his head and leaving the trunk on the sand.

While the victorious Turnus was dealing death on the plain, Aeneas was taken into the camp by Mnestheus and faithful Achates. Ascanius was with them. Aeneas was bleeding and leaning on his long spear at every other step. He was in a fury, tugging at the arrow-head broken in the wound and demanding that they should take the quickest way of helping him, make a broad cut with the blade of a sword, slice open the flesh where the arrow was embedded and get him back into battle. But now there came Iapyx, son of Iasus, whom Phoebus Apollo loved above all other men. Overcome by this fierce love, Apollo had long since offered freely and joyfully to give him all his arts and all his powers, prophecy, the lyre, the swift arrow, but, in order to prolong the life of his dying father, Iapyx chose rather to ply a mute, inglorious art and know the virtues of herbs and the practice of healing. There, with the grieving Iulus, in the middle of a great crowd of warriors, stood Aeneas, growling savagely, leaning on his great spear and unmoved by their tears. The old man, with his robe caught up and tied behind him after the fashion of Apollo Paeon, tried anxiously and tried in vain all he could do with his healing hands and the potent herbs of Apollo. In vain his right hand worked at the dart. In vain the forceps gripped the steel. Fortune did not show the way and his

patron Apollo gave no help. And all the time the horror of
battle grew fiercer and fiercer on the plain, and nearer and
nearer drew the danger. They soon could see a wall of dust in
the sky. The cavalry rode up, and showers of missiles were
falling into the middle of the camp. A hideous noise of shouting rose to the heavens as young men fought and fell under
the iron hand of Mars.

At this Venus, dismayed by her son's undeserved suffering,
picked some dittany on Mount Ida in Crete. The stalk of this
plant has a vigorous growth of leaves and its head is crowned
by a purple flower. It is a herb which wild goats know well
and feed on when arrows have flown and stuck in their backs.
This Venus brought down, veiled in a blinding cloud, and
with it tinctured the river water they had poured into shining
bowls, impregnating it secretly and sprinkling in it fragrant
panacea and the health-giving juices of ambrosia. Such was
the water with which old Iapyx, without knowing it, bathed
the wound, and suddenly, in that moment, all the pain left
Aeneas' body and the blood was staunched in the depths of
the wound. Of its own accord the arrow came away in the
hand of Iapyx and fresh strength flowed into Aeneas, restoring
him to his former state. It was Iapyx who was the first to fire
their spirits to face the enemy. 'Bring the warrior his arms,
and quickly!' he cried. 'Why stand there? This cure was not
effected by human power, nor by the guidance of art. It is not
my right hand that saved you, Aeneas. Some greater power,
some god, is driving you and sending you back to greater
deeds.' Aeneas was hungry for battle. He had already
sheathed his calves in his golden greaves and was brandishing
his flashing spear, impatient of delay. When the shield was
fitted to his side and the breastplate to his back, he took
Ascanius in an armed embrace and kissed him lightly through
the helmet, saying: 'From me, my son, you can learn courage
and hard toil. Others will teach you about fortune. My hand
will now defend you in war and lead you where the prizes

are great. I charge you, when in due course your years ripen and you become a man, do not forget, but as you go over in your mind the examples of your kinsmen, let your spirit rise at the thought of your father Aeneas and your uncle Hector.'

When he had finished speaking, he moved through the gates in all his massive might, brandishing his huge spear, and there rushed with him in serried ranks Antheus and Mnestheus and all his escort, streaming from the camp. A blinding dust then darkened the plain. The very earth was stirred and trembled under the drumming of their feet. As they advanced, Turnus saw them from the rampart opposite. The men of Ausonia also saw them and cold tremors of fear ran through the marrow of their bones. But before all the Latins, Juturna heard the sound and knew its meaning. She fled, trembling, but Aeneas came swiftly on leading his dark army over the open plain. Just as when a cloud blots out the sun and begins to move from mid-ocean towards the land; long-suffering farmers see it in the far distance and shudder to the heart, knowing what it will bring, the ruin of trees, the slaughter of their crops and destruction everywhere; the flying winds come first, and their sound is first to reach the shore – just so the Trojan leader from Rhoeteum drove his army forward against the enemy in wedge formation, each man shoulder to shoulder with his neighbour. Fierce Osiris was struck by the sword of Thymbraeus. Mnestheus cut down Arcetius, Achates Epulo, and Gyas Ufens. Tolumnius himself fell, the augur who had been the first to hurl a spear against his enemies. The shouting rose to the sky and now it was the Rutulians who turned and fled over the fields, raising the dust on their backs. Aeneas did not think fit to cut down men who had turned away from him, nor did he go after those who stood to meet him in equal combat or carried spears. He was looking for Turnus, and only Turnus, tracking him through the thick murk. Turnus was the only man he asked to fight.

Seeing this and being stricken with fear, the warrior maiden

Juturna threw out Metiscus, the driver of Turnus' chariot, from between the reins and left him lying where he fell, far from the chariot pole. She herself took over the reins and whipped them up to make them ripple, the very image of Metiscus in voice and form and armour, like a black swallow flying through the great house of some wealthy man, and collecting tiny scraps of food and dainties for her young chattering on the nest; sometimes her twittering is heard in empty colonnades, sometimes round marshy pools – just so did Juturna ride through the middle of the enemy and the swift chariot flew all over the field. Now here, now there she gave glimpses of her brother in triumph, but then she would fly off and not allow him to join in the battle. But Aeneas was no less determined to meet him and followed his every twist and turn, tracking him and calling his name at the top of his voice all through the scattered lines of battle. Every time he caught sight of his enemy, he tried to match the speed of his wing-footed horses, and every time Juturna swung the chariot round and took to flight. What was Aeneas to do? Conflicting tides seethed in his mind, but no answer came, and different passions drove him to opposing thoughts. Then the nimble Messapus, who was running with two pliant steel-tipped javelins in his left hand, aimed one of them at Aeneas and hurled it true. Aeneas checked himself and crouched on one knee behind his shield, but the flying spear sheared off the peak of his helmet and carried away the plumes from the top of it. At this his anger rose. Treachery had given him no choice. When he saw Turnus' horses pull the chariot round and withdraw, again and again he called upon Jupiter and the altars of the broken treaty, and then, and not till then, he plunged into the middle of his enemies. He was terrible in his might and Mars was aiding him. Sparing no man, he roused himself to savage slaughter and gave full rein to his anger.

What god could unfold all this bitter suffering for me? What god could express in song all the different ways of death for men and for their leaders, driven back and forth across the plain, now by Turnus, now by Trojan Aeneas? Was it your will, O Jupiter, that peoples who were to live at peace for all time should clash so violently in war?

Aeneas met Sucro the Rutulian – this was the first clash to check the Trojan charge – but Sucro did not detain them long. Aeneas caught him in the side and drove the raw steel through the cage of the ribs to the breast where death comes quickest. Turnus, now on foot, met Diores and his brother Amycus who had been unhorsed. As Diores rode at him he struck him with his long spear; Amycus he despatched with his sword. Then, cutting off both their heads, he hung them from his chariot and carried them along with him, dripping their dew of blood. Aeneas sent Talos, Tanais and brave Cethegus to their deaths, all three in one encounter, then the gloomy Onites, who bore a name linked with Echion of Thebes and whose mother was Peridia. Turnus killed the brothers who came from the fields of Apollo in Lycia, then young Menoetes, who hated war – but that did not save him. He was an Arcadian who had plied his art all round the rivers of Lerna, rich in fish. His home was poor and he never knew the munificence of the great. His father sowed his crops on hired land. Like fires started in different places in a dry wood or in thickets of crackling laurel; or like foaming rivers roaring as they run down in spate from the high mountains to the sea, sweeping away everything that lies in their path – no more sluggish were Aeneas and Turnus as they rushed over the field of battle. Now if ever did the anger seethe within them; now burst their unconquerable hearts and every wound they gave, they gave with all their might.

Murranus was sounding the names of his father's fathers and their fathers before them, his whole lineage through all the kings of Latium, when Aeneas knocked him flying from his chariot with a rock, a huge boulder he sent whirling at him, and stretched him out on the ground. The wheels rolled him forward in a tangle of yoke and reins and his galloping horses had no thought for their master as they trampled him under their clattering hooves. Hyllus made a wild charge, roaring hideously, but Turnus ran to meet him and spun a javelin at his gilded forehead. Through the helmet it went and stuck in his brain. As for you, Cretheus, bravest of the Greeks, your right hand did not rescue you from Turnus; nor was Cupencus protected by his gods when Aeneas came near, but his breast met the steel and the bronze shield did not hold back the moment of his death. You too, Aeolus. The Laurentine plains saw you fall, and your back cover a broad measure of their ground. The Greek battalions could not bring you down, nor could Achilles who overturned the kingdom of Priam, but here you lie. This was the finishing line of your life. Your home was in the hills below Mount Ida, a home in the hills of Lyrnesus, but your grave is in Laurentine soil. The two armies were now wholly turned to face one another. All the Latins and all the Trojans – Mnestheus and bold Serestus, Messapus, tamer of horses, and brave Asilas – the battalion of Etruscans and the Arcadian squadrons of Evander were striving each man with all his resources of strength and will, waging this immense conflict with no rest and no respite.

At that moment Aeneas' mother, loveliest of the goddesses, put it into his mind to go to the city, to lead his army instantly against the walls and throw the Latins into confusion at this sudden calamity. Turning his eyes this way and that as he tracked down Turnus through all the different battle lines, he noticed the city, untouched by this great war, quiet and unharmed, and his spirit was fired by the sudden thought of a greater battle he could fight. Calling the leaders of the Trojans together, Mnestheus, Sergestus and the brave Serestus, he took up position on some rising ground and the whole of the Trojan legion joined them there in close formation without laying down their shields or spears. Aeneas addressed them standing in the middle of a high mound of earth: 'There must be no delay in carrying out my commands. Jupiter is on our side. No man must go to work half-heartedly, because my plan is new to him. The city is the cause of this war. It is the very kingdom of Latinus, and if they do not this day agree to submit to the yoke, to accept defeat and to obey, I shall root it out and level its smoking roofs to the ground. Am I to wait until Turnus thinks fit to stand up to me in battle and consents to meet the man who has already defeated him? O my fellow-citizens, this city is the head and heart of this wicked war. Bring your torches now and we shall claim our treaty with fire!'

When he had finished speaking, they formed a wedge, all of them striving with equal resolve in their hearts, and moved towards the walls in a solid mass. Ladders suddenly appeared. Fire came to hand. They rushed the gates and cut to pieces the first guards that met them. They spun their javelins and darkened the heavens with steel. Aeneas himself, standing among the leaders under the city wall with his right hand outstretched, lifted up his voice to accuse Latinus, calling the gods to witness that this was the second time he had been forced into battle; twice already the Italians had shown themselves to be his enemies; this was not the first treaty they had violated. Alarm and discord rose among the citizens. Some wanted the city to be opened up and the gates thrown wide to receive the Trojans and they even dragged the king himself on to the ramparts; others caught up their weapons and rushed to defend the walls: just as when a shepherd tracks some bees to their home, shut well away inside a porous rock, and fills it with acrid smoke; the bees, alarmed for their safety, rush in all directions through their wax-built camp, sharpening their wrath and buzzing fiercely; then as the black stench rolls through their chambers, the inside of the rock booms with their blind complaints and the smoke flies to the empty winds.

Weary as they were, a new misfortune now befell the Latins and shook their whole city to its foundations with grief. As soon as the queen, standing on the palace roof, saw the enemy approaching the city, the walls under attack, fire flying up to the roofs, no Rutulian army anywhere to confront the enemy and no sign of Turnus' columns, she thought in her misery that he had been killed in the cut and thrust of battle. In that instant her mind was deranged with grief and she screamed that she was the cause, the guilty one, the fountainhead of all these evils. Pouring her heart out in sorrow and madness, she resolved to die. Her hand rent her purple robes, and she died a hideous death in the noose of a rope tied to a high beam. When the unhappy women of Latium heard of this, her daughter Lavinia was the first to tear her golden hair and rosy cheeks. The whole household was wild with grief around her, and their lamentations rang all through the palace. From there the report spread through the whole city and gloom was everywhere. Latinus went with his garments torn, dazed by the death of his wife and the downfall of his city, fouling his grey hair with handfuls of dirt and dust.

Meanwhile, on a distant part of the plain, the warrior Turnus was chasing a few stragglers. He was less vigorous now, and less and less delighted with the triumphant progress of his horses, when the wind carried to him this sound of shouting and of unexplained terror. He pricked up his ears. It was a confused noise from the city, a murmuring with no hint of joy in it. 'What is this?' he cried in wild dismay, pulling on the reins to stop the chariot. 'Why such grief and distress on the walls and all this clamour streaming from every part of the city?' His sister, who was driving the chariot in the shape of Metiscus and had control of the horses and the reins, protested: 'This way, Turnus. Let us go after these Trojans. This is where our first victories showed us the way. There are others whose hands can defend the city. Aeneas is bearing hard on Italians in all the confusion of battle; we too can deal out death without pity to Trojans. You will kill as many as he does and not fall short in the honours of war.'

Turnus made his reply: 'O my sister, I recognized you some time ago when first you shattered the treaty with your scheming and engaged in this war, and you do not deceive me now, pretending not to be a goddess. But whose will is it that you have been sent down from Olympus to endure this agony? Was it all to see the cruel death of your pitiable brother? For what am I to do? What stroke of Fortune could grant me safety now? No one is left whom I love as much as I loved Murranus, and I have seen him before my own eyes calling for me as he fell, a mighty warrior laid low by a mighty wound. The luckless Ufens has died rather than look on my disgrace, and the Trojans have his body and his arms. Shall I stand by and see our homes destroyed? This is the one indignity that remained. And shall I not lift my hand to refute the words of Drances? Shall I turn tail? Will this land of Italy see Turnus on the run? Is it so bad a thing to die? Be gracious to me, you gods of the underworld, since the gods above have turned their faces from me. My spirit will come down to you unstained, knowing nothing of such dishonour and worthy of my great ancestors to the end.'

Scarcely had he finished speaking when Saces suddenly came galloping up on his foaming horse having ridden through the middle of the enemy with an arrow wound full in his face. On he rushed calling the name of Turnus and imploring him: 'You are our last hope of safety, Turnus. You must take pity on your people. The sword and spear of Aeneas are like the lightning and he is threatening to throw down the highest citadels of Italy and give them over to destruction. Firebrands are already flying to the roofs. Every Latin face, every Latin eye, is turned to you. The king himself is at a loss. Whom should he choose to marry our daughters? What treaties should he turn to? And then the queen, who placed all her trust in you, has taken her own life. Fear overcame her and she fled the light of day. Alone in front of the gates Messapus and bold Atinas are holding the line and all round them on every side stand the battalions of the enemy in serried ranks. Their drawn swords are a crop of steel bristling in the fields. And you are out here wheeling your chariot in the deserted grasslands.'

Turnus was thunderstruck, bewildered by the changing shape of his fortune, and stood there dumb and staring. In that one heart of his there seethed a bitter shame, a grief shot through with madness, love driven on by fury, and a consciousness of his own courage. As soon as the shadows lifted from his mind and light returned, he forced his burning eyes round towards the walls, looking back in deep dismay from his chariot at the great city. There, between the storeys of a tower came a tongue of flame, rolling and billowing to the sky. It was taking hold of the tower, which he had built himself, putting the wheels under it and fitting the long gangways. 'Sister,' he said, 'the time has come at last. The Fates are too strong. You must not delay them any longer. Let us go where God and cruel fortune call me. I am resolved to meet Aeneas in battle. I am resolved to suffer what bitterness there is in death. You will not see me put to shame again. This is madness, but before I die, I beg of you, let me be mad.' No sooner had he spoken than he leapt to the ground from his chariot and dashed through all his enemies and their weapons, leaving his sister behind him to grieve as his charge broke through the middle of their ranks. Just as a boulder comes crashing down from the top of a mountain, torn out by gales, washed out by flood water or loosened by the stealthy passing of the years; it comes down the sheer face with terrific force, an evil mountain of rock, and bounds over the plain, rolling with it woods and flocks and men – so did Turnus crash through the shattered ranks of his enemies towards the walls of the city where all the ground was wet with shed blood and the air sang with flying spears. There he made a sign with his hand, and in the same moment he called out in a loud voice: 'Enough, Rutulians! Put up your weapons, and you too, Latins! Whatever Fortune brings is mine. It is better that I should be the one man who atones for this treaty for all of you, and settles the matter with the sword.' At these words the armies parted and left a clear space in the middle between them.

But when Father Aeneas heard the name of Turnus, he abandoned the walls and the lofty citadel, sweeping aside all delay and breaking off all his works of war. He leapt for joy and clashed his armour with a noise as terrible as thunder. Huge he was as Mount Athos or Mount Eryx or Father Appenninus himself roaring when the holm-oaks shimmer on his flanks and delighting to raise his snowy head into the winds. Now at last the Rutulians and the Trojans and all the men of Italy, the defenders guarding the high ramparts and the besiegers pounding the base of the walls with their rams, they all turned their eyes eagerly to see and took the armour off their shoulders. King Latinus himself was amazed at the sight of these two huge heroes born at opposite sides of the earth coming together to decide the issue by the sword. There, on a piece of open ground on the plain, they threw their spears at long range as they charged, and when they clashed the bronze of their shields rang out and the earth groaned. Blow upon blow they dealt with their swords as chance and courage met and mingled in confusion. Just as two enemy bulls on the great mountain of Sila or on top of Taburnus bring their horns to bear and charge into battle; the herdsmen stand back in terror, the herd stands silent and afraid, and the heifers low quietly together waiting to see who is to rule the grove, who is to be the leader of the whole herd; meanwhile the bulls are locked together exchanging blow upon blow, gouging horn into hide till their necks and shoulders are awash with blood and all the grove rings with their lowing and groaning – just

so did Aeneas of Troy and Turnus son of Daunus rush together
with shields clashing and the din filled the heavens. Then
Jupiter himself lifted up a pair of scales with the tongue
centred and put the lives of the two men in them to decide
who would be condemned in the ordeal of battle, and with
whose weight death would descend.

Turnus leapt forward thinking he was safe, and lifting his
sword and rising to his full height, he struck with all his
strength behind it. The Trojans shouted and the Latins cried
out in their anxiety, while both armies watched intently. But
in the height of his passion the treacherous sword broke in
mid-blow and left him defenceless, had he not sought help in
flight. Faster than the east wind he flew, when he saw his own
right hand holding nothing but a sword handle he did not
recognize. The story goes that when his horses were yoked
and he was mounting his chariot in headlong haste to begin
the battle, he left his father's sword behind and caught up the
sword of his charioteer Metiscus. For some time, while the
Trojans were scattered and in flight, that was enough. But
when it met the divine armour made by Vulcan, the mortal
blade was brittle as an icicle and shattered on impact, leaving
its fragments glittering on the golden sand. At this Turnus
fled in despair and tried to escape to another part of the plain,
weaving his uncertain course now to this side now to that, for
the Trojans formed a dense barrier round him, hemming him
in between a huge marsh and the high walls.

Nor did Aeneas let up in his pursuit. Slowed down as he
was by the arrow wound, his legs failing him sometimes and
unable to run, he still was ablaze with fury and kept hard on
the heels of the terrified Turnus, like a hunting dog that
happens to trap a stag in the bend of a river or in a ring of red
feathers used as a scare, pressing him hard with his running
and barking; the stag is terrified by the ambush he is caught
in or by the high river bank; he runs and runs back a thousand
ways, but the untiring Umbrian hound stays with him with

jaws gaping; now he has him; now he seems to have him and the jaws snap shut, but he is thwarted and bites the empty air; then as the shouting rises louder than ever, all the river banks and pools return the sound and the whole sky thunders with the din. As he ran Turnus kept shouting at the Rutulians, calling each of them by name and demanding the sword he knew so well. Aeneas on the other hand was threatening instant death and destruction to anyone who came near. Much as that alarmed them, he terrified them even more by threatening to raze their city to the ground, and though he was wounded he did not slacken in his pursuit. Five times round they ran in one direction, five times they rewound the circle. For this was no small prize they were trying to win at games. What they were competing for was the lifeblood of Turnus.

It so chanced that a bitter-leaved wild olive tree had stood on this spot, sacred to Faunus and long revered by sailors. On it men saved from storms at sea used to nail their offerings to the Laurentine god, and dedicate the clothes they had vowed for their safety. But the Trojans, making no exception for the sacred tree-trunk, had removed it to clear space for the combat. In this stump the spear of Aeneas was now embedded. The force of his throw had carried it here and lodged it fast in the tough wood of the root. He strained at it and tried to pull it out so that he could hunt with a missile the quarry he could not catch on foot. Wild now with fear, Turnus cried: 'Pity me, I beg of you, Faunus, and you, good Mother Earth, hold on to that spear, if I have always paid you those honours which Aeneas and his men have profaned in war.' So he prayed and he did not call for the help of the god in vain. Aeneas was long delayed struggling with the stubborn stump and no strength of his could prise open the bite of the wood. While he was heaving and straining with all his might, the goddess Juturna, daughter of Daunus, changed once more into the shape of the charioteer Metiscus and ran forward to give Turnus his sword. Venus was indignant that the nymph was

allowed to be so bold, so she came and wrenched out Aeneas'
spear from deep in the root. Then these glorious warriors,
their weapons and their spirits restored to them, one relying
on his sword, the other towering and formidable behind his
spear, stood there breathing hard, ready to engage in the
contest of war.

Meanwhile the King of All-powerful Olympus saw Juno
watching the battle from a golden cloud and spoke these
words to her: 'O my dear wife, what will be the end of this?
What is there left for you to do? You yourself know, and admit
that you know, that Aeneas is a god of this land, that he has a
right to heaven and is fated to be raised to the stars. What are
you scheming? What do you hope to achieve by perching
there in those chilly clouds? Was it right that a god should
suffer violence and be wounded by the hand of a mortal? Was
it right that Turnus should be given back the sword that was
taken from him? For what could Juturna have done without
your help? Why have you put strength into the arm of the
defeated? The time has come at last for you to cease and give
way to our entreaties. Do not let this great sorrow gnaw at
your heart in silence, and do not make me listen to grief and
resentment for ever streaming from your sweet lips. The end
has come. You have been able to harry the Trojans by sea and
by land, to light the fires of an unholy war, to soil a house
with sorrow and mix the sound of mourning with the marriage song. I forbid you to go further.'

These were the words of Jupiter. With bowed head the
goddess Juno, daughter of Saturn, made this reply: 'Because
I have known your will, great Jupiter, against my own wishes
I have abandoned Turnus and abandoned the earth. But for
your will, you would not be seeing me sitting alone in mid-air
on a cloud, suffering whatever is sent me to suffer. I would
be clothed in fire, standing close in to the line of battle and
dragging Trojans into bloody combat. It was I, I admit it, who
persuaded Juturna to come to the help of her unfortunate

brother, and with my blessing to show greater daring for the sake of his life, but not to shoot arrows, not to stretch the bow. I swear it by the implacable fountainhead of the River Styx, the one oath which binds the gods of heaven. And now I, Juno, yield and quit these battles which I so detest. But I entreat you for the sake of Latium and the honour of your own kin, to allow what the law of Fate does not forbid. When at last their marriages are blessed – I offer no obstruction – when at last they come together in peace and make their laws and treaties together, do not command the Latins to change their ancient name in their own land, to become Trojans and be called Teucrians. They are men. Do not make them change their voice or native dress. Let there be Latium. Let the Alban kings live on from generation to generation and the stock of Rome be made mighty by the manly courage of Italy. Troy has fallen. Let it lie, Troy and the name of Troy.'

He who devised mankind and all the world smiled and replied: 'You are the true sister of Jupiter and the second child of Saturn, such waves of anger do you set rolling from deep in your heart. But come now, lay aside this fury that arose in vain. I grant what you wish. I yield. I relent of my own free will. The people of Ausonia will keep the tongue of their fathers and their ancient ways. As their name is, so shall it remain. The Trojans will join them in body only and will then be submerged. Ritual I will give and the modes of worship, and I will make them all Latins, speaking one tongue. You will see that the people who arise from this admixture of Ausonian blood will be above all men, above the gods, in devotion and no other race will be their equals in paying you honour.' Juno nodded in assent. She rejoiced and forced her mind to change, leaving the cloud behind her and withdrawing from the sky.

This done, the Father of the Gods pondered another task in his mind and prepared to dismiss Juturna from her brother's side. There are two monsters named Dirae borne to the goddess of the dead of night in one and the same litter with Megaera of Tartarus. The heads of all three she bound with coiling snakes and gave them wings to ride the wind. These attend the throne of savage Jupiter in his royal palace, and sharpen the fears of suffering mortals whenever the King of the Gods sets plagues or hideous deaths in motion or terrifies guilty cities by the visitation of war. One of these Jupiter sent swiftly down from the heights of heaven with orders to confront Juturna as an omen. She flew to earth, carried in a swift whirlwind. Like an arrow going through a cloud, spun from the bowstring of a Parthian who has armed the barb with a virulent poison for which there is no cure, a Parthian, or a Cretan from Cydonia; and it whirrs as it flies unseen through the swift darkness – so flew the daughter of Night, making for the earth. When she saw the Trojan battle lines and the army of Turnus, she took in an instant the shape of the little bird which perches on tombs and the gables of empty houses and sings late its ill-omened song among the shades of night. In this guise the monster flew again and again at Turnus' face, screeching and beating his shield with her wings. A strange numbness came over him and his bones melted with fear. His hair stood on end and the voice stuck in his throat.

His sister Juturna recognized the Dira from a long way off by the whirring of her wings, and grieved. She loosened and tore her hair. She scratched her face and beat her breast, crying: 'What can your sister do to help you now, Turnus? Much have I endured but nothing now remains for me, and I have no art that could prolong your life. How can I set myself against such a portent? At last, at last, I leave the battle. Do not frighten me, you birds of evil omen. I am already afraid. I know the beating of your wings and the sound of death. I do not fail to understand the proud commands of great-hearted Jupiter. Is this his reward for my lost virginity? For what purpose has he granted me eternal life? Why has he deprived me of the state of death? But for that I could at least have put an end to my suffering and borne my poor brother company through the shades. So this is immortality! Will anything that is mine be sweet to me without you, my brother? Is there no abyss that can open deep enough to take a goddess down to the deepest of the shades?' At these words, covering her head in a blue-green veil and moaning bitterly, the goddess plunged into the depths of her own river.

Aeneas kept pressing his pursuit with his huge spear flashing, as long as a tree, and these were the words he spoke in his anger: 'What is the delay now? Why are you still shirking, Turnus? This is not a race! It is a fight with dangerous weapons at close quarters. Turn yourself into any shape you like. Scrape together all your resources of spirit and skill. Pray to sprout wings and fly to the stars of heaven, or shut yourself up and hide in a hole in the ground!' Turnus replied, shaking his head: 'You are fierce, Aeneas, but wild words do not frighten me. It is the gods that cause me to fear, the gods and the enmity of Jupiter.' He said no more but looked round and saw a huge rock, a huge and ancient rock which happened to be lying on the plain, a boundary stone put there to settle a dispute about land. Twelve picked men like those the earth now produces could scarcely lift it up on to their shoulders, but he caught it up in his trembling hands and, rising to his full height and running at speed, he hurled it at his enemy. But he had no sense of running or going, of lifting or moving the huge rock. His knees gave way. His blood chilled and froze and the stone rolled away under its own impetus over the open ground between them, but it did not go the whole way and it did not strike its target. Just as when we are asleep, when in the weariness of night, rest lies heavy on our eyes, we dream we are trying desperately to run further and not succeeding, till we fall exhausted in the middle of our efforts; the tongue is useless; the strength we know we have, fails our body; we have no voice, no words to obey our will – so it was with Turnus. Wherever his courage sought a way, the dread goddess barred his progress. During these moments, the thoughts whirled in his brain. He gazed at the Rutulians and the city. He faltered with fear. He began to tremble at the death that was upon him. He could see nowhere to run, no way to come at his enemy, no chariot anywhere, no sister to drive it.

As he faltered the deadly spear of Aeneas flashed. His eyes had picked the spot and he threw from long range with all his weight behind the throw. Stones hurled by siege artillery never roar like this. The crash of the bursting thunderbolt is not so loud. Like a dark whirlwind it flew carrying death and destruction with it. Piercing the outer rings of the sevenfold shield and laying open the lower rim of the breastplate, it went whistling through the middle of the thigh. When the blow struck, down went great Turnus, bending his knee to the ground. The Rutulians rose with a groan which echoed round the whole mountain, and far and wide the high forests sent back the sound of their voices. He lowered his eyes and stretched out his right hand to beg as a suppliant. 'I have brought this upon myself,' he said, 'and for myself I ask nothing. Make use of what Fortune has given you, but if any thought of my unhappy father can touch you, I beg of you – and you too had such a father in Anchises – take pity on the old age of Daunus, and give me back to my people, or if you prefer it, give them back my dead body. You have defeated me, and the men of Ausonia have seen me defeated and stretching out my hands to you. Lavinia is yours. Do not carry your hatred any further.'

There stood Aeneas, deadly in his armour, rolling his eyes, but he checked his hand, hesitating more and more as the words of Turnus began to move him, when suddenly his eyes caught the fatal baldric of the boy Pallas high on Turnus' shoulder with the glittering studs he knew so well. Turnus had defeated and wounded him and then killed him, and now he was wearing his belt on his shoulder as a battle honour taken from an enemy. Aeneas feasted his eyes on the sight of this spoil, this reminder of his own wild grief, then, burning with mad passion and terrible in his wrath, he cried: 'Are you to escape me now, wearing the spoils stripped from the body of those I loved? By this wound which I now give, it is Pallas who makes sacrifice of you. It is Pallas who exacts the penalty in your guilty blood.' Blazing with rage, he plunged the steel full into his enemy's breast. The limbs of Turnus were dissolved in cold and his life left him with a groan, fleeing in anger down to the shades.

Appendix 1

Silvius: According to Jupiter's prophecy at 1.257–77, Rome is to be founded in four stages. Aeneas will build his city at Lavinium and live for three years. His son Ascanius Iulus will reign for thirty years and transfer the city to Alba Longa. After their descendants, the Alban kings, rule for three hundred years, Romulus (Quirinus), son of Mars and Ilia, will found his city at Rome. But here at 6.763, where Aeneas begins his survey of the Alban kings waiting in the underworld, Ascanius, being still alive, is not in the parade, and the first to be mentioned is Silvius, a son of Aeneas not yet born.

Alban kings: Virgil offers five names to cover the years from about 1053 to 753 B.C.

Romulus: Romulus restored his grandfather Numitor to the throne which Numitor's younger brother had usurped. Romulus then founded Rome in 753 B.C.

Caesar: Julius Caesar, 102–44 B.C., adopted his grand-nephew Octavian as his son and heir.

Augustus: Name adopted by Octavian in 27 B.C.

(Numa): From the village of Cures, he gave Rome religion and laws. His traditional dates are 715–673 B.C.

Tullus: Tullius Hostilius, the warrior king, 673–642 B.C.

Ancus: Ancus Marcius, 642–617 B.C., here only appears as a king who courted popular favour.

Tarquins: L. Tarquinius Priscus, 616–579 B.C., and L. Tarquinius Superbus, 534–510 B.C.

Brutus: L. Junius Brutus led a rising against Tarquinius Superbus to avenge the rape of Lucretia. Later, as one of the first two consuls of Rome, in 510, he executed his own two sons who tried to restore the Tarquins. The rods and axes carried by the consuls signified their right to flog and execute. This passage alludes also to the other avenging Brutus who assassinated Julius Caesar in 44 B.C.

Decii: P. Decius Mus, father and son of the same name, were famous for self-immolation, each taking his own life to secure victory for Roman armies, the father in 340 B.C. in the Latin War and the son in 295 B.C. in battle against the Samnites.

Drusi: Livia, wife of Augustus from 38 B.C. till his death in A.D. 14, was a member of this notable Roman family.

Torquatus: T. Manlius Torquatus led the Romans against the Gauls in 361 B.C., and in 340 B.C. in the Latin War he executed his own son for disobeying orders in engaging and defeating an enemy champion.

Camillus: M. Furius Camillus recovered the gold said to have been the price of the Gaulish withdrawal from Rome in 390 B.C. This passage may also be read as an oblique tribute to Augustus, who, after long negotiations, recovered in 20 B.C. the standards lost to the Parthians at Carrhae in 53 B.C.

(Pompey):   Gnaeus Pompeius and Julius Caesar are the two spirits in gleaming armour. Caesar defeated Pompey at the battle of Pharsalus in 48 B.C.

(Mummius):   L. Mummius sacked Corinth in 146 B.C.

(Paullus):   L. Aemilius Paullus is here credited with the conquest of Greece for his defeat of Pyrrhus, king of Epirus, at the battle of Pydna in 168 B.C.

Cato: M. Porcius Cato, Cato the Elder, 234–149 B.C., was famed as the custodian of traditional Roman virtues.

Cossus: A. Cornelius Cossus defeated Tolumnius, king of the Veientes, in single combat, perhaps in 246 B.C.

Gracchi: Tiberius Sempronius Gracchus (died 133 B.C.), and his brother Gaius Sempronius Gracchus (died 121 B.C.), the two reforming tribunes, were members of this famous Roman family.

Scipios: Scipio Africanus Maior defeated Hannibal at Zama in 202 B.C. Scipio Africanus Minor destroyed Carthage in 146 B.C.

Fabricius: Gaius Fabricius Luscinus fought against Pyrrhus, king of Epirus, in 80–79 B.C. The power he found in poverty is an allusion to his rejection of Pyrrhus' gifts.

Serranus: Gaius Atilius Regulus was sowing seed (*serere*: to sow) on his farm when he was called to the consulship in 257 B.C. He therefore acquired the name Serranus.

Fabii: Anchises at 6.845 calls out to his friends the members of the great Fabian family to ask why they are all in such a hurry to reach the light of life that they are hustling one weary spirit along with them, and then he realizes that the problem is not weariness. This is the great Q. Fabius

Maximus Cunctator (*cunctator:* delayer) who used Fabian tactics against Hannibal in 217–216 B.C. in the Second Punic War. He is not tired. It is his nature to delay!

Marcellus: M. Claudius Marcellus, consul five times, killed the Gaulish chieftain Viridomarus in single combat in 222 B.C., thus becoming the third Roman, after Romulus and Cossus, to win the Supreme Spoils (*Spolia Opima*). Augustus was eager to make sure that there would not be a fourth (see Livy 4.20.5). The younger M. Claudius Marcellus (42–23 B.C.) was the son of Augustus' sister Octavia, and was adopted by Augustus in 25 B.C. An ancient life of Virgil (*Vita Donati* 32) describes how, when Virgil was reading this passage to Octavia and Augustus, Octavia swooned when he reached line 882.

Appendix 2

Most of the scenes on the shield are incidents from Italian
wars (see lines 626 and 678), all depicted with vivid evocation
of the colours, textures and materials used in this imaginary
work of art and the sounds evoked by it.

Around the outside of the circle are six scenes described in
forty-one lines:

  (i) The wolf suckling Romulus and Remus, who are to found
      the city in 753 B.C.
 (ii) The rape of the Sabine women as planned by Romulus
      and the subsequent war and reconciliation.
(iii) The punishment of Mettus Fufetius, dictator of Alba
      Longa who will make a treaty with Tullus Hostilius, king
      of Rome 673–642 B.C., and then desert him in battle.
 (iv) Two famous scenes from the Etruscan attack on Rome in
      508 B.C.
  (v) At the top of the shield the attack of the Gauls in 390 B.C.
      and the origin of some traditional features of Roman
      religion. The matrons of Rome were permitted to drive
      in carriages to the games and temples in return for giving
      their gold and jewels to enable Camillus to build a temple
      to Apollo after the defeat of Veii in 396 B.C.
 (vi) Presumably at the bottom of the shield, scenes in the
      underworld showing Catiline whose conspiracy was put
      down by Cicero in 63 B.C. and M. Porcius Cato who fought
      for the Republican cause against Caesar and committed
      suicide after his defeat at Thapsus in 46 B.C. Like his great

ancestor Cato the Elder (6.841) he was regarded as a model of the uncompromising Republican virtues.

In the centre of the shield, in a ring of silver dolphins feathering with white foam the silver sea and its golden waves, is depicted Augustus' victory over Antony and Cleopatra at Actium in 31 B.C. and his triple triumph of 29 B.C. (Dalmatian, Actian and Alexandrian). To this Augustan theme Virgil devotes 54 lines.

Appendix 3

THE JULIAN FAMILY

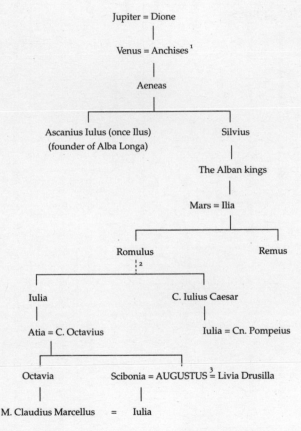

Jupiter = Dione
|
Venus = Anchises [1]
|
Aeneas
|
Ascanius Iulus (once Ilus)   Silvius
(founder of Alba Longa)
|
The Alban kings
|
Mars = Ilia
|
Romulus   Remus
[2]
|
Iulia   C. Iulius Caesar
|
Atia = C. Octavius   Iulia = Cn. Pompeius
|
Octavia   Scibonia = AUGUSTUS [3] = Livia Drusilla
|
M. Claudius Marcellus = Iulia

1. Anchises' grandfather Assaracus seems to be mentioned in a Julian connection at
   1.284, 6.778, 9.259, 643.
2. This gap is variously filled (see S. Weinstock, *Divus Julius*, p. 183 n. 1.).
3. Augustus was born C. Octavius in 63 B.C. He was adopted as Julius Caesar's son by
   Caesar's will in 44 B.C. under the name of C. Iulius Caesar Octavianus (called
   Octavian in English), and took the name of Augustus in January 27 B.C.

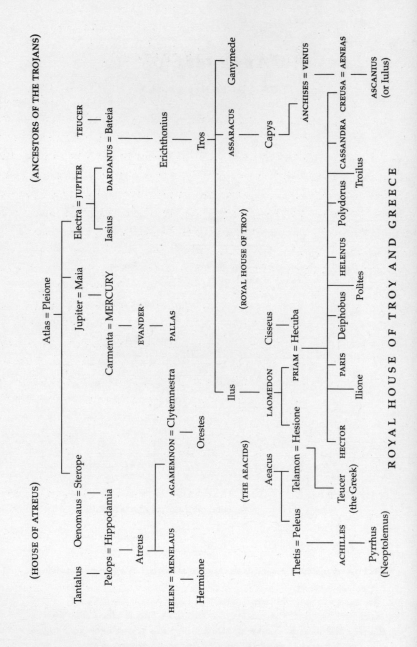

ROYAL HOUSE OF TROY AND GREECE

Maps and Gazetteer

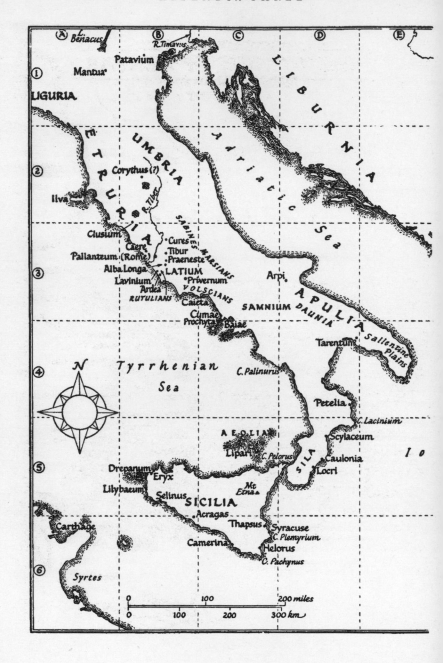

THE VOYAGES OF AENEAS

F G H J K

AGATHYRSIANS

DACIA

R. Danube

GETAE

Caspian Sea

THRACE

MACEDONIA

Aeneadae

EPIRUS

THESSALY

Samothrace

Arisba

PHRYGIA

Rhoeteum

Troy Thymbra

CHAONIA

Buthrotum

Larisa

Meliboea

Lemnos

Antandros

Lyrnessus

MAEONIA

Dodona

Epirus

DOLOPIANS

Aegean

Gryneum

Actium

MYRMIDONS

DRYOPES

PTHIA

EUBOEA

Scyros

LYDIA

Leucas

Oechalia Narycum

Chalcis

Sea

Claros

ian

Ithaca

BOEOTIA

Aulis

C. Caphereus

Samos

a

Same

Corinth

Megara

Thebes

Elis

Nemea

Athenae

Gyaros

Pheneus

Mycenae

Salamis

Myconos

Zakynthos

ARCADIA

Argos

Delos

Lerna

Tiryns

Paros

Donusa

Strophades

Sparta

Olearos

Naxos

Amyclae

C. Malea

Cythera

Carpathos

CRETE

Gortyn

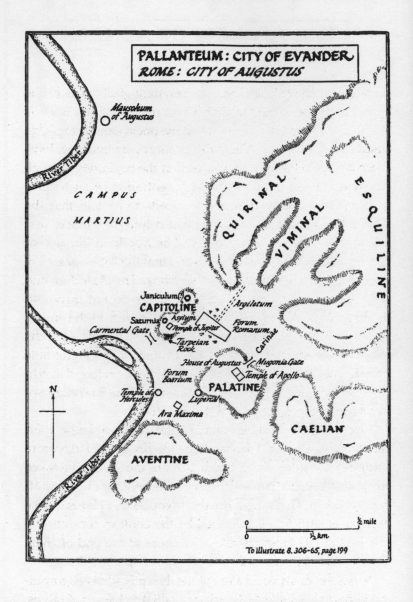

PALLANTEUM: CITY OF EVANDER
ROME: CITY OF AUGUSTUS

Mausoleum of Augustus

River Tiber

CAMPUS MARTIUS

QUIRINAL

VIMINAL

ESQUILINE

Janiculum(?)
CAPITOLINE
Saturnia
Asylum
Temple of Jupiter
Carmental Gate
Tarpeian Rock

Argiletum

Forum Romanum
Carinae

House of Augustus
Forum Boarium
Temple of Apollo
Mugonia Gate

PALATINE

Temple of Hercules
Lupercal

Ara Maxima

N

CAELIAN

River Tiber

AVENTINE

0   ½ mile
0   ½ km

To illustrate 8. 306-65, page 199

340

I started to compile a glossary of mythological terms in the *Aeneid*, but soon decided that it was not necessary. Such is Virgil's command of narration that the poem usually explains itself as it goes along. Where this is not so, explanations have been added to the text, for example at the beginning of Book Six where there is an unusual concentration of such difficulties. Here, the modern reader needs to be told that the Chalcidian citadel is the Chalcidian colony of Cumae; that Phoebus in line 18 is the same god as Apollo in line 9; that Androgeos was the son of Minos and that the Athenians were held to be the descendants of Cecrops. The *Aeneid* is first and foremost a narrative, and narratives do not thrive on interruptions. A glossary would drive readers to the end of the book. Even footnotes would take the eye to the foot of the page and the mind to scholarly furniture. It is a regrettable interference with the text of Virgil, but I have preferred to add such information to the body of the work where it is necessary rather than check the flow of the narrative.

Geography is another matter. The ancients knew their Mediterranean world better than we do. I have therefore supplied an index and maps which are meant to give topographical information which may be helpful for understanding the poem. These therefore omit peoples and places whose locality is sufficiently indicated by the context, for example the lists of the Latin enemies of Aeneas at the end of Book Seven and his Etruscan allies at 10. 163–214.

Virgil has many equivalent or nearly equivalent geographical terms at his disposal. Greeks are called Achaeans, Argives, Graians, and Pelasgians; Troy is Dardania, Ilium, Pergama (strictly its citadel), and its people are Phrygians, Teucrians, even Laomedontiadae, as well as Trojans; Etruscans are also Lydians, Tuscans and Tyrrhenians. Where Virgil seems to be using these terms purely for metrical convenience, the translation speaks of Greeks, Trojans and Etruscans. But the variants are preserved where they are used to some effect, rhetorical at 2. 324–6 for example, or emotive (the term 'Phrygian' usually carries a contemptuous allusion to the alleged effeminacy of the Trojans). In particular Italy is variously referred to as Ausonia, Oenotria, Hesperia (the Western Land), and sometimes these terms are used in prophecies not understood by those who hear them. This oracular obscurity is preserved in the translation since the progressive revelation of the divine will is an important aspect of the plot of the poem. The Tiber, for instance, is called the Lydian Thybris at 2. 781–2 and Aeneas can have no idea what is meant. The Italian river is always referred to by this Greek form of its name until 6. 873.

In the index below these equivalents will be noted but they will not occur on the maps. So too rivers and mountains appear in the list below, but normally not on the maps.

Names in brackets do not appear on the maps; names with map references appear on the map of The Voyages of Aeneas; other names appear on the map of Pallanteum/Rome.

Strophades 5G
Syracuse 6C
Syrtes 6A

(Taburnus – mountain in Samnium)
Tarentum 4D
Tarpeian Rock
(Tetrica – mountain in Sabine country)
(Teucrians – Trojans)
Thapsus 6C
Thebes 5H
Thrace 2GHJ
Thymbra 4J
Tibur 3B
Timavus 1B
Tiryns 5H
(Trinacria – Sicily)
(Troad – the region around Troy)
(Tuscans – Etruscans)
(Tyre – Phoenician city)
(Tyrrhenians – Etruscans)

Umbria 2B

(Velinus – lake in Sabine country)
(Vesulus – mountain in Liguria)
Volsci 3BC

(Xanthus – river in the Troad)

Zacynthus 5F

Publius Vergilius Maro (70–19 BC) was born in the north of Italy and completed his education in Rome. He also wrote the *Eclogues*, completed in 37 BC, and the *Georgics*, which he finished in 29 BC. He then devoted the rest of his life to the composition of his greatest work, *The Aeneid*.

Since retiring from the Latin Chair at Newcastle University, David West has transated the *Odes* and the *Epodes* of Horace and written commentaries on *Odes I* and on *Odes II*.

SEVEN WONDERS OF THE WORLD

The Aeneid   Virgil
Anna Karenina   Leo Tolstoy
Don Quixote Part One   Cervantes
Faust Part One   Johann Wolfgang von Goethe
Hell   Dante Alighieri
Madame Bovary   Gustave Flaubert
The Odyssey   Homer